We were not orphans

NUMBER TWENTY-NINE

Jack and Doris Smothers Series in Texas History, Life, and Culture

We were not orphans

STORIES FROM THE WACO STATE HOME

By Sherry Matthews

Foreword by
ROBERT DRAPER

Oral histories edited by
JESSE SUBLETT

Research by
BEAU LEBOEUF

University of Texas Press
AUSTIN

Publication of this work was made possible in part by support from the J. E. SMOTHERS, SR., MEMORIAL FOUNDATION and the NATIONAL ENDOWMENT FOR THE HUMANITIES.

Requests for permission to reproduce material from this work should be sent to:
    Permissions
    University of Texas Press
    P.O. Box 7819
    Austin, TX 78713-7819
    www.utexas.edu/utpress/about/bpermission.html

♾ The paper used in this book meets the minimum requirements of ANSI/NISO Z39.48-1992 (R1997) (Permanence of Paper).

LIBRARY OF CONGRESS CATALOGING-IN-PUBLICATION DATA

Matthews, Sherry.
  We were not orphans : stories from the Waco State Home / by Sherry Matthews ; foreword by Robert Draper. — 1st ed.
    p.   cm. — (Jack and Doris Smothers series in Texas history, life, and culture ; 29)
  ISBN 978-0-292-72559-1 (cloth : alk. paper)
  1. Waco State Home (Waco, Tex.) 2. Orphanages—Texas—Waco—History. 3. Child welfare—Texas—Waco. 4. Child abuse—Texas—Waco. 5. Children—Institutional care—Texas—Waco. I. Title.
  HV995.W252M38 2011
  362.73′2—dc22

                                                2010039658

Contents

Foreword

On January 1, 1923, an obscure chapter in Texas history commenced when, by legislative mandate, the State Home for Dependent and Neglected Children in the city of Waco received its first inhabitants. From that day until the Waco State Home officially closed in 1979, thousands of Texas children passed through its gates and thereby became part of a Dickensian saga that has remained untold until now.

The Waco State Home was the de facto safety net for children who had committed no crime other than the offense of being born poor. Some of them were left on the street by parents who then sped off and were never seen again. Many were badly malnourished; for some, their most recent meal had been, literally, a handful of dirt. Others had been sexually abused, and still others had been utterly abandoned, dumped with their siblings like a litter of mutts. These were children as young as three years old, and already their fate was sealed—or would have been, were it not for the Waco State Home.

Upon admission, the new arrivals were deloused, shorn of long hair, and then led to barracks-style dormitories. Life, for them, became one of martial discipline. The Home sat on a hundred-acre working farm; the boys milked the cows and slaughtered the hogs, while the girls canned, cooked, laundered, and scrubbed. Beyond occasional field trips, life for this pauper tribe was encompassed within the austere womb of the campus—governed, with almost no state supervision, by the Home's superintendent and his rough-handed charges.

On a baseline level, the institution more than fulfilled its objectives. Its young inhabitants were well schooled, well fed, and well versed in the virtues of labor. The rigors of the Home—environs that had to be kept spotless, beds that had to pass military-style inspection, elbows that had to stay off the dining table, *or else*—instilled a lasting sort of toughness. As one alumnus later recalled, "When I joined the air force, it was like a country club in comparison." Indeed, a number of State Homers later joined the military, just as many went on to start families, enjoy financial success, and, for the most part, prevail over their desperate beginnings. For giving them a chance—for saving their lives—they have the Waco State Home to thank.

Where the Home failed was as a small-*h* home. Human kindness, mercy, and love were not among the campus's offerings. The matrons who enforced the rules were often poorly educated and given to primitive methods—making a bed-wetting boy wear a dress, forcing a girl who had let a boy kiss her stand on a staircase for a period of days, calling a child a "retarded idiot." The term "corporal punishment" does not do justice to the savagery of the beatings memorialized in these pages. And as for the widespread instances of sexual abuse, one female victim can speak only in painful understatement when she says, "I live with all the memories every day of my life."

The voices that speak out in *We Were Not Orphans: Stories from the Waco State Home* are at a loss to explain the cruelties, and even the remarkable internal documents uncovered by Sherry Matthews and her associates provide only hints. Did the Home become a cautionary tale of best intentions undercut by ignorance and frontier strictness? Or did conditions on the campus become a breeding ground for sadism? Whatever the cause, abuse was endemic.

Decades later, the trauma is still evident—and so is, in some cases, it must gently be said, denial. "I just look at it for what it was," one alumnus tells us—and who can blame him for leaving it at that? After all, the children of the Waco State Home had no plan B. They could try to escape it (and indeed many did try), but in the end, their lot was to endure and then get past it—and thereafter regard the wounds as one would a dueling scar, proof that any burden in life can be borne.

Still, the collective story that emerges here is far from a horror show. The single most stunning feature of these monologues is the resilience of childhood. Even in a climate of brutal lovelessness, boys still reveled in juvenile pranks and girls still obsessed over their hair. Laughter, furtive and fumbling romance, raucous gatherings at the escarpment towering over the Bosque River known as Lovers' Leap, everyday subversion of the rules—these elements are persistent, and therefore miraculous. For just as this tale is replete with obvious villains (the sadistic Coach Whigham, the perverted Pop Taylor) and at least one heroine (the much-loved English teacher Mabel Legg), *We Were Not Orphans: Stories from the Waco State Home* is inspirational for one reason: the storytellers. They dared, after all, to be children.

Robert Draper

Acknowledgments

Writing this book was a brief but intense journey involving hundreds of people in a cooperative effort that has amazed everyone, including me. A few thought me crazy to undertake such a project, but I knew that the stories I had heard, and others yet to be discovered, were nothing short of incredible. And I knew that they deserved not only the covers of a book but an audience as well.

I thank University of Texas Press sales and marketing manager Dave Hamrick, who was the first to express interest in shepherding the book to publication; my discerning editor William Bishel; manuscript editor Victoria Davis; and designer Derek George. I also thank copy editors Kip Keller and Ron Silverman and the wonderfully supportive outside "readers," including Denise Gamino, who helped make the book better.

The single person most responsible for this book is my brother Bing Smith. His persistence in getting me to attend a Waco State Home reunion allowed me to discover the children of the Home, now adults, and their stories. He was a diligent researcher, poring over documents all over Central Texas—from the Waco Public Library to the Texas State Library and Archives Commission—as well as obituaries online and, finally, Harold Larson's valuable private collection. I thank and honor my brother for taking this journey with me.

I am deeply appreciative to the talented writer, author, and musician Jesse Sublett for his intelligence, encouragement, great wit and humor, and, most of all, the respectful way he turned taped interviews into the written word. Working with Jesse is always a joy, and he provided wise counsel to someone publishing a first book.

I cannot adequately express my appreciation to Beau LeBoeuf, an outstanding researcher. He had the persistence to go through scraps of paper others might have ignored, and his skill in ferreting out precious nuggets of information from volumes of material helped produce the Epilogue.

Closure for the book came with the important discovery of Rebecca Canning Brumley, who shared her records and memories of the last years of the Home. The book is far better because of Rebecca and her thoughtful, caring perspective.

Harold Larson's private collection of materials related to the Home, along with his thorough documentation and cataloging, helped us make sense of disparate records and other bits of information. Without the help of his niece and executor, Sheryl Scott, the book would be a less thorough record. I owe my deep gratitude to Sheryl and to her uncle for his lifelong, meticulous archiving of the rich history of the Home.

Special thanks go to my sisters, Susan Hodges and Nancy Norman, who supported me every step of the way.

I would like to acknowledge Laura Saegert and Sergio Velasco, of the staff at the Texas State Library and Archives Commission, who provided easy and efficient access to long-ignored records of the Home. My thanks go as well, and for the same reason, to Ellen Brown, of the Baylor University Library.

I wish to thank Chelsea King for her gracious help in securing releases, photographs, and approved stories from dozens of alumni scattered all over the country.

Excellent professional expertise and counsel came my way from entertainment and media attorney Larry Waks, professor and mentor David McHam, book packager Janice Shay, and writers Sarah Bird and Wes Smith.

Designer Gretchen Hicks scrutinized thousands of old and forgotten photographs, and production artists Tom Grodek and Marcus Davis managed to preserve many of them.

My gratitude goes to my champion Dick Clark, and to Ave Bonar, Bill Gilliland, Glenda Goehrs, Jan Justice, Jill McRae, Mark Young, and many friends for their contributions to the making of this book.

Finally, I must acknowledge again the children of the Waco State Home, all of those who, as adults, shared their stories. Without them, there would be no book.

We were not orphans

*The administration building at the Waco State Home, which was built in 1925 on a
ninety-three-acre tract near downtown Waco. Harold Larson's private collection.*

Prologue

I suppose I could say that my relationship with the Waco State Home began when, at three years old, I watched my three older brothers being taken away to live at the Home.

Six long years went by before they were able to return, and as a child, I traveled to Waco from East Texas to visit them with my mother. The family tragedies that sent them to the Home are not part of this collection of stories. My one surviving brother, Bing, says he remembers his time in the Home as the most miserable years of his life and has no story to tell.

For several years, though, Bing invited me to attend the annual Waco State Home reunions held on the last Saturday in June. I hesitated to go, for the Home was a painful memory for our family. I finally decided to go with my brother in the summer of 2004, more than fifty years after I had last visited the Home.

Even after so many years, the Home was strangely familiar to me as Bing and I drove past the gate and onto the sprawling grounds. No longer the Waco State Home for "dependent and neglected" children, the facilities had been turned into a psychiatric residential treatment center for youth. We joined other alumni and the host assigned to conduct the tour. The stately, two-story brick buildings, trimmed in slightly yellowing white wood, were spaced generously over the tree-covered lawns, and the entire facility resembled a college campus.

I had never been inside the buildings. Most of them had been built by the 1930s, with residential-style cottages added in the 1960s. Perhaps five or six of the original buildings remained, and of those, only a few were still in use. One was the baby cottage. My brother wanted me to see where he had lived when he first arrived, so our host took us inside. Bing said little as we walked through the rooms, except that the cottage had changed considerably from how he remembered it.

I then asked whether we could see the boys' dormitory where my other brothers, Donald and Jack, had lived. The building was still standing, though it had been condemned and the doors padlocked. Windowpanes were broken and held together with tape, plaster drooped from the ceilings, and the peeling walls revealed their many colorful layers of paint.

I learned that Donald had had his own private space, a small windowed alcove adjacent to the large, dormitory-style bedroom where about thirty other boys slept. Donald received special treatment because he was "the artist," and his interest in art and music was apparently encouraged.

Some of the alumni expressed dismay that Donald's last remaining mural for one of the dorms had been painted over. There was much speculation about who had taken his paintings that years ago hung on the walls of the dining room and many of the dorms.

Most of the once-handsome old buildings were padlocked and empty. Security escorts, quiet and subdued, almost as if they were ushering at a funeral, arrived to open each abandoned building on the tour to allow those attending the reunion to revisit their pasts.

Former residents eagerly took their families into the dilapidated buildings, climbing the dirty, crumbling stairs to show off their old rooms to their children and grandchildren. They posed for photos beside the windows where their beds had been, and more than one tilted their heads and tucked a cheek into their cradled hands to mimic a child's sleep. They conducted their own minitours of their childhoods for their families and reminisced with one another about what had happened in this building or beneath that tree.

They remembered their dorm parents, the ones who were nice, the ones who were mean. They laughed as they shared memories of homemade rolls and fresh dairy ice cream on Sunday, of beloved teachers who inspired them to write poetry, of learning how to make a bed that could pass military inspection, of sneaking out of the dorms at night to meet a sweetheart down by the creek. Some wanted to see the creek down by the woods but were told it was off-limits.

I admired a woman whose slightly graying hair was swept into an elegant circular braid atop her head. She told me that after she left the Home, she had let her hair grow long because of an incident that occurred when she first arrived.

"When I got here, I had never cut my hair, so it was hanging past my waist. Every night I brushed it before I went to bed. One night I saw the dorm mother watching me, and the next day she came in and told me that I was spending too much time on my hair. Before I realized what was happening, she took a pair of scissors and whacked off all my hair above my ears in this ugly, jagged cut. I was devastated."

The woman, now a college professor, had worked hard as a student at the Home, and with both private scholarships and tuition paid by the state, she had earned her doctorate.

There were similar stories, "secret stories" that were whispered to me in almost childlike fashion, as though the matron or the warden might still hear them.

Most of the stories shared with me that day were, however, surprisingly positive. Many told me that the Waco State Home was the best thing that had ever happened to them. They spoke of a good education, bountiful supplies of food, square dancing and piano lessons that won them national honors, and athletic programs that took them to state championships.

And they talked about the great affection they had for one another. The people who shared their childhoods became the families they had lost. They claimed deep, lasting friendships that had survived the years and even led to marriages between alumni that have been remarkably successful and enduring.

"I can't think of a single kid I didn't like when I lived at the Home," a man told me. "They were all good kids, and most of them were just grateful for a decent place to live."

From outward appearances, the Waco State Home was a "decent place to live." Originally established by the Texas Legislature in 1919 as the State Home for Dependent and Neglected Children, it occupied the site of the World War I–era Camp MacArthur. Its name was changed in 1937 to the Waco State Home.

In 1979, the facility was transferred to the Texas Department of Mental Health and Mental Retardation, reorganized as a treatment center for emotionally disturbed children, and named the Waco Center for Youth.

Early records indicate that the facility did not operate as, and was not intended to be, an orphanage. This distinction was important, too, for the children who lived there. Even today, alumni are quick to correct anyone who makes the mistake of calling the Waco State Home an orphans' home. "We were not orphans," one of them said. "Many of our parents were living. They just couldn't take care of us."

Some of the children at the Home were eventually adopted, but not many, because parents did not want to lose permanent control of their children or see siblings separated from each other. Admission to the Home meant the state assumed temporary custody of the child, who would remain a ward of the state until age twenty-one or until other arrangements were made.

Most of the children remained at the Home until graduation from high school, though some left early to return to their families or live with other family members. Some were transferred to State hospitals or sent to the Gatesville or Gainesville correctional facilities. Some simply disappeared and were never heard from again. There is even one newspaper report, from the early seventies, of two teenage boys who ran away from the Home and whose bodies were later found in an empty railroad car near the Home. Their murders were never solved.

The state owned and operated institution was a self-contained village housing an average of 300 children. A school was on campus until the mid-1950s, after which the students were bused to public schools in Waco. The Home provided competitive sports, church services, movies, and, in later years, a swimming pool and tennis courts.

Much of the nearly hundred-acre tract was reserved for farm operations, which, over the years, included a working dairy and creamery, a canning plant, sheds and barns, hay fields, cow and sheep pastures, and a slaughterhouse for hogs. Two other farms, called the Bosqueville Farm and the Lake Waco Farm, were located within five miles. The children supplied the labor for the farms, which produced much of the food for the Home. They were kept busy from early in the morning until evening, so there was little unsupervised time.

A PROJECT IS BORN

In 2008 my sisters Susan and Nancy joined our brother Bing and me at the annual Waco State Home reunion. I had often thought about the alumni stories and decided to find out if there were any interest in a book collection.

At the reunion, I spoke with Harvey Walker, then president of the Waco State Home Ex-Students' Association, who invited me to make an announcement during the business meeting about my plans for a book. Little did I know at the time of the bravery that quiet, unassuming Harvey had displayed years earlier in a protest to get an abusive 300-pound employee known as "the beater" fired.

I made the announcement about the book project and added that any profits from the book would go to the alumni association for scholarships or for whatever they wished.

I later realized that I had forgotten something very important: they could tell their stories anonymously if they wished. However, in the end, not a single person who submitted a story requested anonymity.

The announcement of the book prompted many more stories that day. The men and women who grew up in the Home were almost philosophical about their experiences. They spoke of disappointments one moment and the healing power of forgiveness the next. Overall, they seemed proud of the Home and their ability to "make the best of the situation." Some even admitted that they had run away from the

The Waco State Home bus, the major mode of transportation for the children, although some recalled being greeted with "here come the orphans" when they arrived at school. Harold Larson's private collection.

Waco State Home to go back to their families, only to return, as one man said, "after I saw how bad it really was back home."

Some came from families devastated by alcoholism and both sexual and physical abuse, but often the reason a child was brought to the home was a simple lack of food or money to pay for the basics.

One woman described her husband, an alumnus of the Home, as a very happy, optimistic man who had attended college and "just feels that no matter what happens to him now, it can't be as bad as his childhood." "Nothing fazes him at all," she said. "He's the most positive person I have ever known."

Another woman described what she called "a wonderful generation story": "My mother lived in the Home for twelve years," she said. "Then, when I was ten, my mother brought me here. So we both grew up here at different times, mother and daughter. Now that's a story!"

Even former staff members attended the reunion and shared stories. Florine Belk Powers, whose mother, Lily Belk, managed the State Home laundry for twenty years, recalled the time two young children from the Home walked all the way across town to visit her mother and got special permission to spend the night.

Jim Myrick, a former coach at the Home in the fifties, proudly told a story about a lost championship. The newspaper had reported a tie, but Myrick and the team learned in the eighties that they had actually won the regional track championship and found the trophy.

On the way back to Austin that day, my sisters and I discussed stories we had heard. Some were almost identical, whispered to us as though the storytellers were sharing a secret. We loved the stories and the people, who seemed eager to share their memories, good or bad.

Soon after we returned home, I learned that the alumni association had more than 250 members, so I sent a letter to every person on the mailing list. All alumni of the Home who signed a release and granted an interview or sent in a written story were promised that their stories would be included.

As we worked with dozens of alumni, we learned that some were very protective of the Home and its reputation. More than one questioned my motives for publishing their stories, especially since I wasn't seeking financial gain.

One man, who had bitter memories of the Home, asked me, "What is the point of telling my story now? It won't change what happened to me."

Another man warned me early into the project that "if this book is a smear job on the Waco State Home, I want no part of it."

The most protective former resident was Harold "Swede" Larson, who lived at the Home from 1938 to 1944. He organized the alumni association in 1950 and began his lifelong self-appointed job as official archivist. He compiled thousands of binders of historical material on the Home. He finally agreed to an interview and invited me to his home in Waco to review his documents, but before we could meet, he died suddenly on October 13, 2009. His wife, Moray, who also grew up at the Home, had died a year earlier.

Before I was able to contact the family, his volumes of red notebooks and binders were given, as he had requested, to Baylor University (which granted me permission to use the collection). Then I discovered that I knew Larson's niece, Sheryl Scott, who lives near Austin, and she graciously offered us full access to Larson's important private documents, including some from his safe-deposit box.

Privacy rights were always on my mind as we dug through boxes and boxes of documents and photographs, whether in Larson's materials, at the Texas State Library and Archives Commission, or in other collections. We carefully protected the privacy of any alumni who did not participate in the book project.

The Epilogue documents and confirms specific cases of abuse by staff members. When alumni read this book, most will learn for the first time what happened to those employees.

Not included in the book are my own family records, which I obtained last year. Because of my reaction to my family's documents, I provided information to alumni so that they could acquire their Waco State Home records. So even as we finished the book, they were discovering more of their own stories.

The dozens of taped oral interviews, told in the voices of men and women who could recall somber, tragic moments as easily as hilariously funny ones, are extraordinary. I don't think that I listened to a single story that did not make me shed a tear or laugh or both.

There are more than fifty finished stories in this book, and we were careful to retain as much of each original taped interview as possible, merely organizing or editing for clarity or coherence. The tone, the nuances of language, and the colorful descriptions of their most memorable moments are theirs, not the editors'. We added nothing of our own. We didn't have to.

The stories, beginning as early as 1924 and ending in 1976, detail not only the lives of alumni while at the Home but also the circumstances that brought them there and their experiences after they left. The stories reveal their places in history and show how the Great Depression, wars, politics, the economy, and changing attitudes toward the poor and indigent helped shape their lives.

As far as we know, there has been no published history of the Waco State Home, despite Larson's voluminous compilation of material. And we have been unable to find any book that contains such a sizeable collection of original, first-person stories from alumni of any public institution housing children. We who love stories and history should be immensely grateful that these storytellers stepped forward to share pieces of their history.

Memories of the Home are contradictory in many ways. Some people told us that certain incidents repeatedly described by others never happened, or they chose not to revisit these events. Most of our storytellers had fond, happy memories of the Home, and they absolutely refused to dwell on the negative. Some alumni told us they had such bad feelings about the Home that they never attended reunions and did not wish to participate in the book project in any way.

I hope that this book honors the cherished memories of those who shared their lives with such candor. I also hope that those who believed they had no voice as children will discover that they found it here.

5 MILES TO WSH
BOSQUEVILLE FARM

N

PARK LAKE DRIVE

pig/sheep pen
slaughter house

pasture

bull pen

hay barn

staff   feed barn   mule
barn   hay shed

cannery

laundry/
boiler room

maintenance   dairy

creamery   calf barn   pig facility

gazebo   dining
kitchen   bus barn   chicken houses

orchard

home
economics   baby cottage   supply   classrooms   gym   bath house

early
tennis courts

girls dorm   girls dorm   administration/school   boys dorm   boys dorm   hay field

barbed wire fence

girls dorm   hospital   pool   boys dorm

later
tennis courts   baseball field   playground/field

staff
housing

vegetable
garden

NORTH 19TH STREET

football field   staff
housing

superintendent's
house   barbed wire fence

2 MILES TO
WSH LAKE
WACO FARM

THE WACO
STATE HOME

1922–1979

WSH
Bosqueville
Farm   Connally
AFB

WSH
Lake Waco
Farm   35

Cameron
Park

WACO
STATE HOME   WACO

Baylor

84

1 MILE

Map of the grounds of the Waco State Home.
Illustration by John Wilson.

Waco State Home Historical Time Line

NATIONAL MILESTONES		WACO STATE HOME MILESTONES

1920 — 19th Amendment gives women right to vote.

1920

1919 — House Bill 112 establishes Waco State Home for Dependent and Neglected Children (WSHDNC).
1920 — Board of Control created, oversees WSHDNC.
1921 — Edgar McMordie appointed first superintendent.
1922 — WSHDNC opens.
1923 — First children admitted to WSHDNC.

1927 — Jennie Burleson appointed superintendent. 136 children at the Home.

1929 — Stock market crashes. Great Depression begins.
1930 — The Dust Bowl begins in Texas.

1930

1931 — Division of Child Welfare created under Board of Control.

1933 — President Roosevelt launches New Deal.
1935 — Social Security Act provides for retirement.
1936 — The Dust Bowl ends.
1938 — Fair Labor Standards Act regulates minimum work ages and hours.
1939 — World War II begins.

1933 — Robert Patterson appointed superintendent.
1935 — 379 children at the Home, 150 on waiting list.
1937 — Home renamed Waco State Home (WSH).
1939 — Department of Public Welfare (DPW) established under Board of Control.

1940

1941 — Great Depression ends. U.S. enters World War II.

1945 — U.S. drops atomic bombs on Japan. World War II ends.

1941 — Arthur Wiebusch appointed superintendent.
1943 — Ben Peek appointed superintendent.

1949 — Texas Board for State Hospitals and Special Schools oversees WSH. State Youth Development Council created.

1950 — Korean War begins.

1950

1953 — Korean War ends.
1954 — Supreme Court orders school desegregation.

1951 — WSH oversight moves to DPW.
1953 — Tornado strikes Waco, killing 144 people, missing WSH.
1954 — James Lands appointed acting superintendent.
1955 — Herbert Wilson appointed superintendent.
1957 — WSH oversight moves to Texas Youth Council.

1959 — Vietnam War begins.

1960

1963 — President Kennedy assassinated in Dallas.
1964 — Civil Rights Act outlaws racial segregation in schools.
1965 — Voting Rights Act guarantees voting rights.
1968 — Martin Luther King, Jr., assassinated.

1963 — James McNabb appointed superintendent.

1965 — Jewel Ludwick appointed superintendent.

1970

1974 — President Nixon resigns over Watergate. U.S. district judge William Wayne Justice issues landmark decision in *Morales v. Turman* regarding rights of institutionalized children.
1975 — Vietnam War ends.
1977 — *Morales v. Turman* decision upheld by U.S. Supreme Court.

1974 — Rebecca Canning appointed superintendent.
1976 — Pat Hickey, Fred Conrad, Robert Drake, and David Gibson serve as interim superintendents.
1979 — Waco State Home closed and renamed Waco Center for Youth under Texas Department of Mental Health and Mental Retardation.

1980

Stories

Children at the Waco State Home during the Great Depression, when stories of children eating dirt or being abandoned on the streets were not uncommon. Harold Larson's private collection.

CHAPTER ONE

The Great Depression

The Great Depression (1929—1941) brought calamity to all of America, but Texas and most of the Southwest were hit with a double whammy—the agricultural disaster known as the Dust Bowl (1930—1936) on top of the general economic downturn. Bread lines, shantytowns, and hobo camps became new symbols of the nation during the desperate times. Yet those years of despair also saw the creation of some of America's most memorable cultural icons, including Hoover Dam, the Empire State Building, John Steinbeck's *The Grapes of Wrath*, the movies *Gone with the Wind* and *The Wizard of Oz*, and the golden age of radio.

President Franklin D. Roosevelt's New Deal created millions of jobs for the jobless, from manual laborers who built highways and housing to artists and writers who documented the times in murals, photographs, and books. In addition, the New Deal saw the passage of landmark legislation, such as the Social Security Act in 1935, which ensured income for the elderly. It also inaugurated a public welfare system to help dependent children, but local politics and a lack of funding stymied implementation for decades.

To further transform society, new regulations were placed on banking and business, workplaces were opened to unions, and child labor was outlawed. Nonetheless, child labor at the Waco State Home remained in place for years, and some children worked the hundreds of acres of farmland instead of attending school.

Although the New Deal brought sweeping reforms, some families were so destitute or desperate that children were reduced to eating dirt, and some parents abandoned their children at churches or gas stations and never saw them again.

As our stories reveal, the Great Depression was the reason many children were sent to live at the Waco State Home. In 1935, the Home was at full capacity with nearly 400 children, and 150 were on the waiting list.

Dick Hudman

1924–1941

I was born in Hubbard, Texas. I had three brothers and a sister. My dad died after being kicked by a mule. My mother couldn't take care of us, so she sent all the boys to the Waco State Home, and my aunt and uncle took in our sister. That was in 1924, when I was two years old. I grew up there.

Miss Jennie Burleson was superintendent. We had some pretty good teachers. Mrs. Legg taught English, and I remember Mrs. Emmons and Mrs. Jones. Charles Romine was coach of basketball, football, and track. Long John Smyers taught shop. Those are the only teachers I can remember.

Dick Hudman, back row, second from right, *and his eighth-grade classmates at Waco State Home, c. 1936. Harold Larson's private collection.*

I have always wondered why Waco High didn't invite some of us to play football. In 1939, we beat their team 75–0. Under Coach Romine in 1938, 1939, and 1940, we went unbeaten and unscored upon.

We all had jobs. Once you reached seven or eight, you worked in the kitchen. The bigger boys were always on the milk gang. You had to sweep and mop the dormitory every day. But the Home was pretty good. Otherwise, I would not have had any education.

In the afternoon, we used to slip off to Cameron Park to play in the playgrounds. We were always going down to the river to swim. When you heard the whistle blow, you would run so you'd get back on time.

If you didn't do things right, they would paddle you. They kept us under control, or at least they tried.

My last two years, I was captain of the track team at Waco High. You had to have an invitation to run track. I ended up getting a scholarship from North Texas State University for track, but that didn't work out so well. I graduated in 1941, and once the war started, the U.S. Army was going to draft you anyway, so during the Christmas holidays, I joined the Marine Corps and reported to them on January 1, 1942.

> They kept us under control, or at least they tried.

Dorothy Sue Robertson Diekmann

1928–1941

I miss the Home. I was out there during the Depression, from age five on through my teenage years. My mother had seven children, one son and six daughters, and she just couldn't take care of us. A lot of people put their children there, and when they got back on their feet, they came back and got them. Some were adopted, but my mother didn't want us to be adopted. She didn't want us separated, so she didn't sign the papers.

My parents were divorced. I was born in Muskogee, Oklahoma, but when I was a baby, my mother brought us back to Dallas. My Aunt Bess was the one who took us in her car down to the Waco State Home. My mother didn't want to go, because she was upset and crying. I'll never forget that.

I remember that Superintendent Patterson took each one of us to our

Dorothy Robertson Diekmann on the grounds of the Waco State Home, 1940.
Photo courtesy of Dorothy Robertson Diekmann.

dormitory. I would walk over to the baby cottage to visit my youngest sister. She was so cute, just a baby. She and I are the only two living now.

My father only came to visit about once a year because he lived in Oklahoma. My mother came more often than that.

As time went by, I made friends with a lot of kids out there. They were all my brothers and sisters: Gladys, Irene, Opal, Harriet, Marilee, Jackie, James, Harry, John, Jack, and so many more. I still remember them and everything about them.

I just loved Mr. Patterson to death. He was like a father to me, to all of us, and he just loved the children. The day he went to another job, I was so sad and cried all day long. I didn't blame him for leaving, though, for I heard he got a really good job.

Then Mr. Wiebusch came, and everything changed. We were all so frightened. There were letters I was supposed to get and never did, but worse things than that happened to the other girls.

There was a caseworker at the Home then, and he didn't misbehave until Mr. Patterson left. I saw in his eyes he was terrible, and I knew to stay clear of him. I think he knew I'd stand my ground. My dorm mother Mrs. Stough told me what to do to protect myself from the workers at the Home, and Mrs. Legg warned the girls who visited her in her home not to let any of the staff touch us.

At first some of the girls thought the caseworker's attentions were cute, but later they were so ashamed. One girl got pregnant, and they sent her away to have the baby, and she came back to the Home. We didn't hold it against her, though, or any of the girls who were abused, because we all thought it was just awful what was happening.

I can tell you one thing. None of that kind of stuff happened under Mr. Patterson. He would never have allowed it. He watched the employees very closely, and those who abused the children couldn't get by with that when Mr. Patterson was there.

I'm glad you're doing this book because people ought to know all the awful things that happened at the Home after Mr. Patterson left.

I enjoyed my life there before Wiebusch. It never dawned on me that I was unfortunate or lacking anything. I accepted the situation. I just really have no regrets that I was put out there. That's what I'm trying to get across.

Mrs. Legg was the best English teacher. She lived in Waco, and she taught us to love poetry and literature. I wrote my own poems while I was out there.

Reading is my hobby now. I read everything—romance, Shakespeare, biographies about special people in the world. I love to read about Lincoln, Jefferson, John Adams, and Lyndon B. Johnson. I love LBJ. I met Lady Bird, and oh, she was superb.

Wiebusch was so mean he didn't let two other girls and me walk across the stage to get our diplomas when we graduated even though we had already bought our dresses for the ceremony. Two weeks before graduation, he sent us to the NYA (National Youth Administration) to do sheet-metal work for almost a year.

I finished the eleventh grade, which was the last grade in high school in those days. It was 1941, the year that the Japanese bombed Pearl Harbor and we got into the war. I moved to Fort Worth and worked at the Consolidated Aircraft plant, which is the Lockheed plant now. I was a riveter. I did rivets, welding, soldering, and all those jobs that men do. When the men came back after the war, they laid the women off. I made good money when I worked there.

After we left the Home, the siblings remained close. I would visit them often. My mother and my aunts lived in Dallas, so I would take the bus to see them.

I met a wonderful man named John Diekmann.

> I just loved Mr. Patterson to death. He was like a father to me, to all of us, and he just loved the children.

He was from New York and in the air force. We met at the downtown USO, where I worked as a greeter. We wanted to wait until after the war to get married. We got engaged the day he left for Europe. He was a draftsman and made the maps they used to bomb Germany and for the D-Day invasion at Normandy. He had his own office in Paris, and he met all the big wheels over there, General Eisenhower, Charles de Gaulle, and General Patton. We got married April 1, 1946, and lived together until he died in 1999.

We had two sons who are still living, John Arthur and Richard Edward Diekmann.

When John left the service, he went to work as a draftsman for General Dynamics. He was an artist, too. He painted beautiful pictures that I've got in my home. He was just a crackerjack.

My brother was in the army and played trombone in the army band. He continued to play after the army, too. He was superb with that trombone. Glenn Miller and the big-band swing guys were his favorites.

The Home set me on the right path. I learned the Bible and all those famous quotes in the Bible. I go to church and I give my portion.

I keep going. My doctor told me, "You're just like a young teenager." I told him that I do yard work, that I love Mother Earth.

I am blessed with my life. I lived my life to the fullest, and I have no regrets at all.

Prentiss "Stick" Andrews

1933–1940

I went to the Home in about 1933, when I was eleven, along with my sister. We came from Dallas. My grandmother had been taking care of us, and my grandfather had passed away. My uncle was taking care of his wife, his two kids, and my grandmother, and he couldn't handle it. He wasn't making that much money, so he had to do something.

He talked to another uncle down in Waco and got us into the Waco State Home. My mother and father both remarried, had a lot of kids, and neither one of them wanted to take us. My parents never came to visit us, but fairly often my uncle would come pick me up for the weekend. He had three daughters. His younger daughter was always cooking, making cakes and pies, so I enjoyed going. One of them ended up opening a pie shop in Pasadena. She could make good pies, I tell you.

Dick Hudman was a good friend. The boys used to play up and down the Bosque River. Once we found a sunken canoe. We pulled it out and patched

Prentiss "Stick" Andrews with a friend on the grounds of the Waco State Home, 1939. Harold Larson's private collection.

it up and played with it a long time. I bought a little .22 rifle at Montgomery Ward, and when we got back to the Home, it turned out that this other guy had stolen a telescopic sight from there. We put it on the gun, and we'd go up and down the river, shooting squirrels out of the trees. It was a lot of fun. The nurses had their own kitchen, and they'd cook them for us. One time I got caught on posted land by a guard, so the superintendent, Mr. Patterson, took my gun away.

We'd set varmint traps in the park, too. We never caught anything, though.

We did a lot of trotlining at Lovers' Leap, and we'd catch quite a few catfish. Mr. Patterson would give us permission to spend the night on the river. We'd sit out there and drink coffee while running our trotlines. We'd lie down on some blankets on the gravel bar and sleep and talk. Yeah, it was fun.

> We'd go up and down the river, shooting squirrels out of the trees.

I worked in the dairy quite a while. When I worked in the boiler room, I helped fire the boilers for the radiators. It was quite interesting. In the laundry, I worked on the mangle [a device that uses heated rollers to smooth out wrinkles in clothes], which just about everybody had to do, and the steam press. It was hot out there.

I had one or two spankings while I was there. Some of us broke into the kitchen one night and got some jelly and bread and peanut butter, all that good stuff. Bill Holder, who was raised in the Home and came back to work there, had a bed check, and so he was waiting on us. I had to go up to the boiler room for my whipping. We called it a "busting." He had me lean over that big pipe there, and he gave me a few licks with a big wooden paddle. It hurt. He was a nice guy, and everybody liked him. He had to do something like that if kids did something that bad.

My sister got spankings just about every day. She was always in trouble. One day, one of the girls stole a pair of her panties. My sister found out, and she went out on the grounds, found the girl, and took them off her in front of everybody.

My sister and I were always close. Every day after supper she'd want to go sit on the steps and talk.

One day one of the boys went down to the river. He wanted to prove that he was good at something, so he told everybody he was going to either swim or drown. He drowned. It upset the other kids. I don't remember his name now.

I went out for football, but I was skinny, and after they ran over me a few times, I decided I didn't like football, so I quit. The only sport I played was washers. I beat everybody in the Home because I was good.

We had a band with quite a few members. Mr. Burnett was the band director. I learned to play the baritone. Some of us kids would have jam sessions once in a while, and I played the bass then. Mr. Burnett would let us practice any time we wanted. We enjoyed that.

Some of the kids washed employees' cars and got paid for it. I had a little paper route and carried the north side of Waco near the Home. I made a little extra money and was able to buy a bicycle to do my route. I left the Home in 1940, while I was at Waco High School. I quit school and went into the service. I was in the National Guard in Waco, Thirty-sixth Infantry Division, and I went into active service at Brownwood.

My wife died last October. I met her in France during the war and brought her over here to Dallas. I had a good, sweet wife. I was real lucky.

One of my friends from the Home was in my army outfit. He was also my best man when my wife and I got married in France.

In later years, we went back to France quite often. One time I let her and my four-year-old daughter go over on a boat, and my wife was seasick the whole time. She stayed in the ship's hospital all the way across. My daughter had the run of the ship.

My wife went to cooking school in Paris. She organized a French club here and had about thirty members. A lot of times, she would invite the whole club over and fix supper for them.

One thing about my family is, I never used to hear any of them say, "I love you." Aunts, uncles, and grandmother—none of them ever said, "I love you." Not just to me—I never heard them say it to their own people. Never heard the words. My aunt and uncle in Waco never said, "I love you" to their kids, and they were good Christian people, real active in the Church of Christ there. My uncle must have given all his money to the church because he didn't have any when he died, as far as I know.

My daughter is sixty years old now, and she's heard me say, "I love you" many, many times.

Oletha "Lee" Dorrough McConnell

1937–1941

I was admitted to the Home in 1937, when I was about twelve years old. There were nine of us children. My uncle was responsible for getting five of us in there. We were just underprivileged. Our home life was very disruptive, and my mother was forced to leave home by my father. Our living conditions in Chandler, Texas, were very, very primitive. My father was very unkind. I don't remember how frequently he came to visit. I don't remember my mother coming to visit at all.

I was delighted to be at the Home. I had all of these schoolmates to play with. I just felt fortunate to have my needs met.

One thing I remember is that we were taught to work. We worked all over the school. We maintained the dormitory that we were in, we worked in the laundry, and we worked in the dining room.

I worked in the dispensary for a while. They had several private rooms and two larger wards—one for male and one for female, of course. They had two nurses, and the doctors came out as needed.

Oletha Dorrough McConnell, age seventeen, wearing a dress made in the sewing room
of the Waco State Home, c. 1942. Photo courtesy of Oletha Dorrough McConnell.

I was working at the baby cottage when my younger brother, Russ, was admitted to the Home. I worked wherever they needed somebody.

When I was at the Home, we made all of our clothes. I still do a lot of sewing. Occasionally, we were allowed to go down to a store to select costumes or gifts or something. We were granted gifts occasionally. I don't know who provided them. A store in town sometimes invited us to come in and select a gift.

We all had our own duties. Some cleaned floors, some did windows. We maintained our own rooms. Each room had two to four girls in it, depending on the room.

We had sports. My brothers were on the football team. Some of us played tennis or basketball.

The Christmas visits with a family in town were enjoyable. I guess I'm a person that sort of goes with the flow. Wherever I am, that's it.

Discipline was merciful. I don't remember any great disturbances or upheavals. Maybe it's convenient forgetting, but I really don't remember anything like that.

There were some girls who did not want to be there. Some handled it day by day, so to speak. There were so many different personalities, so many interests. I'm sure there were restrictions for some of the girls who disobeyed the rules or acted up, but I really don't dwell on that, and I do not remember.

> I guess I'm a person that sort of goes with the flow. Wherever I am, that's it.

Superintendent Wiebusch was the thorn in the ointment. He was not a nice person. I'm sure that he was responsible for a lot of the discord that was present during that time.

I enjoyed school. I'm one that is interested in learning, so I just progressed. I received a good, basic education. I learned to work, and that has sustained me over the years.

The English teacher, Mrs. Legg, was more or less the mother of the school. She was a grand person, and she influenced all of us.

After I graduated from the high school, I attended business school. I went into clerical work and traveled all over. I took employment with the Department of Defense in different places, like Hawaii and Guam. I did not stay more than a couple of years in one place until I went to Alaska.

I have always been in a group, so to speak. I lived at the YWCA. I went into the Army Reserves. That was the way I got to Alaska, when I went from active duty to reserves.

I remember the Home as one big, kind, generous family. All of our needs were met, so we were cushioned from the outside, so to speak. We were not permitted to make decisions like an average family does. I find that I have difficulty making decisions, and I'm sure that's the reason for it. All of our decisions were made for us: "Girls, go over here and fold this laundry, put this up. We're going to go here at a certain time, be ready," that sort of thing.

I live in Freeport, Florida, now with my daughter.

Roy Dorrough

1938–1950

I was born in Chandler, Texas, in 1932. There were nine kids. Times were hard. Where we lived, you could see daylight through the cracks between the boards in the walls.

My father was mean. Nobody liked him. When I was three or four years old, he would go off to town and we'd have to fend for ourselves—eat whatever we could find, things like that.

My mother was a gentle person. She took up for my father like you wouldn't believe. They fought a lot, and finally my mother was forced to leave us. My oldest sister ran away when she was a teenager.

We stayed with an aunt for a while, but they didn't have room for us or

Roy Dorrough standing by the calf barn at the Waco State Home, 1948. Harold Larson's private collection.

the money to support us, so the county people picked us up, and we were taken to the Waco State Home.

They put us in the hospital under quarantine for two weeks to make sure we didn't have any diseases. I cried my eyes out. I wanted my dad.

My mother came to visit us once. Just one time. My dad came out every four years, maybe four or five times total. He would stay a couple of hours, and then he was gone.

You stayed in the baby cottage until you were five or six. My older sister worked there, so I could get anything I wanted.

Ms. Cashion, who was in charge of the boys' upstairs dorm, was the most loved matron out there. Whenever Ms. Cashion spoke, you listened. You moved when she said, "Move." Every boy that graduated and left or ran off and came back to visit, the first person they'd run to was Ms. Cashion. They loved her that much.

She busted my hide quite a few times, though. That was no fun.

Ms. Ball was the relief matron on the weekend. We hated Ms. Ball. She'd whip you with a hairbrush. She had a rotten personality.

At the hospital, you had two nurses, Miss Noonan, who was an angel, and Ms. German, who was awful. She was ugly. We hated her.

We had movies upstairs in the big room. There was a big, honest-to-God projector, and they showed the movies up on the stage on a big screen. We enjoyed that.

We'd have rock fights with each other for fun. We never got in trouble for it because we never got caught. We'd also go up to the shed where they stored the onions, tomatoes, potatoes, and other crops. The boys would divide up into teams, like four against four, something like that, and throw those onions and tomatoes and potatoes at each other. You'd come out of there stinking like you wouldn't believe. We'd run out of there fast and get in the shower, and they'd never catch us.

We had a big hay barn. It held around 5,000 bales at a time. We'd go in there, dig tunnels, and smoke cigarettes. It was hot as hell, and it was dangerous. It could've made one hell of a fire, too.

The only way you could get caught was if Mr. Whigham came around sniffing us. He'd say, "You've been smoking. You've been campused."

I started working at the farm after I turned eleven. Everybody was issued a hoe. We grew our own vegetables. We had a berry patch, too.

They gave the boys striped overalls to wear. It was embarrassing. It made us stick out like a sore thumb around the regular kids whenever we went to town. At one point, my first wife wanted to buy the kids some striped coveralls to wear, but I said, "I will kill you if you do." I scared the devil out of her.

We were tough kids. When I played football my senior year, I weighed 129 pounds. Our heaviest guy—we called him Buck—weighed 165 pounds. Buck made all-district, and Billy, our fullback, made all-district, too.

Our football team was out of this world. In 1938 to 1939, before the war, we played Hillsboro, beat them 14 to nothing. In 1938, we were unbeaten, untied, and unscored upon. In 1939, we were unbeaten and untied. Waco High would not play us. They were scared to death of us.

We played anybody and everybody. We had just barely enough to make a team. We did it by robbing the eighth grade to get enough boys, and the district let us get by with it. By my senior year, we had good equipment. Before that, I think the state was afraid to let go of a dollar. We practically had to beg to get anything.

I ran away twice. The first time, I didn't get very far, and the second time, I made it as far as Gatesville. I found the family who had taken me in the previous Christmas. I worked, but I didn't expect any pay. I was just a kid. I just wanted three meals a day and

I started working at the farm after I turned eleven. Everybody was issued a hoe.

a place to sleep. I didn't know it, but the man called the Home, told them where I was, and they came out there and got me.

A couple from Crawford, Texas, almost adopted me. I was about fifteen, which is really too old to be adopted. The man owned a ranch near Crawford, and he had a son serving in the navy. I'd been there two weeks when the son received his discharge and came home. The man took me to one side and said, "You don't fit what we're looking for." He was looking for a certain type, and I didn't fit his criteria. That's as close as I ever came to being adopted.

I was told that when all the abuse at the Home was going on, they had a court hearing in Waco, but I don't think they ever indicted anybody. Superintendent Wiebusch was a horse's butt, believe me. I remember one time an ex-student named JC came to see Ms. Cashion. He came straight to Ms. Cashion's dorm upstairs. He was on the stairs, and Wiebusch was right behind him and said, "You can't go up there."

JC said, "Yes, I can. I'm going to see Ms. Cashion."

Wiebusch shoved JC back down the stairs and out the door. Ms. Cashion came out and asked us what all the excitement was about. We told her JC came to see her but Mr. Wiebusch wouldn't let him. Here she goes down the stairs. She cornered Wiebusch and read him the riot act. Wiebusch did not bother anybody who came to see her after that. We all laughed about that one.

Wiebusch hired Roy Lawrence and all his old cronies, and all hell broke loose. I mean it was a living hell for everybody, boys and girls.

Some of the girls out there were gorgeous, and everybody in town wanted to get to them. Wiebusch and these dudes, these clowns he hired, they did their thing with the girls. One of our guys caught one of Wiebusch's cronies with a girl from the Home. The next day, the crony told our guy, "You can leave now and we won't chase you, but you have to leave right now and keep your mouth shut." He left.

When I got into the eleventh grade, I had a chip on my shoulder. I wanted to join the army, but I wasn't old enough. I tried my damnedest to get Mr. Whigham to sign a waiver so I could get in, but he wouldn't do it. I was mad as a hornet. I hung around there, hoping they'd make me leave, but they didn't. My sister told me later she was ready to take me in, but I didn't know that at the time.

So I quit school, and they put me to work out there at the Home, worked my butt off. I wasn't getting paid for it either.

Every night we'd come in, and Mr. Whigham would come zipping through and say, "Boy, we're gonna have a heck of a football team this year, with Murphy as fullback, Charlie at quarterback, and Roy." I'd say, "No, I'm not gonna play."

Every night he'd pull that. I got tired of it. Finally I went to Mr. Whigham and said, "Can you get me back in school?" And he grinned and said, "Yeah, we'll get you back in tomorrow morning."

So I finished school and then joined the army. I can see kids out there who didn't finish high school, can't hold a job, down on their luck, half of them drunks or drug users, and I say, "There but by the grace of God . . ."

I did not like old man Whigham, but I respected him. If not for him, no telling what would have happened to me. I'm happy. I'm doing what I want to do. I'm retired. No problems, no worries.

When I signed up for the army in 1950, I volunteered for Korea, but they sent me to Germany. I was a wheeled-vehicle mechanic, also a truck driver and a motor sergeant. When I got out, I went to work for Lennox Air Conditioning, although it was Lennox Furnace Company back then. I was running the big metal cutting shears in the shop—the biggest set of shears in the shop, cutting quarter-inch sheets of metal plate. "Cling! Cling!" all day long. I didn't like that.

Then I went to work for General Dynamics on the B-58 program. That was the big bomber that carried the atomic bomb. The company was called Convair back then. That was one beautiful plane.

After I got laid off from Convair, I went to work for

Cummins Sales and Service, and I've been a diesel mechanic ever since.

Fort Worth, Dallas, Shreveport, Monroe, back to Dallas, then I joined the navy. I went to Vietnam twice, got hit by Agent Orange. I still have a problem from that and prostate cancer, which is now in remission. I think it's gone. I hope.

I went to Iraq for a year and half, had a blast over there. I was rebuilding starters on Humvees at Balad Air Force Base.

I live in Mansfield, Texas. I've got three grown boys. The youngest has one boy, and he lives in Austin. I've got another one who lives about 200 yards from me, and he has a boy. My oldest boy lives here with me, and he's got two boys, too.

You better believe I'll be at the next reunion. There's a girl living in Houston. She graduated a year before I did, and I love her to death. I haven't seen her in, God, I don't know how many years. I conned her into coming to the reunion. I hope she comes. I told her that if nobody will take her, I'll come down there and get her. If she doesn't make it, she'll get the biggest butt-chewing you ever heard in your life. Because a promise is a promise.

Russell Dorrough

1939–1952

I was five years old in 1939, when I was sent to the Home. I had two sisters and two brothers already there, out of nine siblings.

My older sister didn't like the Home too much, so she ran off. She went out to my oldest sister's place in Henderson County. Whenever the state vehicle would show up looking for her, she'd disappear into the woods until they left. They finally gave up.

I graduated in 1952. I'd say that I was the smartest boy in my class. There were only two boys; the rest of the class was girls. My oldest brother left the Home and joined the army. He was part of the first occupation forces in Japan. My brother Roy graduated in 1950. Shortly

Russell Dorrough, right, with his friends, including John Wilson, left, in front of the big boys' dormitory. Harold Larson's private collection.

after that, he joined the army. My remaining sister graduated sometime in the forties. She also joined the army [WACs].

My dad was able to come visit us twice, I think. One time they let Roy and me go home for a couple of weeks. We used to say, "One of these days, we're gonna get to go home forever."

I was told by my sisters and brothers that my dad was kind of mean, but he was never mean to me. I loved him dearly, and I loved my mother, too. I didn't get to see her again until after I got out of high school and joined the air force. That would've been about 1954. My dad died in 1956.

I grew up with the other kids at the Home, and they were family. That was really the only home I ever knew. For the most part, we were very well treated. We got our education, good food, clothing, and shelter.

Mrs. Gertrude B. Cashion was the matron at the upstairs dormitory. She had an eagle eye, and if one of us so much as picked up a rock, she could holler out her window, and I swear you could hear her all the way to the river. If we threw the rock, we'd get a lick that night before bedtime.

I moved from the Hackney dorm downstairs, then to the Whigham dorm upstairs. At each dorm level, we had chores to do. We had to clean the dorm as younger kids and mow the lawns and other yard work as we got a little older.

I remember excitedly awaiting spring and warm weather so we could go barefoot. By the end of summer, my feet would be so tough, I think I could have walked on fire and not even flinched.

We had our own dairy, where we processed our milk and made ice cream. That's the best ice cream I've ever had. Mr. McClain was in charge of the dairy. He was the spitting image of Gary Cooper. He was a tall, good-looking man and a really nice guy. The older boys had to go out at five in the morning to milk cows. The younger boys milked in the afternoons.

My first experience on the morning milking shift was going to the kitchen to pick up empty milk cans and taking them back to the dairy barn to wash and sterilize them. After a couple years of that, I graduated to "herding boy." I had to be the first to the dairy to wake up the cows for milking.

The state leased two farms near the lake. The high school boys worked those. We raised all our vegetables, which were brought back to the Home. Some were served as fresh vegetables, and the rest were canned for future use. We also raised grain and grass and baled hay. The grain was mixed and fed to our livestock and chickens. On weekends we would butcher at least four hogs, sometimes a beef steer or a bunch of chickens.

The last year, I was in charge of feeding the pigs. We exhibited the best ones at the Fat Stock Show in Fort Worth. Our pigs took either first or second place in each of the four categories, and one of them took reserve grand champion.

The only pets we could keep were pigeons. We used scrap lumber and chicken wire and built a pigeon house. We even took some of them to the state fair and turned them loose, and they were there waiting for us when we got home.

In high school, I believe we had some of the best teachers in the whole state. My favorite was my English teacher, Mrs. Vernon Legg. When I first started going back for reunions, I'd always get a big hug from her. I was her prize student. I'd say to everyone, "Yeah, she learned me everything I knowed about language," and she'd whop me one.

A couple of years before I left, Mrs. Balch taught us square dancing. That was fun. We went to square-dance exhibitions all over Houston, Austin, and Fort Worth. We were good! The high point of my square-dancing career was when we went to the Watermelon Festival in Atlanta, Texas. The original square took first place, and they got a plaque. My square took

> The main thing I got from the Home is that I learned a good work ethic.

second. We got a big watermelon that weighed 120 pounds. We were also on Fort Worth television. We gave an exhibition dance during the Fort Worth Stock Show at the [Will Rogers] Coliseum.

We played all kinds of sports—football, baseball, basketball, volleyball, and track. My senior year, 1952, we won the district mile relay. At this relay, I ran the third leg. We broke the record that had stood for fourteen years. We then went to Dallas to the SMU campus for the regional meet. I still have my letter jacket.

The girls had their dormitories, the boys had ours, and "never the twain should meet," but there were several ways to get between the dormitories without being seen. There was a boiler room, where steam was piped through tunnels to the dormitories. Some kids found if they lifted the cover off some of those tunnels, they could go from one dormitory to the next. I even tried it once, but it wasn't real comfortable in there.

As we got older, we could leave the campus on Saturday and Sunday afternoons. To make any kind of money at all, we would go to the golf course and caddy or work for somebody—mowing yards or something.

The best money I ever made caddying was $1.50. Sometimes we'd go to the gun club for skeet tournaments and make a little bit better money.

Also we could go downtown. All we had to do was go to the theater and say, "We're the State Homers," and they'd let us in free. Dan, who grew up in the Home, came back from the army and saved up enough money to buy a Dairy Queen. He ended up having a whole string of them, so we could drop by and get a free hamburger.

On trips back from town, there was an old sporting-goods store where we'd always stop and look at the airplane model kits.

On Sundays we would have church services in the auditorium, and Baylor University's divinity students would come out and practice on us.

We knew if we were going to do something that we shouldn't be doing and got caught, we would get licks. They were heavier licks than even Miss Cashion could give. It was mostly that or getting what they called "campused" for two weeks. Or we couldn't go to the Sunday-night movie in the auditorium. It wasn't tough, but it was strict.

The local Soil Conservation Service [SCS] would select farmers who were having problems and needed help. Local contractors, fuel suppliers, and equipment suppliers would come in and build fences, build barns, or dig the pools for stock tanks. The Future Farmers of America boys at the Home would go out and help. It was really fascinating to me. That's how I got interested in SCS.

I personally believe that growing up out there was the best thing for us because we had food, clothing, shelter, and education. The main thing I got from the Home is that I learned a good work ethic. When I joined the air force, it was like a country club in comparison. I had twenty-three years in the air force. After retirement, I went to school at East Texas State University at Commerce, got my degree, and went to work with the SCS. I am now retired from there after twenty-one years.

Sue Williamson Stolz

1938–1949

My father was dying with kidney problems, and my mother had a nervous breakdown. This was during the Depression. I was born in 1931, the oldest of four little girls. For a while, we each lived with an aunt and uncle. My youngest sister, who was just a baby, was adopted. The idea of us all being separated just killed my grandmother, so she checked around and arranged for us to be admitted to the Waco State Home. That was 1938, when I was seven years old.

My mother went to live with a sister in Dallas. We lost touch with the youngest sister, Mary, until we were teenagers. We started corresponding with her, and we have remained close all these years.

At first I hated the Home. I thought it was the end of my life.

Eventually, I started to have fun and made a lot of friends, but it was not like a family. I missed having a family. I remember, until I was ten years old, every night I prayed, "Lord, please let me have a family again, and also,

Sue Williamson Stolz, right, and her sister Betty on their Waco State Home trip to the State Fair of Texas, 1940s. Photo courtesy of Sue Williamson Stolz.

please let me wake up in the morning with curly hair."

Now when I hear about kids in foster homes being mistreated and other things like that, I realize we were really fortunate.

They had a good school. By the time I was there, I had already been to several schools, but they kept me in first grade because they did not know what else to do with me. Later, when they changed from an eleven-year school to twelve years, I got to skip the fourth grade.

When I was in ninth or tenth grade, I competed in the University Interscholastic League, where schools all over the state competed in different subjects. It was my first year taking typing, and I thought I would never get the hang of it, but I ended up going to the state competition. I came in second place, only because I was typing so fast I left out a line; otherwise, I would have been first place. I won a scholarship to a business college in Austin.

My favorite teacher was Mrs. Legg. She was very strict, but she was a good teacher. My sister sent me a poem that a boy had written about her. It is a beautiful poem.

At the reunion I attended, Mrs. Legg was 100 years old, and it was surprising how good her memory was. It was wonderful to hear her talk and hear the kids stand up and tell the different things she did.

Mrs. Legg was better than most teachers are today, I think. I hate to say it, but I think we learned more than kids learn today. We didn't have computers and things like that, but we were educated by the time we graduated.

Mrs. Bramlett taught history in the ninth grade, and everybody enjoyed her class.

I took speech lessons and took private piano lessons for two or three years and gave recitals. My redheaded piano teacher would rap you on the fingers with a pencil whenever you made a mistake, which did not make me happy at all.

> My husband said, "Do you know how lucky you were?"

Actually, I don't know why they picked me to take piano lessons, because I was more of a sports girl. I liked playing baseball and basketball. All those years I had to take piano lessons in the auditorium, I could hear the kids playing outside, and I thought, "Wow, I am wasting my life." Now all I can do on the piano is find middle C.

When I was in tenth or eleventh grade I was voted Future Farmers of America Sweetheart. It was supposed to be a secret until they made the official announcement, but this boy named Roy told me. I asked him what that meant. What would I have to do? He said, "You'll have to look pretty, make speeches, and kiss all the boys." I said, "Okay!"

When they announced that I had won, they started yelling for a speech. I said, "When I asked Roy what my duties would be, he told me I had to look pretty, make speeches, and kiss all the boys, and I intend to fulfill all my duties!"

I still have my jacket. It is a little bit tight, but I still have it.

The worst punishment I ever got was to stand in the hall. I do not remember what I did to get punished. I never got a spanking, although I know some did. I do not think we were ever mistreated. I have nothing bad to say about the Home.

The food was delicious, except I did not like eating spinach. I was skinny, but I ate a lot. I worked in the dining room, and at breakfast I would go in the back and scrape the cream off the milk and put pure cream on my cereal. It was so good. I loved Saturdays because we had beans, cornbread, macaroni, and tomatoes.

I loved summer camp, too, because we would have lunchmeat, cucumbers, and other food on a long buffet table.

When I got older, I waited on the table where the teachers and other workers ate. Every Saturday they would leave a tip. Fifty cents was a lot of money back then.

I would save my tips for the state fair in Dallas. My sister and I would go there and have a ball. We have a lot of pictures of us at the fair, having a good time.

I only went home with a family for Christmas once. I did not care for that. It made me feel ill at ease.

Every Christmas, we got to make a list of things we would like to have. You could have only one item that cost a dollar. I wanted a pair of skates and a permanent wave. I thought about it and thought about it, but I could not make up my mind between the two. Did I want to be beautiful or have fun? I ended up putting both on the list.

So I got the roller skates, and just two or three months later, they put a beauty shop in the Home so girls could learn to cut and fix hair. Every week I went there and got my hair fixed. So I got both things I wanted.

The last six months of my senior year, I had a job. I worked, and did all my schoolwork at night. I am not bragging, but I could do all my schoolwork without really trying. Besides that, I was making money. By the time I graduated, I had a few hundred dollars saved up, so I was blessed.

I graduated when I was eighteen with a 94.6 average. I could have had a scholarship to college, but that would mean going to another town and finding another job, and I was already making twenty-five dollars a week.

Back then, there were only three options for a girl. You could be a nurse, a secretary, or a teacher. I was already a secretary, and since I did not want to be a teacher or a nurse, I did not attend college.

I worked at an accounting firm, then at a lumberyard. My first husband, Ray, is the father of my sons. We divorced in 1985. I married my second husband, Edward, and moved to Dallas. We both worked for the electric company and retired in 1987. Edward died in May of 2008. Then in July, my son Gordon died of melanoma, so that was a tough year. Gordon worked at Baylor Hospital for thirty-three years, then at the Methodist hospital. Even though he was only at the Methodist hospital for five years, the hospital put up a stone memorial and planted a tree in his honor.

A couple of years ago, I told my husband, "You know, we had good clothes, a good school, good food, and we had to go to church on Sunday. We got to go swimming twice a week during the summer. We got to go down to the coast on vacations, down to Austin, too. We had a movie every Friday night at the Home, and on Saturday we got to go to a movie in town." My husband said, "Do you know how lucky you were? I never got to see a movie until I was sixteen years old." He thought we just had it made.

Betty Williamson Gatlin

1939–1950

I was six years old when I was admitted to the Home. I had three sisters. One of them was adopted, and the rest of us went to the Home. Before that, we stayed with our aunts.

I don't remember exactly how we ended up being transferred to the Home, but it was because of the Depression. My parents just couldn't provide for us. My father wanted us to stay together, and my mother said the most important thing for us was to get an education, which we did. Our parents and other relatives came to visit us often.

One thing I will never forget is the evening I was playing in the yard and Mrs. Shelton called me over and asked me to walk down the sidewalk for her. I did not know why she asked. The next day, she took me into the superintendent's office and explained that something was very wrong with my foot. It turned out to be polio.

Left to right: *Betty Williamson Gatlin with her sisters Dorothy Mae and Sue. Photo courtesy of Betty Williamson Gatlin.*

I had to have a series of surgeries on my foot and spent the rest of my years at the Waco State Home wearing a cast or a brace and using crutches. Because I was not always as mobile as other kids, I was always doing things with my hands, like knitting and crocheting, so they called me "Grandma." I am still Grandma to everybody now, except I am actually a great-grandmother.

I started off at the baby cottage and moved on to the other dorms as I got older. I have nothing but good memories of the houseparents at each of the dorms. They were all kind to me.

The school was very good. We had the best teachers in the world. I was very fond of my English teacher, Mrs. Legg. I also kept in touch with Mrs. Rose, my eighth-grade teacher.

Because of my polio, I wasn't in sports or the band, and I didn't do all the jobs that some of the girls did, but we were always busy. We went to camp every summer for two weeks, and that was great. One summer, I had just had surgery on my foot, and I said I couldn't go. They told me, "Yes, you're going. You can walk. If there's a place you can't walk, we'll carry you." So I went and had a great time.

Going home with a family for Christmas was really fun. I remember going to stay with the Kunschik family in Austin one Christmas. Governor W. Lee O'Daniel took another student, and they took us all on a tour of the Governor's Mansion.

All our clothes were made at the sewing room. I would pick out the patterns I liked, and they would sew them for me. If the patterns were a little out of date, it didn't matter, because we weren't out in public a lot anyway.

The people in Waco were nice to us when we interacted with them. Of course, some people stared because I had crutches, and sometimes they would ask if I had broken my leg, but that happens wherever you go.

I graduated in 1950 and attended the Four-C Business College in Waco. When I graduated, there was a job waiting for me at William Cameron and Company. In 1954, I married Richard Gatlin, another student from the Waco State Home. We had three kids. When our kids were growing up, once in a while they would accuse me of raising them the same way Richard and I grew up in the Home, but I said, "That's all I know." They turned out wonderful.

Richard passed away last year, and it is still too painful to talk about. But I will say that my husband would want me to pass on his own appreciation for the Waco State Home.

I still stay in touch with my friends from the school, and I've been to every reunion except one. I only have good memories. Some of the kids were unhappy, some were renegades. When they wanted to run away, I would say, "Where are you going to go? Look at what you have here. Look at how good you've got it right here."

When I think about the Waco State Home, my main emotion is gratitude. Because of a caring person like Mrs. Shelton looking out for me, I got the care I needed.

At this time I am seventy-seven years old, and I am still walking.

> Because of a caring person like Mrs. Shelton looking out for me, I got the care I needed.

William "Bailey" Yarbrough

1939–1943

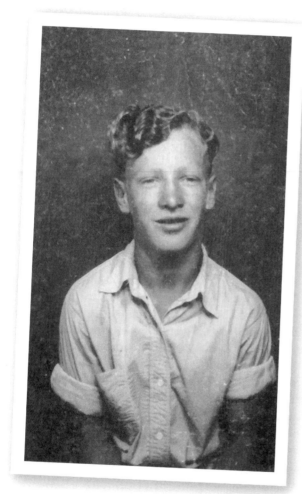

My father had cancer and just could not take care of my brother and me. He put us in the Waco State Home in February of 1939. He died in July of that year, so he got us admitted just in time. It was the Depression. This happened to a lot of kids back then.

My brother was eighteen months older, so he went straight to the big boys' dorm and worked on the dairy farm. He kept running away, though. The third time he ran away, they did not go after him. He was only there about three years.

When I got there, I was ten years old. I started out in the little boys' dorm. They had a matron for upstairs and another for downstairs, about thirty-five or forty kids on each floor. I hated it at first.

The kids still went to school at the Home when I was there. After I left, they let them go to school in town. The school system seemed pretty good.

The high school was in the same building as the administration building.

On the back side of it was the auditorium. We watched movies in the auditorium, and we also had our church services there. The boys sat on one side, the girls on the other. They did not let the boys and girls mix very much.

The superintendent lived in a house by the gate. The last time I was there, the house was still there.

We had a dining room, our own clinic, and a laundry room. Mrs. Belk ran the laundry room. She was a good lady.

We had a dairy with our own pasteurizer. Each boy had to get up and milk six cows every morning. Farmer McClain ran the dairy. He was a good man. I liked him. The big boys also had to work in the chicken barn. There was a big vegetable garden, too.

During World War I, there was an army camp there called Camp MacArthur. There were still trenches and ropes on the property where the soldiers trained. We would swing on those ropes and play cowboys and Indians in those trenches. The Cyclone fence around the grounds was from the army camp, too.

When we got older, we got to go to the Waco golf course and caddy and make a little spending money. In those days, you could go down to Cameron Park and rent a bicycle for half a day and ride through the park or wherever you wanted to go. For a dollar, you could have the bike for the whole day.

We had a radio in our dorm. Mostly, we listened to programs like *The Lone Ranger* and *The Shadow*.

One morning, the matron came in and woke us up and said the Japanese had attacked Pearl Harbor and we were at war. I was thirteen years old.

The older buildings at the Home had a covered passageway between them called a pergola. Usually, they are used for weddings and gatherings that need a little shelter from the rain or the hot sun. When you got in trouble, Ms. Cashion, the upstairs matron, would restrict you to the pergola, and if she said you had to stay there, you had better stay or you would really be in trouble.

I learned how to play baseball there. I played

football, too. We used to play against Crawford, where George W. Bush has his place. We also played the Gatesville State School, Hubbard, Mexia, and a Masonic home in Dallas. Our team was called the Hornets.

A big guy named Roy Lawrence was the coach and athletic director. He was also the person who did the whipping. He had a big board, and he would really bust you with it. Judge Patterson was superintendent when I first got there, but then Wiebusch took over. Wiebusch and Lawrence whipped some girls pretty badly. There was an investigation, and Mrs. German, the nurse, denied that this particular girl had any bruises. Officials from Austin came to the Home and met with the girl. The girl pulled up her skirt and pulled down her drawers, and the bruises were plain to see. Wiebusch, Lawrence, and German all got fired.

I did not like the Waco area. It was hot and humid in the summer, and in the fall it rained a lot. There were mosquitoes and lots of chiggers.

One time these girls found a cute little kitten and brought it into the dorm, and we ended up being quarantined because of diphtheria. The whole place, all the kids and the employees, were put under quarantine, no vacation or anything. I was told cats get diphtheria from eating field mice.

My uncle came and got me in September 1943, when I was fifteen. He wanted me to work on his ranch in McGregor. My brother was at another ranch in Abilene.

I worked at the Grand Canyon for a while. I was employed by Fred Harvey, who owned all the concessions there at the time. I worked at Bright Angel Lodge, El Tovar, on the trail. I even worked as a bellhop for a while. In 1946, I went to Flagstaff and signed up for the Army Air Corps.

I was stationed at the Yokota Army Airfield in

I hated it when I first got there, but I decided it was one of the best things that ever happened to me.

Japan for three years. In 1948, the Air Corps became the U.S. Air Force, so when I was discharged, I was discharged from the USAF. When I got out, I went back to work at the Grand Canyon and got married.

My brother joined the army and was in World War II and Korea. At one time, he was stationed just thirty-five miles from Yokota.

I got my GED at South Plains College and went to work for a little oil company, then worked for Amoco. After thirty-two years, I retired. I have a pretty good retirement, and I have two children. I have been married for fifty-seven years. So I would say things turned out pretty well for me.

I made a lot of friends at the Waco State Home. I went to see a few of them at the last reunion I attended, a few years ago. I stay in touch with some, too. One of the guys came by to see me just the other day.

Most of them have passed on, though. Another one passed away in the last year. I do not think I will go again. I will be eighty-one in November of 2009, so I am getting too old to go.

At the last reunion, I saw my old friend Dan. He was one of the kids at the Home who wound up a millionaire. He had a string of Dairy Queens.

My feelings about the Waco State Home are pretty positive. I hated it when I first got there, but I decided it was one of the best things that ever happened to me. There is no telling where I would have wound up otherwise.

My experiences there helped me get through life. They taught you right from wrong. One lady was real good about teaching us the Bible when we were little. The kids took care of each other. The big kids took care of the little kids.

I have been back in West Texas ever since I went to work for the oil company. I like it here. It gets cool at night, and the wind blows a lot. There are no chiggers here, either.

Charles Goodson

1939–1952

I went out to the Waco State Home in 1939, and when I left, I had been there longer than anyone out there, employees and all.

I was born in a dirt-floor tent at Gilmer, Texas, on the old Cherokee Trace. I remember Mama sweeping the dirt floor with a broom she had made. My brother, who was about fourteen, was doing the hunting and stuff for us so we'd have something to eat. He killed birds, armadillos, possums, just anything to feed us. He stored our meat supply in the tent by salting it down so it would not spoil.

I was told that we were starving to death when the state picked us up. I suppose someone noticed that we were not eating regularly, so the state came out and took my sister and me to the Waco State Home. I was about three years old. We had another sister, who was in the Mexia State School.

I remember absolutely nothing about my father. I was told that Daddy would lie underneath the wagon while Mama picked cotton, but I can't back any of that up.

Charles Goodson, photographed by his wife many years after he left the Waco State Home. Photo courtesy of Charles Goodson.

My father would not work, but it is the opposite with me. I am seventy-two years old now, and I work five or six days a week. One thing God has blessed me with is my health. I have been strong all my life.

My mother came out to the Home when my sister graduated. My brother brought her. That was the only time I saw my mother in the thirteen years I was there. I did not know what she looked like. I knew she was my Mama because of her features, but other than that I did not know her.

My sister kind of mothered me at the Home. She was tougher than a damned boot, and she would fight those boys if that was what it came to. Nobody picked on me. I was just a little boy, and my sister was three years older.

I started out in the baby cottage and went through the whole shebang.

I was never in any serious trouble, but I never cared to learn in school. I am not that educated now, but I read four books a week, mostly westerns, and I read all the classics, too. My bookcase must have 1,500 books in it.

You had your chores out there. At about twelve or thirteen years old, the boys went to work in the dairy barn. We called Mr. McClain "Farmer." I owe a lot to him. That guy taught me a lot, and he cared about me. He lived in Waco after he left the Home. I talked with a boy a few years ago who told me the last thing out of Farmer McClain's mouth was my name, Charles Goodson.

Mr. McClain was a great man, a great individual. I guarantee you that he looked just like Randolph Scott and had the same features. He was tall and rawboned and had a heart of gold. He cared about us boys and never raised his voice at any of us.

Johnny Wilson and I worked in the kitchen after working in the dairy barn. I believe it was on a Friday when we were told to go to the hay barn to get a sack of onions. The onions were on a wire at the top of the barn. In order to get to the onions, you had to climb up the hay. While we were up there, three other boys walked in, and we began throwing onions at them and got into a big onion fight. I noticed a wasp nest up in the rafters, so we started chunking onions at it. We couldn't knock it down, so I said, "Let's get a pole and burn it down."

We found a long pole, tied a rag on it and set it on fire. While trying to burn the nest down, a part of the rag burned off and fell into the hay. We tried to put it out, but when it was nearly extinguished, I dropped the pole and the fire started on the other side. It was out of control, so John and I got our onions and tried to look as innocent as possible.

The barn burned down. For fear of serious consequences, we never told a soul. We made a pact between us to keep our mouths shut, and nobody knew about what happened until after we got out of the Home. They said the cause of the fire was spontaneous combustion.

When I left the Home, the superintendent, Ben S. Peek, looked me straight in the eye and told me I would never amount to anything.

I'm not saying that he was a bad guy. He wanted me to stay and finish high school. He cared about us. You don't realize that when you are a boy. You don't realize that anyone cares about you besides your friends. We all said the people at the Home were mean and cruel because they whipped us and that kind of thing, but we all needed it. One matron trying to corral thirty or forty boys, you understand, was a hell of a job. I see all of that now. At that time, I couldn't see any of it. I just thought they were cruel and enjoyed whipping us.

I was always the show-off and the smart aleck. I liked to make the girls laugh, and consequently I took all the whippings and other punishments. When you got them, you didn't dare cry, because if you did, you would be a sissy.

When you were little, the matrons did the spanking, but after you got up to age eleven and twelve, they

> When Mr. Peek told me I would never amount to anything, he did not know what was in my heart.

had Mr. Whigham. We always called him "the Beater." He was a sadist. This guy loved it. We heard he came from the Gatesville School for Boys. He came out to the Home to discipline the boys—keep us in line and that kind of thing. But we hardly ever got out of line. We would have a fight every once in awhile, but everybody got along pretty well most of the time.

Whigham would whip you with all of his might. He was a big man, weighed about 250 pounds. He was also a good coach to the boys. He got us into baseball and things like that, so he had his good side. But his bad side was very bad.

I deserved every whipping I got out there except for the ones Mr. Whigham gave me. He just needed someone to whip so he could show off his authority.

He was really the only bad person out there, as far as I am concerned. We got along with everybody else. The rest were decent people.

I was already gone when some of the guys ganged up on Whigham and whipped him. I was real proud that that happened. I heard about it at a reunion. These boys just decided they had taken enough from him, so they took him down to the ground and beat the fire out of him. I don't know it for a fact, but I heard he retired and left the Home afterward.

I left the Home when I was about fifteen. The girl I was dating was two years older, so she graduated at midterm when I was in the tenth grade. We've been married now fifty-five years.

As I look back on it now, I am sorry I burned down that barn. The state fed me three meals a day and provided me with clothes, shoes, soap, toothpaste, church, and a hospital. We had so much more than any other children on the outside. All that I am, I owe to God first and the Waco State Home second.

When Mr. Peek told me I would never amount to anything, he did not know what was in my heart. Now with six figures in the bank due to hard work five or six days a week, I intend to hunt and fish and spend money in my retirement.

Doris Goodson Bray

1939–1952

I remember standing in the courtroom when the judge declared us wards of the state. I was five years old. Both of our parents were there, divorced after thirty-three years and seven kids. Our mom remarried, and her new husband didn't want the two little kids, my brother Charlie and me, so we went to the State Home.

When we got there, we were assigned to the baby cottage. Charlie was on one side with the boys, I was on the other side with the girls. We'd meet in the living room before bedtime so I could kiss him good night. We'd lie there and look at each other across the room until we fell asleep.

Doris Goodson Bray, first row, third from right, *on a senior trip to Dallas, which included her first airplane ride, with Superintendent Ben S. Peek,* far left, *Harvey Walker,* fifth from left, *Betty Ann Moreno Dreese,* second row from top, left, *and other students, c. 1950. Harold Larson's private collection.*

The first year we were there, Governor Pappy O'Daniel made an appeal over the radio to come and take the little kids home for Christmas.

A family in Waco took me, and they became my friends for life. It was 1940. I'll always remember that Christmas in their home.

The governor took Charles home, plus a little girl from the Corsicana State Home. When the governor came to get him, he came in with a highway patrolman wearing his gun. We were all lined up waiting, sitting in our little chairs. My brother said, "Look at that big gun," and walked over to the patrolman to get a closer look. The governor told the patrolman to take it out and show it to my brother.

Charles said his prayer over the air for the governor's radio show. He said, "Now I lay me down to sleep, I pray the Lord my soul to take." Then he paused and said, "That's all I can remember," and that was that.

Charles was a beautiful child, big eyes and real blond hair. He looked like a little angel. He stayed ten days at the Governor's Mansion. He got a tricycle and clothes for Christmas.

I always looked after Charles. My mother used to say, "Here comes the cat wagging the kitten." She was talking about me because here I'd come carrying my brother, and he was bigger than I was. I was always a little thing.

I waited tables in the dining room so I could see my brother, because we were so segregated. Once I saw a boy hit Charles on the head when he was eating. A little while later, I saw the boy at the water fountain. When he leaned over the fountain to get a drink, I clasped my two hands together and hit him real hard on the back of the neck and broke his two front teeth out. He never hit my brother again.

They asked me why I had done it, and I said he hit my brother and nobody could hit my brother. They didn't do anything to me.

> I always looked after Charles. My mother used to say, "Here comes the cat wagging the kitten."

Superintendent Peek wanted Charles adopted, but my mother wouldn't sign, so I signed for him. He was eight, and I was twelve or so. I thought he should have a better life in a real home, so I was happy to sign for him.

A single woman adopted him. He stayed one year, and then she got married, and her husband had three boys. She didn't think it was fair to her new husband, so she brought my brother back to the Home. He stayed in touch with her though, and he really liked her.

My brother ran away one time, and I told them where he was, so they brought him back. I didn't tell him until we were grown. I wanted my brother back because I was afraid something might happen to him.

Charles had a girlfriend in the Home, and she was two years older. She graduated and moved to Dallas, so my brother, who was not yet sixteen, left the Home. He went to Houston and found our mother and two brothers. Charles married his girlfriend from the Home when he turned eighteen, and they're still together.

Charles did an apprenticeship with a plumber, a really good man, and when he went to Austin to get his license, the tester told him he'd done very well, that whoever taught him knew what they were doing. He's a master plumber, and he has a good business and has had a good life. Mr. Peek told him when he left that he would never amount to anything because he hadn't finished school. But he was wrong.

Charles comes down every year and takes me on my vacation. Last year he took me to Virginia.

Most of the good conditions at the Home came under Superintendent Peek. He made it a much better place. He was always doing things for kids, taking us to town for things, helping us out. If we had been working extra hard, canning beans or something like that, he would come tell us he was taking us to

Robinson's ice cream shop on Waco Drive. They had homemade ice cream, the best I've ever had in my life. Peek would have six girls in a car—three in front, three in back—because that was how many would fit in his car.

A lot of the girls were better off than I was because they got money from home. Peek would take them to town to buy shoes. Then they didn't have to wear those ugly steel-toed, lace-up shoes the rest of us had to wear that were left over from World War II munitions plants.

Charles and I grew up in the Home. We knew the ropes and could take care of ourselves. The difference in attitude with kids often resulted from those who grew up in the Home at an early age and those who arrived later in life. If we went there as babies, we came up through the ranks and did what they told us to do. Some came when they were as old as thirteen. Those kids often had problems and ran away.

It would have been better if more of the dorm parents had raised children of their own. Many of them just didn't know how to cope with all the kids they had to handle. Mrs. Tucker, for example, didn't understand anything about kids.

I heard about Whigham, the man who beat the kids. I don't know why Mr. Peek didn't get rid of Whigham sooner. Maybe he didn't know what was going on, since he wasn't in the dorms, and the boys who got the beatings would never tell for fear they'd get it worse the next time.

We were very well educated at the Home. They made us go to symphonies at Baylor all the time, even though we didn't want to. I remember we'd sit there and make fun of the hats women wore.

We were better off going to school on campus than attending the public schools because we had such great teachers at the Home. I especially remember Mrs. Legg. She was an outstanding teacher. I can recall things she said to me to help me with the lessons. She made us want to learn, and we had the time to do it. If you did well in her class, you thought you were

something. I can still remember every detail of *Lady of the Lake*.

We also had training in other subjects, and that helped us get jobs after we left the Home. We had a teacher who taught shorthand, another who taught typing. You could go into the typing room anytime you wanted and practice after class. They had a beauty school, and a lot of the girls learned how to do hair and provide other beauty services.

I acquired a lot of skills before I left the Home. We did all the cleaning in the dorms—the waxing, scrubbing, and polishing of every inch of them. We didn't have to paint them, but we did everything else.

I served six tables with six boys each in the dining hall, and I could have become a waitress, but I didn't want to do that. I worked in the laundry and learned everything about that business. I didn't want to do that either.

Peek knew a lot of people in town, and he helped us if we wanted to go to college.

When I graduated from high school, I attended Baylor for a year, living at the Home and riding the bus to college. Then I found a roommate and a place to live and went to work at General Tire Company in Waco as a secretary. I was paid well, and it was a good job.

I met my husband one night at a party at my boss's house. He was an executive at General Tire. He'd seen me walking through the plant. I looked like a million dollars then, and the guys would all whistle when I walked through.

I knew after our first date he was the man I wanted to marry. We just celebrated our fifty-eighth year together. We have a son who's fifty-five and a daughter age fifty. They both live in Waco, so we see a lot of them and the grandchildren.

We've had a good marriage because my husband had the three things that were important to me. He didn't drink, he didn't smoke, and he didn't run around. I told him, "If I ever catch you running around on me, I'll kill you. I won't do it while you're awake, because you're too big for me, but I'll do it when you're sleeping." He never did, so we're both still here.

Mother came to visit us twice at the Home, once when I was ten and once when I graduated from high school.

My father never came to see me. When he died, I stood at that casket where my father lay, and I said, "Oh, God, what you missed. You had wonderful children, and all had a good life, and we all survived without you." And I walked off.

I was a lot better off at the State Home than I would have been with my parents. We had clean clothes, we made our own beds, we learned how to clean and maintain our dorms. We had plenty of good food. And most of all, we had good schools.

Working in the Waco State Home cannery, where as many as 6,000 gallons of fruits and vegetables were packaged in a single year. Harold Larson's private collection.

CHAPTER TWO

The War Years

Although President Franklin D. Roosevelt, who had struggled to pull America out of the Great Depression, tried to keep the nation out of another world war, the bombing of Pearl Harbor in 1941 made it virtually impossible for the country to remain neutral. Men left home and family for the battlefields. Women, some aided by child care for the first time, tasted the independence of the workplace. Wartime production was what finally ended the Depression.

Radio delivered wartime news and propaganda, soothed by the sounds of big band, bebop, blues, and jazz.

Along with the heroism of the 1940s, there were ugly episodes. Thousands of Japanese American citizens, despite no evidence of treasonous activities and without any hearings or trials, were sent to internment camps, and atomic bombs were dropped on civilian populations in Hiroshima and Nagasaki. The House Un-American Activities Committee conducted witch hunts for suspected communists, ruining hundreds of lives in the process.

By the end of the decade, the Cold War had begun, and the Soviet Union, which had been an ally during the war, became enemy number one.

African Americans, Hispanics, and Native Americans who had fought in the war began to demand equality once they returned home. However, despite some tentative steps forward, real progress toward equality would not be realized until the sixties. Mexican *braceros*, recruited to work in agriculture during the war, remained in the United States and began to assimilate into American life.

The GI Bill expanded college opportunities for thousands of returning veterans. And new legislation established the school lunch program and increased federal funding for low-cost housing.

The following stories offer many personal experiences of the effect of the war and its aftermath, both before and after the alumni arrived at the Waco State Home.

And though college tuition was free to graduates of the Home, many young men left as military enlistees rather than college students.

Margaret Morren Edwards

1940–1949

There were fifteen in my family, ten boys and five girls. I was the youngest. My mother had been paralyzed from a stroke, and she couldn't get around anymore. My aunt took in my sister, my brother, and me and brought us to the Home in 1940.

My brother was thirteen, my sister was eleven, and I was eight. My brother kept running away to be with our mother. They brought him back the first two times, but the third time they realized my mother needed him more than he needed to be in the Home. So he took care of my mother.

In 1943, he signed up to go in the navy, but before he left, he went out on a date one night, and coming home, he had a wreck. The car turned over four times, and he only lived four days.

When my sister got out, she brought Mom and Dad down to see me. I had another brother stationed there at Connally Air Force Base. He'd come get us for the weekend.

Margaret Morren Edwards, age thirteen, photographed at a studio in downtown Waco, c. 1940. Photo courtesy of Margaret Morren Edwards.

I wasn't upset to be there, because a bunch of other kids were there and the matrons made sure that we felt welcome.

A lot of the kids at the Home wanted to be adopted, so when I was old enough, they asked if I wanted to be adopted. I told them no, I had a mother and dad.

In the little girls' dormitory, we had to learn to make our own beds and take care of ourselves. At about age eleven, I went to another dormitory. There were thirty of us. Each one of us quilted a block and put our name in the middle, and when it was done, we gave it to our matron as a friendship quilt. She was so proud of it. We learned to clean house, can foods, do laundry, cook, and wait on tables. We learned a lot from being in the Home. We were taught to respect other people.

We waxed the floor every week. One time we tried to warn the matron, Miss Tucker, that we had just waxed the floor and it was slick. She walked across it anyway, fell, and broke her pelvis. Later on, she came walking through there again. We warned her again, but she wouldn't listen. She fell and broke her arm. So we just gave up.

We never went to school in town. Later on, the kids got to go to the town school.

We had a show on Saturday nights. Sunday we went to church and Bible training. We also had homemade ice cream every Sunday.

We went to summer camp at Inks Lake for a week or two weeks. We also went to Galveston.

We got to order what we wanted for Christmas. They also had a peppermint stick about five feet long. They cracked it all up and told us to get as much as we wanted. So we did. Quite a bit of it was left, and they'd take the rest to the kitchen and make homemade peppermint ice cream.

I was a good girl. I tried to be the best I could be. I only got three spats in the years I was there. We may have gotten spats with a paddle, but we didn't get whippings like some of the boys.

Every evening we could all go up to the front of the schoolhouse, and the boys and girls got to meet each other. We'd sit and talk. A lot of times, they'd bring this watermelon truck, and we would all sit there and eat watermelon. There was a bench in front of a little bush in front of the schoolhouse. You could sit on the bench with a boy, but you couldn't touch. The bench isn't there anymore, but the bush is still there.

We had boyfriends. The one I was going with left in 1948, I believe. I'm still friends with him today. His sister and I talk all the time. We send Christmas cards every year and stuff like that.

Once, my sister and her girlfriend wanted to go to town and see a movie, so they tied sheets together and went out the window. When they were climbing over the fence, this other girl's dress got caught on the barbed wire. Next morning the matron told the girls, "I know some girls slipped out last night. One of them got scratched, so raise up your skirts." So my sister got in trouble. Their punishment was that they weren't allowed up front to see the boys for a week or two.

They never taught us anything about the birds and the bees. All they said was, "Don't ever hold a boy's hand, or you're gonna get pregnant." That's how naïve we were. We learned a lot after we got out. I had six boys after I married.

I played softball and volleyball. I'd still play now if my legs would let me run. I really do love sports. After graduation, I went to beauty school, and they paid for that. I went to Austin, took my test, and passed. We had a style show, and we had to fix three people's hair. People in town came to the show, and a lady came up to me and said, "How would you like to come work for me when you get out of the Home?" So I did.

After I got out of the Home, this girl I knew from the Home called and invited me to go on a double date with her. She said, "Whatever you do, don't you tell

> All they said was, "Don't ever hold a boy's hand, or you're gonna get pregnant."

him you're from the Home." I said, "Forget it, I don't want to go." I wasn't ashamed of being from there.

I think they should have left the Home the way it was when we were there. There are lots of children in this world that need a home like that. At least they wouldn't be out on the streets.

I am glad I was there and proud of it. I don't know where I'd be if I hadn't been there. I might be dead.

I keep in contact with a lot of the boys and girls from the Home. They really and truly are just like brothers and sisters. The last homecoming we attended, we went on a tour, and I took my two sons with me. They took pictures of everything. The big girls' dormitory was still there. It surely did look small compared to when I was there.

Bobby Graham

1940–1951

I was born in 1933. My mother died when I was about three years old. I had three brothers. There was no way my father could work and take care of us, so we were shuttled between my maternal grandparents and my aunt and her husband. Unfortunately, none of my family had enough income to take care of us as well as they wished.

One day in 1939, I believe it was, some vehicles pulled up in the yard. The sheriff and people from the child welfare department had come to take us to the Waco State Home. My grandfather stood on the front porch with a double-barreled shotgun, saying, "Not over my dead body."

The law won, however, and my grandfather cried like a baby as we were

Bobby Graham, right, and friend on the river at Camp Val Verde,
summer of 1950. Harold Larson's private collection.

hauled off to start a new life a world away from our family.

My younger brother and I were sent to the baby cottage, and my older brothers went to the dormitories. I used to try to slip away to see my brothers, even though I didn't know where to find them. My whole world was upside down.

As time went by, I moved through the dormitories and adapted to the regimental operations of the Home.

When I was in the seventh grade, Mrs. Hawthorne, our teacher, came up with the idea of a class project to enter in the State School Fair. The project was a book on the Congressional Medal of Honor winners from Texas during World War II. We sent off letters and solicited photographs. The project turned out well. We won first place and a $100 prize. One man wanted to buy the book we made, but we decided to donate it to the Texas History Room at Baylor University. I was selected to make the presentation speech. I really felt proud.

I lost my oldest brother, James, in 1943, when he climbed a highline tower and slipped and fell. Between the jolt of electricity and the fall, he did not survive. I remember Mrs. Cashion, the matron, waking me up about one a.m., then taking me into the living room and telling me that James had died.

Everybody had jobs to do in the Home. The boys took care of the farming, hogs, chickens, and dairy. The girls worked in the canning plant, dining hall, kitchen, and laundry.

The boys used to go down to Lovers' Leap to swim in the river, where I had my most embarrassing experience while living at the Home. I was not a very good swimmer. Everybody swam to the other side and kept urging me to swim across as well. Just as I made it across, someone said, "We have to go. It's milking time."

There was a lot of discipline and not much love, but the discipline paid off for me.

I was too exhausted to swim back right away, so I told them to go on and walked upriver to find a narrow spot to swim across. I had no luck.

There was a telephone crew in a field replacing a pole. I walked up to them in my birthday suit and asked if they were going back across the river. One of them gave me a raincoat to wear.

They dropped me off at the road behind the Home, and I walked back down to the river to get my clothes. The other boys had already finished milking and returned to check on me. When they got there, my clothes were still there but I was not. They thought I had tried to swim back and drowned.

Another unforgettable experience was in my senior year when I got to take my first airplane ride. Mr. Kultgen from Bird-Kultgen Ford chartered a plane to fly the class to Dallas to spend the day and then fly us back.

I did not graduate with my class. A friend and I were reprimanded for violating the rules. They were going to run my friend off, but they told me that I could stay. I said we were both guilty of the same thing and if he left, I would leave, too. So I left. I went back to school the next year and graduated from Cayuga High School in 1952.

In retrospect, the Waco State Home was probably the best thing that happened to me. There was a lot of discipline and not much love, but the discipline paid off for me.

I was drafted in January 1953 and spent the next twenty-four years in the army. After my discharge from the army, I worked for the Texas Department of Corrections until I retired at the age of sixty-two, in 1995.

The man who had the most impact on my life was Mr. James Wharton, the dean of boys at the Waco State Home. He was the type of man who could get the most out of a person, not by whipping you or threatening you, but by treating you as a human being.

John Wilson

1940–1953

My mother and father, Frank and Ruth Wilson, had three girls and five boys. The three youngest kids were sent to the Waco State Home. I was five, my brother was about nine, and my sister was three. That was in 1940.

Norman Clark and I started out in the baby cottage at the same time. The older girls would bathe us. We had a long sink, and they would put us in there and give us our baths. We flew kites, played hide-and-seek, marbles, and jacks—things that were popular back then.

I was about thirteen when we moved to the upstairs dorm. That November, my brother talked me into running away from the Home with him. It

John Wilson, top right, *Russell Dorrough,* bottom right, *and friends on the grounds of the Waco State Home. Harold Larson's private collection.*

was real cold, and we had no coats. He said we should go to Bremond, about fifty miles southeast of Waco. He had gone there the last time he ran away, and he said the people there were real nice.

We headed out North Nineteenth Street and walked all the way to Circle Road before we started thumbing rides. Sometimes we would duck under a bridge to keep from freezing while waiting for another vehicle to come along. We finally got a ride in the back of a truck.

We made it to Bremond and knocked on the door of this house. We were freezing, and they had a wood-burning heater going. They got us warmed up and fed us, and then we went to bed. They had feather beds, and it felt good. I think we stayed there about three days, and then the superintendent of the Home showed up and took us back. They made my brother leave the Home because he had run away twice. That left just my sister and me.

Saturday nights we had a movie, but if you misbehaved, you had to stand in the corner. I missed a lot of movies because I misbehaved a lot, or so they told me. Most Saturday nights, I was there standing in the corner while the movie played.

The Home had these long covered porches, and if you misbehaved during the week, you had to stand up against the brick wall out there. I had to do that a lot, too.

Overall, we had some good matrons and some that just ran over us. They would punish you for the smallest thing.

As I got older, I got involved in sports. I played basketball, baseball, football, and ran track. Mr. Whigham told me there were two things he remembered most about me: I could really play baseball, and I had a bad temper. I said, "Is that the best you can do?"

He said, "Well, yeah, those are the two things that really stood out."

But eventually I learned to adjust in school. As I got older, I had to get up at four in the morning to help milk the cows. We even did our own butchering. I learned how to butcher hogs, calves, and chickens.

I worked in the kitchen with a baker from Palestine, Texas. He taught me how to make the rolls for Sunday lunch. Whenever he missed a Sunday, I would step in and make the rolls. Everybody thought I was the best baker around. You put some butter in them, and, boy, they were good!

My job was scrubbing out those big cooking pots. We pasteurized our own milk, so I had to go to the dairy barn, load up the milk, haul it over, and put it in a big vault in the kitchen. Occasionally, I had to push a laundry basket to the dorms to pick up soiled clothes and take them to the laundry. Mr. Tucker was in charge of the laundry. He did all the washing, and the boys distributed the clean laundry to the dorms.

In the summer, we baled hay and stored it in the barn. We also picked peaches, watermelons, and tomatoes. It was hot, and I always got badly sunburned, but that was what we had to do every summer.

Rayborn and Mabel Balch worked at the Home. Mabel taught square dancing and organized two square-dancing teams. We were outfitted with costumes with donations from local civic clubs. After much practice, she began showing us off by taking us to square-dance festivals in Amarillo, Corpus Christi, Dallas, Fort Worth, Atlanta [Texas], and in Oklahoma. We also danced at the inauguration of Governor Allan Shivers.

When we were about sixteen, they would let us mow yards to make a little money. On Sunday afternoons, the gun club would come pick up two or three of the boys and take us out to operate the little trap shooters. That was another way we made money. I also caddied at the golf course at Lake Waco. Most of the time I would carry two bags for eighteen holes and make three dollars.

The year I graduated, 1953, the big tornado came through Waco and killed 144 people. That summer, while I was waiting to leave for college, they put some of us to work at the General Tire factory cleaning up tires that had been in the tornado.

When I was about fifteen, one of my older brothers came to the Home one Saturday and talked me into getting in the car. He had hired this man to take us to Abilene to see my mother and dad. They were living in a tent. I remember the dirt floor. They had to get water from one of their neighbors. They had lanterns and a wood stove. She was ironing clothes with one of the old-fashioned irons you heated on a stove. I was there about a week before Ben Peek, the superintendent, showed up and took me back to the Home.

Seeing the conditions my mother and father were living in convinced me that I wanted to go to college and make something of myself. When I graduated, in 1953, they came out to the Home. They wanted me to come to Abilene and support them. I told them the state was sending me to college at Sam Houston State University and I would not be going to Abilene to work for them or take care of them.

For two years I attended college at Sam Houston and worked at a Dairy Queen. The state sent Norman Clark to college there, too. He had a job at a drugstore.

BJ, who was one of my roommates at the Home, had learned how to play the fiddle while he was at the Home. I remember it drove me crazy while he was learning how to play, but he mastered it, and he had a band in Houston. I went to Houston and told him I was tired of going to college. I wanted him to help me find a job.

BJ was "between checks" himself, so we lived on pork and beans, bread, and red Kool-Aid until I found a job at Foley's department store. I went into the Marine Corps for two years, and then I went back to Foley's.

Norman Clark and Harvey Walker showed up one day and said, "Why don't you come to North Texas? We're going to school up there."

So I quit that job and enrolled at North Texas. I met my wife there. When we got out of school, she and I moved to Atlanta, Texas, and had four daughters. Now we have thirteen grandchildren. September 13, 2009, marked forty-four years of living in Atlanta, and we love it! So life worked out well.

At the Home, we were like brothers and sisters to each other, even more so than our own families. We just grew to love each other. I think that is really the only way we made it through those years. Of course we lost contact, and a lot of the kids would not attend the homecomings. I think a lot of them were ashamed to let people know where they had grown up. It took me a while to start coming, but I became a regular. I learned not to be ashamed of where I had grown up. I still keep in touch with a few friends from the Home.

The way we were treated by some of the matrons made me bitter, and I had a bad temper, but I learned to get over it. I think the Marine Corps took that out of me.

My sister left the Home the year after I graduated. She never came back to the homecomings, and she died in December of 2008 in New Orleans. All of my family is dead now, Mother and Dad and the other seven children. I am the last one remaining.

I wish I had known my brothers and sisters better. I never saw them at all during the last years of their lives. We never even called each other. Sometimes I would look around and see these happy families, and I wished I had a family like that.

I became determined that when I got married and had a family, I would take good care of them. I would see that we all stuck together. Life has been good since then.

> At the Home, we were like brothers and sisters to each other, even more so than our own families.

Edith Wills Swadley

1940–1954

We were living in Orange, Texas, when my father left us: a crippled mother, two girls, and four boys. The oldest, my sister, ran away and got married. My mother just couldn't take care of us anymore, so my grandfather and one of my aunts called the sheriff, and they took my four brothers and me to the Waco State Home.

I was a little over three years old when they took us to Waco. They didn't have room for us right away, so we spent our first night in the Orange jail. We all slept in jail cells!

At the Home, they kept us busy all the time. We'd snap peas and do canning, laundry, ironing. I was ironing when I was nine years old.

The laundry at the Waco State Home, where Edith Wills Swadley
worked from age eleven. Harold Larson's private collection.

The education was good. There wasn't the competition you have in public school. There were teachers we really liked. Some of them were special people, like the cook in the girls' dorm and the music teacher, who was a sweet, genuine person. I took piano lessons from her. I went to church services mornings and evenings.

We were also exposed to all sorts of culture, whether we wanted it or not. A particular dorm would be selected to attend the opera, plays, ballet, and the symphony. You had to go. You didn't have a choice.

Mostly, I have bad memories of the place. The matrons were not good to us, and the state misrepresented how we were being treated. No one really knew how we were being treated. It was not good. I have bad feelings about the matrons.

When I was living in the girls' dorm after the baby cottage, there was a big closet under the stairs where they stored personal things our parents sent us. Mom sent me a doll, and instead of letting me have it, the matron hung the doll on the wall above the bed. When I moved up to the next dorm, she wouldn't let me take it. That was cruel. When you're in a place like that, anything your parents send to you is special, and that doll was very special to me.

Another time I remember well is when my brother came to visit. I remember going to the large dining room, and I saw him across the room in the boys' area. Without thinking, I yelled at him, and the matron hit me on the head with an umbrella. The same matron would make a fist and hit students with the joint of her middle finger.

One Christmas when I was living in the senior girls' dorm, the matrons found all these empty boxes and had us put Christmas wrapping paper on them and put them under the tree. The people from the state were coming to visit, and they wanted it to look as if we were getting a lot of Christmas presents. To me that was cruel, too.

I'm sure we had good times, and as far as we knew, we were having a good time. We didn't know any different. Some of my best memories of the Home are of the friends I made there. The boys and girls were separated, so we didn't see each other often. We had boyfriends. You had to sneak around to see them, and we did.

In the senior girls' dorm, guys would sneak over and get on the roof with their girlfriends. Everyone knows that already, so I'm not letting the cat out of the bag. That was probably the most exciting thing at the Home except for going to summer camp. Summer camp was always fun. We did get the opportunity to attend college. That was another good thing. I graduated when I was seventeen and attended Sam Houston State University for two years. Back then it was called Sam Houston State Teachers College.

I moved to Houston, got a job at the Methodist hospital working in the business office, and then worked in the business section of the fire department. After getting married, I quit my job to devote more attention to the family. We raised two boys.

I suppose growing up in that environment had an effect on the type of parent I was. We were never really shown any love or affection at the Home, and consequently, I was probably not as loving as I should have been to my children when they were growing up. When you grow up with thirty other girls in a dormitory, the environment is just very different.

My brothers joined the service after they left the Home. We've all remained close.

I stay in touch with a number of friends from the Home. There's a lady from San Antonio I talk to on the phone either every day or every other day. We

> The matrons were not good to us, and the state misrepresented how we were being treated.

were closer to each other in the Home than we were to our own families.

I haven't been to a reunion in several years. So few people go now, and so many have passed on.

When my youngest brother came to Houston after being in the service, he and Donald Smith, who lived at the Home, had an antique shop. Donald was a painter. He was very artistic.

Unfortunately, a lot of people don't talk about growing up in the Home because it's too painful. I do because it's the past and we have to look to the future and we have to learn from our mistakes.

Norman Clark

1941–1953

My mother and father divorced when my two sisters and I were very young. My mother had no education and was unable to secure a well-paying job. It was during the Depression, and everybody was having a difficult time.

We started off in Shamrock, Oklahoma, and later lived in the Corpus Christi area. My mother was just trying to survive, and we weren't able to. At first they placed us with an elderly couple. We stayed with them for a few months, but it didn't work out. Fortunately, the welfare people came by and took us to the Waco State Home.

I was about five years old, and my sisters were older. I remember being

Norman Clark, second from left, with other members of the Waco State Home track team. Harold Larson's private collection.

placed with many other children about my age in the baby cottage. The girls used to come up and give us baths and put us to bed. We used to kid about that in later years. A girl would come up and say, "I used to give you a bath."

My mother came to visit us once or twice. She wasn't financially able to come often. My dad just disappeared altogether. Eventually, you sort of lose the feeling you have for a mom and a dad. It's something that I missed and wished I could have had. It's why I have been sensitive to that with my two sons.

It's amazing how quickly you can acclimate, though. I adapted quickly to the Home and the way they did things, maybe because we were all experiencing a similar situation.

We always had jobs to do. As you grew older, you took on larger responsibilities. I worked in the dairy two times a day except Sunday and baled hay all summer. I slaughtered hogs, too. We knew what we were supposed to do; we did it, and then went on to something else.

We got our education there. They brought in teachers from outside the Home. Some of the teachers would recognize that you had certain abilities, and they would work with you in that area. For example, I used to love to sing, and I still do. On Sundays, I would take care of the singing in the church. We had church services twice on Sunday, morning and evening.

We were involved in all kinds of sports. I enjoyed playing football, basketball, and baseball and running track.

The matrons lived in the dorm with their own private room and bath. Probably the most unfortunate aspect of the situation was that the matrons were not well educated and didn't know much about rearing children or how to handle them. Somehow, you managed to get through that.

A lot of us always got away with things the matrons weren't even aware of. You were supposed to stay on the campus, for example, but we would figure out ways to get out and go somewhere. Mainly on Saturday and Sunday, we enjoyed going down to swim in the river in the park in Waco. The matrons weren't even aware we were gone.

Everybody was afraid of Miss Cashion. She'd sit out there in her rocking chair all day watching us. She wouldn't say anything unless somebody came up and complained: "That guy's hitting me" or "He's throwing rocks at me." Then she'd call you over and make you sit on the bench for an hour. That's the way she handled it. At the close of day, she would line children up that had not behaved and spank them with a large board as others watched.

I never had the inclination to run away. If you ran away several times, you'd be sent somewhere like the Gatesville State School for Boys or somewhere else that was a little tougher than where we were.

Discipline wasn't severe. If you got into trouble, they would give you a spanking or "campus" you. They wouldn't let you go anywhere. For example, you weren't allowed to attend the movie at the end of the week. You had to stay in the dorm.

I graduated from high school there in 1953. I went to a university, but I wasn't happy with it, and I didn't have any extra money, so I joined the air force. After my discharge, I attended North Texas State in Denton on the GI Bill, graduated from there, and later received my master's degree. I roomed with three or four guys from the Home, so it was more or less like brothers.

After graduation from the university, I took a job in Denton and later moved to Arlington. I was there for about twenty-five years and later retired there.

I still have several good friends from the Home. We stay in touch. It was a different way of growing up than in a normal family, but I was never uncomfortable about it until I left and realized what a normal family situation was like. I longed for that and wished I could have had it. At the same time, I was thankful

> Eventually, you sort of lose the feeling you have for a mom and a dad.

that someone came along and saved my life, so to speak, and encouraged me to go on to college.

My first job after graduation was with Moore Business Forms in Denton. My area of interest was human resources administration, dealing with personnel issues. Later, I was employed with the City of Arlington in human resources. I retired in 1998.

Raising my own children seemed to come naturally to me, but I learned a lot from my wife, too. I have two sons, both of whom are well educated. We have a wonderful life. My wife, Betty, has now passed away, and my two boys live nearby. We see each other regularly. We have Christmas and special days together like a normal family.

Growing up in the Home was an interesting experience when I think about it. I take the position that it actually saved my life. People react to it differently. When I graduated from North Texas, I was dating Betty. We married in 1963. Her mother was real uncomfortable about our relationship because of my upbringing. Later on, she said it scared her to death when Betty and I got married, but she was thankful the way things worked out. It changed her mind altogether.

A lot of guys I graduated with have had similar situations. Johnny Wilson and I were good friends. We went to school and graduated from North Texas State together. I introduced him to his wife. We talk once in a while.

I don't attend the homecoming every year, but I try to go every two or three years.

Looking back, I am thankful for the steps that were taken, for they probably saved my life or at least gave me the opportunity to achieve what I have. I am grateful for the many fortunate events that allowed me to gain a solid education and meet my wonderful wife. I am proud of my two sons, who are well educated and enjoy the work they have selected. Most important, I am thankful for my wife, who helped me have a wonderful life. Others from the Home have done well, but many were not as fortunate.

James Smith

1942–1947

The Waco State Home was the best thing that ever happened to me. My mother died, and my father did his best to raise my brother and me, but we gave him hell. Then my father died, too. I was fourteen years old, running in the streets and chasing women. They picked me up and put me in the Home instead of the penitentiary. Up until then, we weren't really getting any education. I got an education and learned how to get along with people.

At first I was reluctant about the Home, but Mr. Ben S. Peek, the superintendent, took a liking to me, and that made me feel better about it. It made me feel like one of the gang.

We went straight to the big boys' dorm because of our age. The only matron I remember is Mrs. Adams. Her husband was the gardener. I believe there were twenty-eight of us in the dorm. That was the only dorm I was in at the Home, except for the girls' dorm. We used to sneak in there once in a while. We would go through the

James Smith, center, and other boys working on one of the Waco State Home farms. Harold Larson's private collection.

tunnel that carried the steam heat to the dormitories to get to the girls. We gave that tunnel a workout. I never got caught. The other way to get in was to climb up the wall. The girls would dangle a sheet out the window, and we would climb up. I had quite a few girlfriends there.

The work at the Home was more about discipline and teaching you what to do and bringing you up in life. The work itself was not very hard. The kids who thought they worked you hard did not want to do anything. They just wanted to sit on their butts. We had to milk cows by hand, and then in 1943, we got the electric milkers. Before that, you had to get up at five in the morning to milk the cows by hand, but when we got the electric milkers, we could sleep an hour later and it cut down on the number of boys you needed to do the job. We would pasteurize the milk and do everything. Then you had to clean the stalls. We killed our own beef, hogs, and raised chickens.

The school was super. The teachers were very good. My old football coach and math teacher was Mr. A. J. Speece. Mr. Ludwick, our principal, treated me right and was the peach of my eye. Mrs. Legg, the English teacher, was another favorite, but she did not care for me because I did not give a crap for English. Mrs. Rose was one of our teachers, too, and she was a sweetheart.

I was the big shot on campus in sports. I played baseball, basketball, football, and tennis. We had a tennis court down by the girls' dormitory. It was on the other side of campus. That is how we would get in the girls' dorm. We would say we were going over there to play tennis. It was a good life.

As to the discipline, if you kept your nose clean, they did not mess with you. If you went around sticking your nose in everybody's business, you deserved to get in trouble.

I wish they had taken me there sooner, because I would have gotten a better education and been able to get a degree from college.

I learned to get along with people and make friends. I only had two fights the whole time I was there. After I kicked the crap out of a couple of kids, they didn't bother me anymore. I used to go out to the Waco golf course and carry two bags for a dollar apiece. Two dollars in those years would last two months. A hamburger was ten cents; a show was eleven cents. We had to make our own money because no one gave us any money there.

I left the Waco State Home in 1947 when I joined the navy, and I've been in California ever since. I was in the navy until 1952. That was during Korea, but I was stationed in San Diego. I played football. I had two appointments to the Naval Academy because of my athletic abilities. They wanted a team that could beat the damn army, but I turned down the appointments both times because my grades were not that good and I did not want to go there and wash out.

After my discharge, I went to work for U.S. Steel, and then went into the trucking business. I retired from that.

I got married in 1955, had two kids. My daughter is married and has two kids, and my son has one kid.

I have stayed in touch with my friends from the Home, but a lot of my close buddies I used to keep in touch with have died. Swede was one of my dear friends. He's the only one who came out here to see me in California.

When I think about the Home, my only regret is that I wish they had taken me there sooner, because I would have gotten a better education and been able to get a degree from college. That is the only thing I miss in my life, not having a college education. I wish I'd been as good at academics as I was in football. At least I got married and have kids. And I've never been in jail.

Betty Louise Huffman Dubose

1942–1948

My family was poor, and my mother was recovering from terrible burn injuries she suffered after fainting and falling into the fireplace. There were eleven kids, although some were old enough to have left home already.

We lived in Kirbyville, where my father was a carpenter, but it was hard for him to find work. He wasn't formally educated. There was no one who could come and help out while my mother recovered, so four of us were taken to the Waco State Home in 1942. I was five years old. The three brothers who went with me to the Home were all older.

My older sister, who was married with two children of her own, got a family friend to take us to Waco. In those days, not everyone had a car.

My oldest brother at the Home left when he was old enough to join the military. One of the twins ran away and did not get brought back to the Home, because he had enrolled in school at Kirbyville and they felt he was old enough to make that decision.

Betty Louise Huffman Dubose, right, *with her brother.*
Photo courtesy of Margaret Morren Edwards.

That left just one of my twin brothers and me at the Home. We were only supposed to be there until my mother recovered, but we didn't go home again until 1948, six years later.

It was traumatic for me at first because I was so young and inexperienced. I had not even started school yet. But I got used to it after a while. I made lots of friends. It became my home and my life, and I forgot everything else.

Someone from the family would come to see us once in a while, about once or twice a year. Everyone was so poor in those days. They couldn't just jump in the car and go visit someone.

Everybody started out at the hospital. They had to check you out for lice and all that stuff. They didn't want to have anything like that out there. It was a clean place, and they kept you healthy and well fed.

I was at the baby cottage until I was eight years old. I never heard of any kids being adopted while I was there. Your parents had to give their signed consent for that. I learned later on, however, that my parents had actually signed for me to be adopted. Twice, a couple came to the Home to adopt a child and I turned out to be the only one available, which is funny because I know I wasn't the pick of the litter.

The prospective adoptive parents would take you home for a weekend to see how you might work out. I had some say in the matter as well. I told the Home that I only wanted to be adopted with my brothers. They were twins, however, and were never released for adoption. Most people only wanted one kid, so I did not go.

Everybody had to contribute to cleaning the dorm. I wasn't old enough, however, to do any of the jobs that the older girls did. I was only twelve and a half when I left, which meant I wasn't allowed to work in the kitchen or the laundry. In the laundry, they had those big presses, and they weren't about to let a little kid mess around with one of those.

I didn't think the discipline was harsh, but I wasn't an unruly kid or a hell-raiser, and I didn't know anybody who was. I knew that if I was told to do something, that I should go ahead and do it. The worst punishment I ever received was being made to stand for an hour or so. I didn't mind that at all. From the place they made me stand, I could hear the shows I enjoyed on the matron's radio. I remember *Stella Dallas* and the scary one, *Inner Sanctum*, which always came on with some spooky music. Sometimes I would pull something so I would have to stand up, then I would get to hear those shows. The matrons most likely knew.

Probably the worst thing was that I almost never got to see my brothers, since they were on the other side of the campus.

We always had movies on Saturday night. Sunday mornings, seminary students from nearby Baylor and from the Methodist seminary would come preach to the kids. One Sunday it would be a Baptist, then the next time it would be a Methodist. I don't remember any other kind of faith, but they always said the same thing. They taught you stuff out of the Bible and religious songs, just like you might have done at home, except on a large scale.

I enjoyed all the kids. You were never alone or lonesome, always had a lot of good friends around you.

I thought we got a good education at the school at the Home. At the end of sixth grade, they promoted me to eighth grade, but when I went back home in 1948, the school in Kirbyville said I could not possibly have learned enough for the eighth grade, so they put me in the seventh grade. They were wrong, of course, because they had me tutor other kids who didn't understand what they were teaching us.

My brother, the twin who had run away, had been petitioning the family to bring my brother and me home. He kept it up until they finally brought us home. But instead of my mother and father being

> If they taught us anything, it was discipline, fairness, and keeping your area clean.

our primary parents, my older sister would be our primary guardian until we were legal adults.

It actually was not a good situation when we came back home. Our parents didn't want us back. We'd been gone a long time, and they were still very, very poor. They seemed to be past the notion of wanting kids around.

My dad actually seemed to be more caring toward the boys, and by then I was the only girl left at home. I guess that's why I had been released for adoption. My father had a farm, and there wasn't much for girls to do except work in the house. He didn't have much use for girls.

My dad was older by then and still having a hard time getting by. The family did receive some financial assistance to help support us. The State of Texas wasn't going to let us starve.

I tell my children that if times got hard again—and at this point, things are getting bad again—I could probably make it and so could my husband, because he grew up under hard times, too. Kids nowadays haven't had to live like that, but we've already been there and done that.

My brother who was at the Home with me lives in Florida now, but he did not want to be interviewed about his experience there. He didn't say why. He was ten years old when we were taken there, and a ten-year-old boy knows more than a little six-year-old girl.

I don't have anything bad to say about the Waco State Home. Now that I've gotten as old as I have, I feel that it was very good for me. But I don't know how it affected other kids. If they taught us anything, it was discipline, fairness, and keeping your area clean. That's what they expected of you.

At the Home, everyone knew me as Betty. Once I left there, I never used Betty again.

I'm still in touch with some friends from the Home. I attended some homecomings in the past, but I'm seventy-three years old now, and it's hard to go that far. The last time I went, two or three years ago, some of us recognized each other right away, but others had to be told who we were.

Margaret Morren Edwards and I stay in touch. I'm also back in touch with Edith Wills Swadley. She was my best friend when I left, and we're still friends.

All in all, the Home was not a bad experience.

John L. Smith

1942–1952

I came to the Waco State Home in 1942, when I was four years old, and I left on the 31st of May 1952, when I was fourteen.

They sent my older sister out there first. The way she tells it, they did that so she'd be there when we got there, to help get us acclimated or something. I came next, then my brother, and finally my sister.

I had two older siblings, a brother and a sister, who went to live with their grandmother in California. I hate to use the words "mother" and "grandmother" because I never had a mother or grandmother.

When I first got to the Home, I cried and cried. I first went to the infirmary, where they checked me out. All I remember is crying. I then went to the baby cottage, and I remember crying there, too. But after that, I got over it and didn't really think about my parents again. It was for the best. My father was a gambler and a roustabout, and my mother wasn't enough to talk about.

Most of us had been through similar experiences and backgrounds, but

John L. Smith, age eleven, in his Captain Marvel T-shirt, when his sister visited the State Home in her boyfriend's Buick Dynaflow, c. 1950. Photo courtesy of John L. Smith.

what is interesting is that hardly anyone ever talked about their background. I didn't remember mine, since I was too young to remember much anyway, but what I do remember is not pleasant.

There are many positive things I could say about the Waco State Home, if only because where we came from, anything would've been a step up. My older brother is able to remember all the lean, mean times before we were taken there, and he says what he remembers more than anything was all the food we had at the Home. We had all we could eat. That gives you some idea of the conditions we had before we were taken to Waco.

There was one bunch of kids at the Home whose parents had just left them on the streets somewhere— just dropped them off and drove away. They actually made it for a few months on their own before the authorities picked them up.

Many of us were physically, mentally, or emotionally fouled up, but we were good kids. This one guy was the best athlete I've ever seen in my life. He could do anything athletic—football, baseball, basketball, shoot marbles, play pool, anything. But this guy couldn't spell "cat" if you spotted him the *c* and the *a*.

Around 1953 or 1954, right before I went into the navy, I ran into him in downtown Waco, and he hustled me into a pool game for money. It wasn't a lot of money he won, but that was all right, because he needed it. I didn't throw off—I was still trying to beat him—but he won anyway. I remember he smoked so many cigarettes all his fingers were stained yellow. He was in terrible shape. I heard he did not make it very long after this.

A kid who suffered from learning disabilities came to the Home, but only for a few weeks, and then was gone. Years later, when I was living in Austin, I was visiting friends of mine who owned a hotel and restaurant. They called the Austin State School because they needed some extra kitchen help, and the guy they sent turned out to be this same guy. I couldn't believe it. He only lasted a few hours on the job. I couldn't say

anything, and there wasn't anything to say. I didn't know if he even remembered me. It still bothers me to think about it.

I remember Donald, the artist, who was friends with my brother. Donald used to play classical music for us. He was really something, very talented. He made these puppets out of papier-mâché and would put on puppet shows. He would pretend to be Dracula and play other scary parts. We just loved all that.

I can see Donald walking down the road as if it were yesterday. He was wearing his big overcoat. The Home issued us those genuine wool coats. He sewed big pockets inside his so he could carry records from the record stores in town. He'd always bring candy for his brothers.

The kids at the Home were all one big family, but it was important that you had a best friend. You had to make a friend or you were out of luck. My best friend was a boy named John.

He and I were really buddies. We did everything together. John and I would sneak out at night, and he would meet this girl. While they were smooching and playing grab ass, I'd sit on the sidelines and keep jiggers. "Keeping jiggers" means being the lookout for somebody else.

John's momma came and got him and his sister in 1949. I hated to see him go, and I was as jealous as I could be. I had lost my buddy. I never saw him again from 1949 until about five years ago at a reunion at the Home. My brother brings this guy up to me and says, "Do you know who this is?" Finally, I recognized him, and now we are mates again.

Discipline? Boy, did we ever have discipline. We were taught dormitory manners. It was "yes ma'am," "no ma'am," "please," "thank you." I still talk that way to this day. By the time we were six years old, they had taught us to make a bed that would pass military inspection. As we got older and progressed through the dormitories, we were given more work and responsibilities. Everybody did their share of work, and that was good.

Let me tell you about this one girl I knew from the Home. Last time I saw her, she was working at a job, raising kids, and taking care of a husband, but she still cleaned out every closet in her house once a week. She took out everything, every single thing, and vacuumed the floor, washed the walls and everything. She did that once a week her whole life. I think that came from what she was taught at the Home, because she was under a lady out there by the name of Mrs. Tucker, who was the head of the big girls' dorm. She told them if you hold hands with a boy, you'll get pregnant, and all that BS.

You were punished if you broke the rules. For example, when you were eating, you did not put your elbows on the table. One day I was at Ms. Belcher's table, and I very casually put my elbow on the table. She said, "JL, I'll see you in my room after the bell." I thought she might forget about it, but she didn't. She wore my ass out, but I must say that Ms. Belcher was a fair lady.

I was steady getting in trouble for doing something, and I think you must have rules and you discipline people for breaking them. I didn't mind that. But beating people until they bleed, which is what some of them did, that was out of line.

We never called the people in charge of our dorm "dorm parents." The word "parent" was not in our vocabulary. We called them "overseers," "wardens," "turnkeys," and things like that.

One of them, Mr. Phillips, was a good and fair man but didn't have it in him to discipline the ones in his care. You get a bunch of thirty wild, crazy-assed boys or thirty wild, crazy-assed girls, they're liable to do anything. You've got to discipline them. But Phillips would kind of let you run where you wanted, and that's what got him into trouble.

When we went off to do things like going swimming, we used the buddy system. For example, if I were number one, my partner was number two, and every so often they'd say, "Find your partner," and we would count off. Well, one day Mr. Phillips took his

boys to the river to go swimming and didn't do the buddy system, and when they got back, there was one boy missing. He'd gone into the water and drowned. Mr. Phillips never got over that incident.

Ben S. Peek became superintendent of the Home about a year after I arrived. I never had many run-ins with Peek, but I remember him well. One thing stands out in my mind. Evidently, he smoked a cigar, or somebody smoked a cigar in that part of the building, because I still remember the smell of cigars and candy. There was a bowl of candy on his desk, and the combination of tobacco and candy was a pleasant smell.

Mr. Whigham came to the Home in the latter half of the 1940s from the Gatesville State School for Boys. Mr. Whigham was a beater. That was his job at Gatesville, and he continued to do this when he came to the Home. Mr. Whigham ran off so many good boys, and we will never know how many lives he ruined. He was a very strange guy. You never knew where you stood with him. Sometimes he would put his arms around your shoulders like he was your pal, but he wasn't. All the teachers would give you whippings, but Whigham beat you.

One time Whigham took another boy and me in the washroom and gave us a busting. You had to drop your pants before he paddled you—and this is rude and crude—but he hit the other boy so hard that shit hit all four walls. I was there; I saw it. He would beat you until your butt bled. This guy was a brutal, brutal, brutal son of a bitch.

Most of us liked sports—baseball, football, and stuff like that—and Whigham liked coaching and was good at it. He got us into a lot of good contests.

We had a little football team, a little ninety-pound team. We had no shoes; we played barefoot. We had some old beat-up jerseys from no telling when, no shoulder pads, our trousers, and an old helmet you could just about fold up and put in your pocket. The other teams would have their shoes, shoulder pads, nice helmets, and everything. But we were pretty darn good for little kids, and we beat everybody in this little Waco league.

Whigham was as happy as he could be when he got us a match with the Masonic Home in Fort Worth. He drove us up to Fort Worth in a driving rain. We get there, eat lunch, go out and play those kids, and they've got all this equipment. They've got everything, and we've got nothing, and it's cold and rainy. It was an exciting game, but they beat us 7–6. When the game was over, we didn't go back to a dressing room, didn't go in and take a shower. We got our bare feet on the bus and drove back to Waco. I'm telling you, we loved it. We got to make a trip to Fort Worth, and we damn near beat those bad son of a guns, and we thought we had just played the national championship.

Whigham would do things like that. He would be so nice and make you feel so good, then the next minute he would be knocking the hell out of you.

I got out in 1952, and the first reunion I went back to was in 1962. Whigham was there. I don't know if he was there for the reunion or if he was still working there. Anyway, I come walking through the gate, and he came running up there to me, hands out, and says, "Oh, JL, good to see you," and I said, "Get away from me, you son of a bitch. Get away from me. I didn't like you back then and I goddamn sure don't like you now, so just stay away from me or I'm gonna hurt you. I'm a grown man now and not a kid." I had to say that and get it off my chest. His old wife got all uppity, and I told her, "Calm down, lady." She always reminded me of the Wicked Witch of the West in *Wizard of Oz*. She was skinny and had black hair in a bun. She was a pitiful-looking old thing.

Whigham was there for a while, got fired, but a few years later was hired back. Then some of the boys ran him off. I was already gone when it happened, but the boys who did it were from my old dorm. A bunch of them got together and whipped the hell out of

> I've seen a mother's love, but I've never felt a mother's love.

Whigham, until he had blood running out of his nose and out of his head. I was talking about it the other night on the phone with one of the boys, and I said, "I wish I'd been in on the count." I really do!

One more little story about Whigham. There was a pair of twins in our dorm, and I had a fistfight with one of them one day and just kicked his ass. Whigham put me in the washroom with the boy and his brother and told them to whip me, or he was going to whip them. They whipped me like they owned me. I probably deserved it, but I mean they wore me out, bless their hearts.

Sometime in the 1970s after Whigham had retired, I was making my calls in Waco, and I saw Whigham walking down the street. I had a brand-new car, and I pulled up alongside him. I wanted to show him I had a new car and was making it. I got out to talk to him and asked him how he was doing. He said, "Oh, JL, I had prostate cancer and they castrated me."

I said, "Hell, we should've castrated you years ago!" He huffed off after that. That son of a bitch was something.

Most of the staff and administrators out there were good people. And the Home was really the best setup there's ever been for kids, if it had been run properly. We were kids who didn't have anything, and they let us live and work. Of course, they didn't teach us any life skills. For example, I didn't know how to dial a phone number or how to mail a letter to someone.

Another thing they didn't give us was the feeling of being loved. In a regular family home, when you go to bed at night, even if it is in a chicken coop or whatever your surroundings are, you have somebody that loves you. They're looking out for you and doing what they can for you. None of these kids I grew up with ever had that. They'd never seen it. I don't even know the concept of what it is to love a mother. You can't explain it to me. I've seen a mother's love, but I've never felt a mother's love. It's a shame.

When I was in the eighth grade, I was in Mrs. Hackney's dorm. She was a real weirdo, and I didn't get along with her at all.

On a Sunday night in the middle of May 1952, just two weeks before school was out and after all the kids were in bed, Mrs. Hackney came and shook me and said, "Come to my room." I had no earthly idea what she wanted. I knew I hadn't done anything wrong. I went in her room, and she said, "Bend across that bed." I said, "What in the world for?" She said, "I'm going to give you a busting." I said, "No, you're not, unless I've done something. What've I done?" She said, "I told you to do it." I said, "I'm not gonna do it." She said, "Will you tell Mr. Peek that?" I said, "I'll tell anyone that."

We went to Peek's house. She said, "Tell him what you just told me." I said, "Mr. Peek, I'm not taking any whippings anymore. I've had about one a day since I've been here, and I'm not going to take them any more." He said, "Then you can just leave." I told him no, that I would leave as soon as school was out.

Little did he know, I had already planned to leave then anyway. My oldest sister had gotten married, and I was able to go live with her. I was lucky they didn't come get me and send me to Gatesville.

I'm damned fortunate, because I made it. I'm married and have two daughters. The oldest is forty-six, married and living in Kansas City, Missouri. Our daughter Della, who's thirty-six, lives with us and is autistic, but she is really something special, very smart, and has a really good memory. She goes places with me a lot. We're running buddies. She keeps me on track.

I never liked the Home or being in the Home, but just because I did not like it does not make it a bad place. It was probably the best thing that ever happened to me. When I look back, I cannot recall one student, then or now, that I did not like. Of all the people I have known or met in my life, the kids from the Waco State Home are the ones that I admire the most. They are my heroes!

Betty Ann Moreno Dreese

1944–1951

I was born in Austin, Texas. My father was Hispanic, and my mother was Irish and English. My mother's folks did not approve of her marrying this handsome Latin man, which made it very difficult for my parents to make the marriage work. My mother's brothers were always interfering and causing problems. My dad was a worker, a pleasant man, a Catholic.

When my parents broke up, my father was shattered, but he managed to afford to send the five kids to St. Mary's Academy in Austin.

We were four girls and one boy, very young. My youngest sister was in diapers. When my father could no longer afford it, the Settlement Home took two sisters and my little brother, but he ran away. An older sister refused to be taken to a home. She was only ten years old. Somehow she managed to get a job as a carhop at a drive-in on the Drag by the University of Texas. While she was working there, she met a young engineering student, and they got married when she was

Betty Ann Moreno Dreese in her basketball uniform and holding a team trophy, on the upstairs porch of the big girls' dorm. Harold Larson's private collection.

fourteen. Her husband got his engineering degree and went on to be president of Hughes Tool Company. They remained together until his death in 2008.

My other sisters were transferred from the Settlement Home to the Presbyterian Children's Home in Itasca, Texas, where both of them stayed until they graduated from high school. They sent me to the Waco State Home.

My father was very depressed about losing his wife and children and over the years, he began to decline in health. He began to drink excessively, but he basically died of a broken heart. My mother was very young and not a responsible mother. She married again and had many more kids. She and her new husband were very poor, but they stayed together. I heard that three of their children were neglected and ended up being taken to the Presbyterian Children's Home.

When I arrived at the Waco State Home, I was six or seven years old. I had a hard time adjusting. In spite of everything, I still cared for my mother, and I thought that as soon as she got on her feet again, she would come back to get me.

I cried constantly. I refused to eat and didn't want to go to school, so they put me in the hospital. I don't remember exactly how long I was there, but it was, I believe, at least three months. A nurse would sit with me and make sure I ate something. They would talk to me gently, trying to help me get over the hurt. They even put me in a room with a window that looked out on the front gate so I could watch for my mother.

I watched and watched, but she never came. The superintendent told me that it was time for me to adjust to the situation. He said something to the effect that if I could not straighten up, I could be sent to Gainesville. He explained that the place in Gainesville was a correctional facility, not a loving atmosphere like the Home.

What helped the most, I think, was when Mr. Speece, the coach, started coming to visit. He told me he could really use me on the basketball team. He even brought me a basketball. Children have a way

of figuring things out. Finally, I knew my mom was never going to return. Somehow or other, playing basketball appealed to me. I got out of the hospital and started going to school and basketball practice.

My mother finally came to visit two or three years later, and it was the only time she came to see me. She was with my stepfather, and there were a lot of other children—I can't say how many. At that time, I knew I did not want to go back with her because I knew she could not take care of me, so it did not hurt so much this time. With all those other children, somehow I knew in my heart that it would never work. I guess I was growing up.

At the Home, they kept us busy all the time, which helped me deal with the stresses I had experienced at such a young age. That kind of discipline is missing from the lives of young people today. My dad came to visit me twice, once before I graduated and then again for my graduation. My older sister lived in Austin and did keep in touch with my father and the rest of the family. The siblings all stayed in touch with each other, and we are still close today. My little brother who ran away ended up in San Angelo, where a couple adopted him, raised him, and sent him to college.

The only time my younger sisters were allowed to come visit me was when I graduated in 1951. Someone from the Waco State Home called the home in Itasca and worked it out. My older sister and her husband came, too. In all those years at the Home, those were the only visits from my family.

I was just average in school. I loved school, but I did not apply myself seriously, and in many subjects, I squeaked by with Bs, Cs, and even a few Ds. The subjects I really liked were athletics, English, music, and science, and in those subjects I did very, very well. I dearly loved our English teacher, Mrs. Mabel Legg. She taught us to love poetry and all the things that make a child's life beautiful. I got to see her at a reunion before she died and thank her for the beautiful example she gave us. There could not be a finer teacher in the world.

I loved science. I took typing, and I really liked business English. The training I received in these subjects would be very valuable to me later in life, after graduation.

We had cosmetology, too. We got perms at the beauty school. When you were hooked up to the heating elements, your hair would get so hot you could feel it cooking. I had 1,000 hours in cosmetology, but I did not want to become a beautician. I continued with my typing classes and other office skills.

We had sports of all kinds. We would play basketball tournaments in other towns. We would ride the school bus and sing all the way home from the game if we won. If we lost, we would cry on the way back.

> We were very, very poor, living in a house with dirt floors. That is why I will be forever grateful for the Home.

The Home had a great choral program, and they developed our voices very early in life. We had a marvelous director. We sang in the choir, we sang at activities, on the bus, in the dorms. We harmonized, like in the movies, and we just sang all the time. I could really belt out a song. I sing to this day.

In the summer, we got to watch movies outside on the lawn. When I look at the movies that we had then and the movies we have today, it is just inconceivable to me to believe we would have regrets about what we had then.

In the summertime, we went to camp and enjoyed swimming, hiking, backpacking, and other activities. The Home had a wonderful Christmas for the children. It was like a fairy tale. There was a huge Christmas tree with all the lights, and everyone had presents.

They had dental care. They taught us hygiene, and today I have beautiful teeth. We didn't have frills, but we had everything we needed.

As for clothes, we had to wear things that were out of style and shoes that made me cry.

We had rules. The discipline was never harsh. If we misbehaved or broke a rule, we would get demer-its, and after you got thirteen demerits, then activities were canceled. You were grounded or you could not attend the movie.

Our routine was like clockwork. We were assigned certain jobs. It was a farm atmosphere. It was very healthy. It is too bad that children today do not have an opportunity to be raised that way.

The food was not what children today would like. For example, we had cooked prunes. We never had much red meat. Even today, I do not eat a lot of meat. I don't think we ever had steak. Today I am not a steak eater, but I do love chicken.

Some of the kids had problems to begin with, as I did—psychological depression. But it soon left. Because they kept us so busy in the cannery, mopping and waxing and buffing the floors, we were worn out. That buffer would run off with me. You could see your face in those floors.

I graduated from the Waco State Home in 1951, when I was just barely seventeen years old. I was the youngest in my graduating class. I was one of two students who sang a solo at the ceremony. I sang "The End of a Perfect Day," and I remember looking out and seeing my father with tears in his eyes. He sent me a letter once, which I carried with me for years and years, which expressed his heartbreak so well. In the letter, he quoted a line from a poem by John Greenleaf Whittier, "For of all sad words of tongue or pen, / The saddest are these: 'It might have been!'"

After graduating, I went to work in the actuary department in the Amicable Insurance Building, the tallest building in Texas at one time. I was working on the eighteenth floor in May 1953 when the tornado struck Waco. I remember going down the stairwells and the building shaking.

During that time, the Gresham family took me in. I lived with them, and they took me to classes at Baylor University, where I would sing. The Greshams were very nice people, but I wanted to be close to my own family, so I moved to Oklahoma, where I would be near my sisters.

My husband, a civil engineer, and I were employed by Saudi Aramco, the largest oil company in the world. We were in Dhahran, Saudi Arabia, for thirteen years. My husband and I went around the world in 1985.

I also attended Clayton College and received a doctorate in nutrition. Today we live in Granbury in a gated community. The grounds are covered with papershell pecan trees, and it is beautiful. I am a substitute teacher and a nutrition consultant.

I feel that I have had a very wonderful life. I've gone back for a couple, maybe three reunions and have felt the love and sincere appreciation of all my classmates. Some really fine people were raised in the Home.

If my mother did anything right, it was allowing us to be sent to the children's homes. I shouldn't say it, but I do think it was a good thing the State of Texas took us away from them, because I can remember being very hungry and on the street with no place to stay. We were very, very poor, living in a house with dirt floors. That is why I will be forever grateful for the Home.

The Waco State Home was the best thing that happened to me. It gave me structure, an opportunity to have an education, good principles, and a foundation for my faith in God.

Harvey Walker

1944–1951

I was born in Littlefield, which is just northwest of Lubbock, about forty miles. My father's name was Bluford Walker. He was a share-cropper near Littlefield. I really don't know much about him. He left when I was about two years old and my sister was a baby. When I was three or four, I remember a man came by in a truck. I assumed he was my father because he wanted my brother Bill to leave with him. Bill got in the truck, but they only made it a little way down the road before Bill changed his mind and came running back home.

We lived with my grandfather on my mother's side. My mother worked occasionally, but once I was in school, she started running around with different men. The first time I remember her leaving us, she was working downtown at what we called a Coney Island cafe. A guy was sitting outside the store on his car fender, strumming a guitar, singing "Wabash Cannonball," and before I knew it, she left with him. She took my sister but abandoned my brother and me. Next time we saw them, they were married. They came to live with Granddad and us for a while because the guy had burned himself badly while in a drunken stupor and they had no other place to stay. He ended up in jail.

After that, my mother would go with one guy after another. We never had sheets on the bed. We had bedbugs. We were living in a small frame house my grandfather had built. During the dust storms, the wind and dirt came seeping through the walls. There was no electricity, no running water. Granddad was a great old guy, but he never did have anything.

When Granddad went out west to visit some of his other kids, he left our mother with a car and some money. As soon as he was gone, she immediately took off, abandoning my brother and me. In the fall, I enrolled myself in the fifth grade. I had no school supplies, so I made a little tablet, drawing the lines on the pages by hand. An elderly couple across the street looked after us, made sure we had something to eat. The authorities found out, took us to court, made us wards of the state, and eventually took my brother, sister, and me to the Waco State Home. That was in 1944, when I was eleven years old.

They placed me in Mrs. Cashion's dormitory. She was a very strict disciplinarian. Mrs. Cashion had a custom-made paddle, and she used it quite often on some of the guys.

Once I sneaked off after school and went swimming in the river by Lovers' Leap. We convinced one of the guys who couldn't swim very well to swim across the river, but then he wouldn't come back across, so we just left him there, buck naked. He came upon a road crew. They gave him a yellow rain slicker and a ride to the other side of the river so he could get

his clothes. It was real late by the time he got back to the Home, so Mrs. Cashion realized we had done something. I got a paddling for that.

While I was in Mrs. Cashion's dormitory, I wanted to raise a steer for my Future Farmers of America project. I went to a rodeo and won one in a calf scramble. They would get a bunch of kids and a bunch of little calves, turn them all loose in the arena, and whoever caught a calf got to keep it. So I caught one, and I raised him, got him fattened up, and took him to the livestock show in Waco. I didn't win any prizes, but I sold him for a profit. I think I spent the money on a Christmas present. I was sweet on a girl at that time, and I suspect I spent it all on her.

We ground and mixed our own feed at the Home. The grinder at the feed barn was driven by a big, powerful electric motor with a belt drive. One day I accidentally stepped on the belt while the motor was running and broke my right ankle in several places. The doctor from Waco came out and put a cast on my ankle. By nighttime, my foot had swollen so much it was really painful, so the doctor had to come back in the middle of the night and put a different cast on it.

Another boy fractured his leg, and they ended up having to rebreak it a couple of times. It never healed properly. So my older brother told me, "By God, that's not going to happen to you. You're going to start using that leg as soon as you get that cast off." So that's what I did. It was painful, but things turned out all right.

Several kids died during the time I lived there. A boy named J. T. Rosson drowned while swimming in the Bosque River. Travis Fagan was the one who found him. That was a real tragedy. One of the girls got leukemia, and one of the boys died from some other disease. Another boy died when he fell off an electrical tower in the cow pasture.

At Christmas, various people in Waco would give money to the Home, and it would be distributed among the kids. I think it amounted to five or ten dollars per person. We would take the money to town and buy ourselves something or a gift for our girlfriends.

Mrs. Cashion had left the Home while I was in the hospital with a broken ankle. When I got out, they moved me to Ms. Hackney's dormitory. She was not as strict as Mrs. Cashion. Her boys were a bit older and were allowed more freedom. They could go places around the campus on their own to do chores. I started working in the dairy barn then, and did so until I graduated.

The most important things about living at the Home were attending school, doing chores, and playing sports. We had our own school, where everyone went until they graduated. This changed in 1955, when we started going to public schools.

School was just the essentials, but because of our English teacher, Mabel Legg, we had exceptional training in this most important subject. I never knew of anyone from the Home having trouble with English classes in college.

Sports were important to almost all the guys and some of the girls. We played football, basketball, and baseball. A few of the guys ran track. The high school didn't have enough students to qualify for the lowest classification of eleven-man football, so the Class B schools in the area had to vote us in for district competition. Still, we usually had only fifteen to twenty guys on the football team, and sometimes had only eleven or twelve ready to play. Almost everyone played both offense and defense. We always managed to win a few games a year and were seldom outscored too badly. We did better in basketball, but never won district during the four years I played.

In the second semester of my junior year, we started a new activity that soon became very popular—square dancing! A well-known teacher and caller, Mabel Balch, helped us learn the basics, then exhibition dancing and couples dancing. We went to many local dances and to a number of large dance events out of town.

Chores for boys, other than keeping our dorms spotlessly clean and neat, were pretty varied. My first assignment as a sixth grader was to perform janitorial duties in the school building—sweeping, taking out trash, etc. Then, in the eighth grade, I moved up to working in the storeroom where everything used at the Home was received, stored, and then distributed based on requisitions sent in from the dorms, kitchens, etc. Only two guys worked in the storeroom—traditionally from Mrs. Cashion's dorm.

In the ninth grade, I joined the group of guys that worked in the dairy barn in the mornings from five a.m. until we finished before breakfast. Other guys, who didn't play sports, worked in the dairy barn in the afternoon. It takes a lot of milk to feed 300 kids plus a lot of employees. We milked thirty to forty cows twice a day.

By the twelfth grade, I had been promoted to running the pasteurizing room, where milk was strained, heated, cooled, put in five-gallon milk cans, and delivered to the kitchen cooler. Some of the milk was run through a separator to provide several gallons of cream every day. All the equipment had to be sterilized by steam after being used.

After breakfast and before school, we had to haul garbage, feed the pigs, take hay to the cows, feed the chickens.

On Saturday mornings there was feed to be mixed and ground, slaughterhouse duties—cows, pigs, and chickens, we did it all—chicken houses and pigpens to be cleaned, plus hauling trash, mowing grass, clipping hedges, etc.

In the summer, we worked on two farms located several miles away, plus a large field and a large garden at the Home. We did everything, but I guess the highlights were baling hay and harvesting watermelons. We also picked tomatoes and peaches on other farms.

The girls worked regularly in the kitchen, dining room, and laundry. In the summer, they canned and prepared for freezing a lot of the things we ate.

All was not work, school, or sports. Every summer, we went to camp for two weeks or took special trips. One year, the older boys baled and hauled hay for several farmers to make money for a week's trip to Galveston. We went swimming in the large public pool in town, went to movies—usually a busload at a time to a drive-in—Cameron Park, events at Baylor, pro baseball games, and, of course, square dancing. Sports involved going to other schools or in town for Little League. The Future Farmers of America boys went to the Texas State Fair every year.

The older boys were allowed to go off campus on Saturday and Sunday afternoons. We mowed lawns, washed cars, caddied at the country club, and anything else to make a little money so we could go to town to movies, buy Levis or something for our girlfriends, or just go for a long walk. We were always back in time to visit the girls late in the afternoon or after supper. Our visiting was restricted to the area in front of the school, but we all enjoyed it.

We gathered for watermelon feasts and singing on the lawn. Some of the older guys and girls were good singers, or so we thought. Occasionally, entertainers would come out and do a show for us. One of them was Hank Thompson, back when he was just getting started.

When I was in the tenth or eleventh grade, I went up to the big boys' dormitory, under Mr. Whigham. Whigham was widely despised and hated by all the boys, but we had to get along with him somehow, since we didn't want to be "chased off." He regularly did force certain boys to leave the Home.

We were afraid of Whigham. He was physically intimidating. When he gave you a paddling, it was severe enough that just the threat of repeat experiences was enough to make some guys leave.

Some of the boys in Whigham's dorm were big and athletic. When my brother, Bill, was in twelfth grade, he and another kid got in trouble with Whigham. He told them he was going to give them both a good paddling. They told him he would regret the hell out of it if he did.

Whigham arranged for them to leave the Home in January, in the middle of their senior year, to attend Tarleton Junior College. None of us knew what had happened until they were gone. My brother told me about it later on.

Then Mr. Whigham made the mistake of beating a kid so badly that it brought blood to his buttocks. I get choked up just thinking about it.

That was the last straw. All of us in that dorm decided we weren't going to put up with Whigham's nonsense any longer. At first, we thought we would just ignore him. We would not talk to him, and we all made sure that none of us were ever alone in his presence. After a day or so, Whigham decided we ought to have a conference with Mr. Peek, the superintendent. So they gathered us all in a schoolroom to talk to Mr. Peek. One of my good friends at that time was a great athlete and good-looking. Everybody liked him. When Mr. Peek asked us what was going on, my friend and I were the ones who spoke up. Before the day was over, Whigham had been terminated, and he was gone.

This happened about four or five months after my brother left. Too bad we didn't do it sooner.

After I left the Home, I found out they hired Whigham at the Methodist Home in Waco, and a few years later the Waco State Home hired him back. I never could believe that. He used to come to the reunions, but we despised him until the day he died.

After I graduated, my sister ran away from the Home and went to live with our mother. She married, and ended up with five kids by the time she was twenty-two.

My brother, Bill, joined the air force after attending Tarleton one semester. After the air force, he went

> That was the last straw. All of us in that dorm decided we weren't going to put up with Whigham's nonsense any longer.

to work for the Federal Aviation Agency as a regional air traffic controller. Bill died of heart failure when he was fifty-three.

I graduated in 1951 and went to college for a few years. I briefly attended the University of Texas and Stephen F. Austin [State] University before I went to North Texas State University. Then, in 1954, I was about to be drafted in the army, so I joined the USAF [U.S. Air Force]. I was assigned to Operational Intelligence in the Strategic Air Command, based at Westover Air Force Base in Massachusetts.

After leaving the USAF in 1958, I got a BBA in accounting at NTSU and went to work for Magnolia Petroleum, a subsidiary of Mobil Oil. I started out in the Dallas office, went through a two-year training program, worked in the New York headquarters, and then spent six years in various other locations. Later,

I went to work for Champlin Petroleum Company in Fort Worth, and then worked for ten years with Delhi International Oil Company, which had operations primarily in Australia. I started with Delhi as comptroller and rose to vice president of finance and administration.

In 1982, I managed a large private foundation until I retired in 1998. It was quite a switch, having worked in big corporations with all sorts of responsibilities and then changing to what was basically a two-person private foundation. I like to say that the other employee did all the work and I did all the thinking. I was responsible for hiring money managers who invested the foundation's money.

My wife, Martha, and I were married in 1967. We have two sons, one granddaughter, and four great-grandchildren.

Yvonne Mabry Barnes

1945–1955

Not only orphans were eligible for entry into the Waco State Home, but also dependent and neglected children. My parents had also been dependent and neglected children. As for my mother, her mother died giving birth to her, and her father abandoned her. When my father was three, his father died, and his mother died when he was fourteen. Both my parents grew up being shuffled between relatives. I think they regarded marriage as a haven where they would be loved and safe, but they were wrong. Neither of my parents graduated from high school, and my father was physically disabled. Shortly before my mother reached her eighteenth birthday and my father his twenty-second, they

Yvonne Mabry Barnes, top row, second from left, Norman Clark, front row, second from left, John Wilson, front row, far right, and other members of the Waco State Home square-dancing group. Harold Larson's private collection.

had two children. I was the oldest. They were divorced when my sister was nine months old.

We lived with an aunt and uncle who were childless, but when I was about nine years old, my aunt died. Then the animosity between my parents erupted and the fighting began. My father learned of the Waco State Home while he was attending a training school, and soon was in the courts having us separated from our mother and installed at the Home. I remember the date being sometime in September of 1945, because it was the beginning of football season. We were taken from our classes at Waco public school and deposited with two old ladies who lived in a two-story house in downtown Waco, where we stayed only a couple of days while the details were worked out. Then we were transported to the hospital at the Home, where we were quarantined, which terrified us. After another couple of days, my sister and I, being close in age, were assigned together to Mrs. Arrowwood's dormitory. She was a grandmotherly, sweet, loving, and caring lady. We were soon assimilated into our new lifestyle. And the saga continued.

We had some really interesting dorm matrons. The older ones were really strict, but they had a lot of responsibility. I remember a Mrs. Stipes, who played boogie-woogie on the piano. I really enjoyed her playing.

If I remember correctly, I rarely got into trouble. My only risk for punishment was talking back, which I never learned to stop. I was punished by having to stand in the hall or on the stairs. Once, when I was really young, my punishment was having to eat out of a tin plate instead of a regular one. I cannot remember receiving any corporal punishment, and I know of no others who suffered severe beatings. We always had really great Christmases. The Home and many social clubs in the Waco area made sure we were all remembered. Our first year at the Home, the people from my father's little town sent us boxes and boxes of toys.

> We did not mingle much with "city" kids.

Our mother and father always came to see us—separately, of course. When we were younger, abandoned tennis courts were near our dorm. Our father bought my sister and me roller skates, and we spent hours skating on the tennis courts and daydreaming about how our lives would be when we were educated and on our own. When we were promoted to the mid-age girls' dorms, our father bought us a bike, which we rode until it would go no more.

Our vacations were usually away from the Home—Galveston, Corpus Christi, Port Aransas, and Inks Lake. Once at Inks Lake, we were going up a steep incline in a bus, and the driver lost control. The bus tumbled over, but did not go down the incline. I had a head cut that required stitches. Some of the other kids were more seriously injured, but they were given immediate medical attention, and all survived with a deep respect for driving on inclines. I remember walking away, and the pavement was really hot on our feet. Some people driving by gave us rides back to our camp.

We did not mingle much with "city" kids. I always felt self-conscious around them and thought they either looked down on us or felt sorry for us. But my thoughts did not linger on my situation, and I accepted where I was and where I was going.

We all had boyfriends, but our social activity was limited to meeting in front of the administration building and giggling with goo-goo eyes. We were terribly innocent and/or naïve. We had movies outside during summer, which was a great treat. In my time at the Home, we were bused somewhere to go swimming, but later, before my sister graduated, they built a pool on the grounds, which was really great.

My sister was a good basketball player at only five feet two inches tall. I played basketball and softball. Once, at a baseball game, I was playing shortstop, with a girl on second base. She was pretty fair-sized, and I told myself, "She's not going to get past me," but she ran flat over me and slammed me to the ground.

The school was excellent. I was a little intimidated

by all the strict structure when I first got there, but I soon adjusted. Mrs. Mabel Legg, our high school English teacher, was a model of comportment, mental agility, and compassion. Another favorite teacher was Mr. Speece, the girls' basketball coach. He taught algebra and history and was really great with the kids. I think he had a lot of compassion for our situations.

High school was fun. My sister and I both were members of the square-dancing group, a really big social activity. Mrs. Balch, the teacher, took care of all of us, many times going out on a limb to see that we had a good time. We were privileged to dance all over the state. We danced on television in San Antonio and got to explore the River Walk. We also did an exhibition in Amarillo. We had fun everywhere we went. My husband and I still square-dance, and it is still fun—sixty years of do-si-dos.

I think my graduating class in 1955 had no more than ten or twelve students. We were all pretty close, like brothers and sisters. That was soon after the Waco tornado, which killed over a hundred people. At the time, I was working downtown near where the tornado hit. The experience was emotionally devastating. My mother was living in San Angelo, where a tornado struck that same day, and my father was living in San Antonio. We had no communications for a couple of days and could not reach our mother or father, nor could they reach us.

The most traumatic event, however, was leaving the Home and moving to Huntsville to attend Sam Houston State University. My roommate at the Home went to Sam Houston State and was my roommate there. I cried and cried for months, especially when my father called. I had thought of WSH as my home for a long time, and I was homesick. My biggest regret is that I did not finish college.

I eventually moved to San Angelo, where I met my husband. We married in 1961. I worked at Angelo State University for six or seven years while I attended classes. My greatest joy working was when I was girl Friday for Grant Teaff, the famous football coach, who was coaching at Angelo State before Baylor recruited him. He and his family treated me as family. They are fine, inspiring people. I really enjoyed working for the college. I enjoyed the atmosphere. It was cool!

My husband and I now live in Brandon, Florida, where I have attended classes at nearby University of South Florida. I really enjoy going to school. I told my old friend JoAnn, "You know what's different about going to school these days? You have to wear short shorts and walk around with a water bottle in your hand."

I have been to three reunions at the Home, but it has been a while. My husband and I have three grown children, six grandchildren, and three great-grandchildren.

The greatest lesson I learned from my experience at the Home is that my family comes first. I have tried hard with my children and really, really hard with my grandchildren. I want them to know they are truly loved, and I think they do know it. We've got a good family. The other day, one of my granddaughters said to me, "You can't do that, Grandma—you're perfect." It doesn't get any better than that.

Tommy Turner

1947–1957

I came to the Waco State Home with my brother Kenneth when I was eight years of age. We, like many children of the WSH, came from a broken home. Our father was an alcoholic and deserted the family. Our mother, with little education and no job experience, could not maintain the family.

When we got to the Home, Kenneth and I agreed to stay together, regardless. We would not agree to adoption if the adopting parents would not take both. Later, I had the opportunity of adoption but declined to be separated from my brother who was four years older.

Mr. and Mrs. C. B. Whigham were my dorm parents twice during my stay in the WSH, once in a younger dorm and again when I was junior high age. Mr. Whigham coached a lot of summer athletics for boys younger than high school age. He was a large man with a loud voice. If he didn't like a boy, he would berate and bully and destroy his self-esteem. He was overbearing. He wasn't a good person.

Tommy Turner, as a sophomore, standing in front of the senior boys' dorm of the Waco State Home, 1955. Photo courtesy of Kenneth Turner.

Mr. Raborn Balch and his wife Mabel were at one time the dorm parents of the older boys' dorm. She also taught square dancing, and he was the dean of boys. Mr. Balch and Mr. Whigham both came to WSH from the Gatesville State School for Boys—delinquents in trouble with law enforcement. Their discipline methods were much too severe for the WSH.

I witnessed many merciless beatings and a few times was told of sexual molestation.

There was a boy in our junior high dorm named David who had a horribly disfigured leg from an auto accident. He was a weight lifter with a strong upper body, so he was by no means weak. He was just not able to participate in most athletics, so Mr. Whigham had little use for him and constantly picked on him.

One day David had already been disciplined, but after bedtime Mr. Whigham pulled him out of bed and took him into the locker room. We heard a struggle, loud voices, and lockers slamming. About six of us, including some of the boys who made up the three sets of twins who lived in the Whigham dorm, rushed to the locker room.

What we saw was a fistfight, not a disciplining, and Mr. Whigham, who had a lump on his head and a bloody nose, had David in a headlock. We attempted to separate the two, and Mr. Whigham hit one of our boys in the face with his fist, starting an all-out brawl. No matter how hard we pounded on Mr. Whigham, he would not let go of David's head, so we kept fighting. No one was seriously hurt, but we gave him a good thrashing that night. We were just tired of him and his brutality, for we'd all been on the receiving end.

Mrs. Whigham heard the disturbance and came to the locker room in her night robe. She saw her husband on his knees on the floor, his white T-shirt covered in blood. She started crying and screaming, "Don't hit him anymore. Let him alone!" and rushed out of the room for help.

> I witnessed many merciless beatings and a few times was told of sexual molestation.

Mr. Whigham tried to scold us, and he was crying a little, but that didn't evoke any emotions in us. We'd had it with him.

There wasn't an ounce of blood on any of us, except David, and that was Mr. Whigham's blood.

Mr. Balch came, talked to the Whighams, and then interviewed each boy individually. We expected to be expelled from the Home, but none were. I believe the Whighams were later reassigned. I was soon moved to the senior boys' dorm, and I never saw Mr. Whigham again. He finally got his comeuppance because we cleaned his plow that night.

I was not known as a troublemaker, but I've always hated to see people mistreated. There were many nights we had heard Mr. Whigham in action, and we'd covered our heads and hoped he didn't come after us next. That night with Mr. Whigham represented a lot of unvented frustration that was finally vented.

During most of my later years at the Home, I didn't have time for fights. I was going to school, playing sports, and too busy working in the dairy or on one of the farms belonging to the Home.

I got up at four or five in the morning and went straight to the dairy to help milk or feed nearly thirty head of cattle before breakfast, then returned to the dairy to work before and after school. On Saturday mornings I had to grind and mix feed for the cattle.

During the growing season we traveled to the Lake Waco farm in that red Dodge truck. It had high sideboards, so we could stack a lot of hay and haul it back to the dairy barn, where we had to lift those bales into the loft. We also planted and harvested acres of peas, beans, corn, and potatoes. Farming was hard work.

My brother graduated in 1953 and attended North Texas State University for a year before joining the air force. Our mother offered to take me to live with her and a stepdad. I declined because the kids at WSH had by now become like siblings.

My favorite dorm parents were Mr. and Mrs. T. C. Brumfield at the senior dorm. Mr. Brumfield had worked earlier for the Texas Prison System and suggested that I look into this after high school.

The campus high school was closed in 1955, so I finished my last two years at University High School. I graduated in 1957 with scholarships, as a member of the National Honor Society, and in the upper part of my class. I didn't go to college because I got a job with Texas Power and Light right out of school. I made my first bit of money, bought myself a new car, and I was high on life.

I later joined the Marine Corps, and upon discharge I went to work for the Texas Prison System in 1961. I had planned to attend Sam Houston State while working, but my penal career advanced so fast. I suppose because I had by then been thoroughly institutionalized by the WSH and the Marine Corps.

At one point I managed five or six factories in the prison system, and I got them air conditioned when the cell blocks were not. Inmates stood in line to work in my area, and I tried to create working conditions that were fair and that gave the men an opportunity to learn a trade. We manufactured garments, including all the inmates' clothing, as well as draperies and stage curtains. We even took raw cotton to cloth in the textile mill.

I often joke that the state of Texas not only raised me but employed me during my adult years and has since provided a retirement for life. I have been married for forty-three years and have two children and two grandchildren.

My son was the first person in our family in many generations to graduate from college. He went to Sam Houston State, and then, against my advice, he got a job in the prison system. I recommended against it because, in my opinion, it's a very negative atmosphere. Your biggest problem isn't being attacked by an inmate; it's inmates attacking each other. There is so much violence in there.

As for the WSH, it probably saved my life and kept me out of jail. I cherish those kids that I grew up with, both boys and girls, who provided many years of fond memories. I enjoy and look forward to the WSH reunion each year. It's like going home.

Betty Emfinger Cupps

1948–1951

W hen we were taken away, we had been living in an abandoned school building, just an old one-room school in the country. I remember there was a great big picture of George Washington on the wall and a big wood stove we used for heat. To this day, I have bad scars on my elbows and knees where I burned myself on that stove. We all got burned by it.

We were neglected. I remember going hungry, and I remember my brother, James, and I eating dirt to fill our stomachs. We never went to the doctor. Once, when I was just big enough to lift an axe, I dropped one on my leg. That's another big scar. My sister said that Dad just poured some cooking oil on it. It really is a wonder that we all made it.

Even before we were taken away from our parents, I remember my mother and father fighting. It was very scary. They threw things at each other—knives and chairs and things like that. I remember realizing I had to be responsible for them. I had to keep them from fighting and take

Betty Emfinger Cupps, age four, and brother James, age six, in front of the administration building, shortly after arriving at the Waco State Home, 1948. Photo courtesy of Betty Emfinger Cupps.

care of them. I always felt I had to take care of everybody else.

One day they took my parents to jail for neglecting us. Both of them had tuberculosis, so they put my mother, sister, and stepsister in a TB hospital. I'm not sure about my father. I know he had TB for the rest of his life. This was in Commerce, Texas, in 1948.

We stayed with my aunt until somebody came and took us to the orphanage. I don't know how long we stayed with my aunt, maybe a week or so. As a four-year-old, a time line doesn't mean much. James and I were the only two who were taken to the Waco State Home at that time, but later on, my older sister went to live at the Home, after she was discharged from the TB hospital.

The way I understand it, when we were still staying with my aunt, my father ran away from jail somehow and came by, but he didn't stay. I was four and James was six. We were so little we didn't understand. I told James we needed to go tell them to let our parents out of jail. We started walking down the road, but once my aunt's house was no longer in sight, we got scared and decided to go back. I remember the feeling of hopelessness. A caseworker came by and took us to Waco.

It's hard to explain, but when you're a child and you've been taken from your home, no matter what kind of place it was, it was home to you. You don't know what's going to happen to you or why.

I thought we were in jail because there were gates and a brick fence around most of the place. Everything about it was self-contained. They raised all their meat and vegetables—everything essential to living was done there. We lived in dormitories, and a matron blew a whistle to tell you to line up, go to bed, go to lunch, and so forth, and you marched wherever you were supposed to go. So it was very much like a prison.

As long as you obeyed the rules, they pretty much left you alone, but nobody ever touched you, patted you, put an arm around you, or told you everything

was going to be okay. Nobody ever explained anything to you or reassured you. There was none of that at all. Imagine taking a baby and telling him, "You go here and do this, you do this, you do that." It was like putting a baby in boot camp.

The first night, they let me stay with James in the little boys' dorm. That's the only thing I remember that gave any indication they were cognizant of our fears. After that, we were separated and not allowed to see each other. Once, we spotted each other and sneaked behind the trash barrels along the fence that separated the boys from the girls. We hid there so we could talk to each other, but we were discovered and given whippings. That was the only whipping I got the entire time I was there. I was a good little girl. I was sort of scared to misbehave. I never wet the bed, and I did what I was told whether I wanted to or not. I didn't want to get in trouble. I witnessed other people getting into trouble, and that was scary enough.

I don't remember the names of the matrons, but when I first got there, our matron was in the hospital. They took us on the school bus to visit her. We were told that one of the really mean girls at the Home had made the matron fall and break her leg.

I don't know if all the things I heard about that girl were true, but she hurt me once. There was a pole, like a Maypole, with long straps, which you would grab and swing on. Since I was too little to reach the straps, this girl lifted me so I could grab the end, and then she flung me real hard so that I fell and hit my head on the center post. She was a rough girl.

Being so young at the time, I don't remember the names of the friends I played with at the Home. I do remember the night when one of the older girls in the upstairs dorm wet her bed. They made her come downstairs and sleep with the little ones. Getting to sleep upstairs was supposed to be a reward for me, since I never wet the bed, but it wasn't. I didn't know any of those girls. I felt out of place.

Some of the guys and some of the girls who grew up at the Home have horrible stories about being beaten. I did see older ones get whippings, but I didn't see that happen to the little girls. The Home was cold and very military-like, but I didn't see any of that. We were really little, and I think we were sort of afraid to misbehave.

I tended to play by myself. There was a tennis court out there that wasn't used much, and I would go out there to play. I didn't have any toys at all. If I found a tissue or a piece of paper, I would roll each side and then roll up the bottom to make two babies in a blanket. I sort of invented things to play with.

I remember clothes being donated to the Home. I remember the matron going through the items to determine what each of us could wear.

I had very few clothes. I had one pair of mismatched pajamas and two outfits—so that I could wear one while the other was being washed—and one pair of shoes. I still remember my feet hurting when I had to wear those shoes. The only thing I remember about chapel is that I had to stand up at the very front, and those shoes made my feet hurt so badly. It wasn't a very spiritual childhood.

I remember saluting the flag. Every morning we all came out and watched the flag being raised. I guess we said the Pledge of Allegiance, I don't know.

We had a kindergarten. I was there about a year, and I could already count to 100 and do some simple math. I knew my ABCs and things like that.

Being adopted was the one thing all the kids really dreamed about. Everyone thought it would be wonderful. Several people came to the Home and wanted to take me for the day and get to know me, but I never went with any of them until I met the couple that ended up adopting me. For some reason, I had been leery of the others, but I was comfortable with this couple.

The woman who adopted me was a teacher from Mexia. She taught first grade, so she knew how to talk to me, and that's probably why I liked her. About a year after they adopted me, they divorced. My mother and I moved to another town and sort of started all

over again. She remarried about a year after that. It wasn't a very happy marriage. It turned out that being adopted wasn't a magical gift like everyone thought. After the divorce, I became more or less the person my mother leaned on, her confidant. She told me things you shouldn't tell a little girl.

Despite all that, I grew up fine, but I had a lot of responsibility put on me at an early age. After I got married, I decided to look for my family. Actually, the only person I wanted to see was James. I did not have much attachment to my two sisters. I knew I had a baby brother who had been adopted, but my mother had told me he had died. James was the only one with whom I had a real bond, but when I contacted him, they all started calling and we got together.

The reunion of our family was not a happy thing for me. I hadn't realized what kind of family I had come from. Your mind can play tricks on you. After the adoption, my new mother asked me about my birth mother, and I told her that she was dead. That was how I remembered it. I even remembered going to her funeral. But when I found out my family was from Commerce, I went there and went straight to my aunt's house and I said, "That's it, that's my aunt's house." I hadn't seen it since I was four years old. The house was closed up and abandoned, with a note on the door stating that if you were interested in buying the property, go to the fire station and talk to the chief. The fire chief was my cousin.

I met him, and he started telling me things. He sent me to see a couple that used to let James stay with them and work for them. They mentioned going to see my mother, which was a big shock to me. They told me she wasn't dead—she was very much alive. She was in an institution for people with intellectual disabilities.

My mother was in the same institution as my older stepsister, Joann. They tested Joann and finally re-

> Being adopted was the one thing all the kids really dreamed about.

leased her, but my mother was still there. I didn't want to go see her, but different people talked me into it.

The doctors I spoke with at the institution confirmed that my mother had intellectual disabilities. They said it wasn't severe. She may have been a borderline case, and if she'd had better family support, she might have been able to live a normal life without being institutionalized. None of us had disabilities. I graduated from college with an A average.

I was basically inundated with bad news. It was overwhelming. To tell the truth, at first I didn't want to be around any of my family. It was unpleasant. They all had scars, emotional scars, and most people who were raised in the Waco State Home weren't taught anything about life skills or how to relate to people.

Most of them didn't learn anything about working except the physical labor they did on the farm. They didn't know how to get out and get a job and do the simplest things. They kept you there until you were eighteen or graduated from high school, and then they opened the door and said, "You're on your own." There was no preparation. Some of them literally slept on the streets for a few nights until they could find something.

My sister ran away from the Home when she was about fifteen or sixteen. She had run away before, and the last time they let her stay gone. She went back to Commerce, and later she went to live with Uncle Leon and his wife, who live in Washington State. Irene made her go to school and saw that she graduated. After graduating high school, my sister married and got the Home to release James so he could come live with them. A few months later, however, they moved to New Jersey. Leon and Irene took him in. James graduated and got a job with the Union Glass Company and has done well for himself.

They have taken me to all of the reunions at the Home. I've gotten to know quite a number of those people, although I didn't remember them at first. Some of them have done well, but so many of them have never been able to make it.

Right now I'm planning a big wedding for my daughter. It's not a huge wedding, but it's a church wedding. My sister and brother both decided to come see me. Now I've got guests, including my daughter from Arizona with all her family, and people from all over will be coming in and staying here with me.

James Emfinger

1948–1960

I was born in Gilmer, Texas, but we were living in Commerce when the state came and split us up. That was in 1948, I believe, which would mean I was six years old.

My parents were having real difficulty providing for us. My father, along with my older sister, had been in a sanitarium for tuberculosis patients. My mother and one of my sisters were sent to Mexia State School, which was for people with mental health and developmental problems.

My younger sister was admitted to the Waco State Home at the same time I was, but she was adopted within a year or two. Since the boys and girls were separated, I didn't get to see her very much anyway. I was happy for her. I think it was during my second year that my other sister was sent to the Home.

My dad came to visit a couple of times. He was very poor. The price of a tank of gas was a lot of money to him, so driving down there from Commerce was a real hardship, but he did come a couple of times. I was real happy to see him. I looked up to my dad.

One of the matrons had a sister in Yoakum, Texas, who took my sister and me home with her for a week or two during the summer. That was nice of her and her husband to do that. We did that a couple of times. They were an older couple, nice people.

There were lots of good times at the Home. With that many kids, we could do lots of different things together, playing games and stuff. One of my first strong memories is seeing a kid being whipped by the matron at my first dorm. I had never seen anything like that before. He was jumping all around, and everyone was laughing because it looked funny. But pretty quickly I thought to myself, "That's going to be me one day," so I quit laughing. That particular matron wasn't actually all that bad.

In general, though, the matrons did things that I would definitely disagree with now. For example, they punished a kid for wetting the bed by making him wear a dress.

After a couple of years, I was moved to Ms. Woodington's dorm. Ms. Woodington was a pretty rough woman, really strict. Looking back, I can see you have to be somewhat firm when you are responsible for that many kids, but she whipped us and made us toe the line. Every two years they moved us to another dorm.

Ms. Belcher, who was in charge of the dorm I lived in when I was about ten, was the toughest matron I ran into. When she got mad, she called us idiots, imbeciles, and morons. She would grab you by the head and bounce your head off the walls.

When she whipped us she would make us pull our pants off down to our underwear and bend over this bench. She used a baseball bat that had been shaved down, and whipped the daylights out of us. She really tore us up. After a whipping by her, we were black and blue on the back, rear end, and legs. The bruises took a long time to fade away. It would take a few weeks before they were all gone.

As I recall, she treated us all the same. She was a big woman—I'd say over 200 pounds—and a really rough person. As I got older and more mature, I realized that poor woman may have had a lot of things bothering her that could make her do things like that.

Her husband was nice to us. He was a really gentle person, but he should've stepped in to control her now and then. Ms. Belcher whipped me a few times. I don't remember how many.

After one of her whippings, I left the dorm and walked downstairs. I felt very bad. It was painful. I walked to the area connecting the dorms that had arches and concrete slabs where you could sit. I walked through the arch that led to our playground. For some reason, I looked up into the sky and saw this vision. I saw myself flying around in the air. I was really enjoying it.

I watched it for a little while, having a great time, and then I noticed something else. I looked to my right and saw the Heavenly Father and Mother watching me with big smiles on their faces. I didn't understand it at the time.

Later I started getting into the Bible. Many scriptures, such as Acts 17:28–29, tell us that we are God's offspring. Hebrews 12:9 says that he is the father of our spirits. I believe that before we came to Earth, we lived in heaven, as spirit children of heavenly parents. They give us these bodies so that we come to Earth to be educated and learn very valuable things. They gave us these bodies to house our spirits.

Many scriptures bear this out, but I didn't learn about this until years and years later, when I was in Alaska. I began talking to missionaries, and I learned these things. If I had told Ms. Belcher about that vi-

> When she got mad, she called us idiots, imbeciles, and morons.

sion, she would have tore me up. She would've said I was lying and whipped me like crazy.

As a child, you get busy playing and doing things that help you forget about bad things, but that kind of treatment definitely does something to you. It did cause me problems later in life. I had low self-esteem. When you're called an idiot, a moron, and an imbecile by an adult, it leaves a mark on you.

The matron at my next dorm was a single woman. I can't remember her name, but she was nice, a good person. She was nothing like Ms. Belcher.

The guys who lived in Mr. Whigham's dorm talk about how rough he was, but I liked him. He always treated me nice and took a lot of time coaching us in different sports. He did have a temper but never treated me badly, never got angry with me or scared me. He did hurt some of the kids. He knocked out James and put scars all over his eyes, but James is a remarkable person, and he forgave Whigham. When Whigham died, James went to his funeral.

They put me in the big boys' dorm instead of Whigham's dorm. The matrons there were Mr. and Mrs. Collier. They were good people—no complaints about them. After Ms. Belcher's dorm, everything went pretty smoothly.

I ran away from the Home several times. The last time, they let me stay with my aunt in Commerce. But I got to missing my friends so much, I asked to go back. At the Home, you could always get up a game of baseball, football, or something. There were a lot of real good times out there. The real rough times were few, and the good times were many.

One time, another boy wanted to take off and asked me to go with him. I didn't especially want to go, but I didn't want him to call me a coward, so I went with him. I guess we thought we were big shots. We went to Cameron Park and got picked up there. The park was just north of the Home. We didn't get very far.

Another time, I stayed with a friend from East Junior High School. It was a bad experience. He had me hide out in his barn because he didn't want his mom to know I was there, and I almost froze to death. I was happy to get back to the Home.

I remember going to the movies and how fun it was in the summer when we had a big watermelon feed. I think everybody was happy when they started letting us go to the public schools in town. We got to see a little more of the world that way.

It was embarrassing to be riding around in buses that said "Waco State Home" on them. When we'd go places, people would see us and say, "Oh, those kids are orphans," and things like that. We all used to say we hated the Waco State Home and the State of Texas, too, but they gave us clothing, they fed us well, we had recreation, and we learned how to work.

I attended Waco High School. I liked it and was looking forward to playing sports, but my sister called me from Washington and asked if I wanted to come and live with her and her family, so I jumped at the chance. That was Christmas of 1959. I had been at the Home for twelve years.

Now that I'm grown up, I want to say I am very appreciative of the Waco State Home and the State of Texas. They did an awful lot for us.

Sudie Powell Goodman

1948–1954

To start from the beginning, I would like to say that I am so grateful to the wonderful citizens of the state of Texas for providing this particular facility.

In case you are not aware of this, I want to share with you how the Home for Dependent and Neglected Children began. In 1919, a precious lady named Mrs. Bennett F. Smith campaigned before the Texas Legislature and explained why the bill creating the Home should be passed. Thank God for women who have a passion for neglected children. She listed ten reasons:

1. It provides for the full carrying-out of the state juvenile law.
2. It will save children from places of vice and immorality and prevent grafters from dealing in humanity.
3. The Home will provide for the grooming of children that they may be acceptable in private homes.

Sudie Powell Goodman and friend at the Waco State Home, their last time together before graduating and going to college, 1954. Harold Larson's private collection.

4. It will save children from pilfering, lying and stealing caused by extreme want and neglect.

5. It will make lazy, indifferent parents interested in keeping their children at home.

6. It will save children from blindness and disabilities caused by loathsome diseases.

7. It will make possible the taking of innocent children from people using them as a means of begging or vice and/or for immoral purposes.

8. These are children with talents as other children and they should be protected, cared for and educated. Act for them; they cannot speak for themselves.

9. No provision has been made for such children, and it is the State's duty to provide for them, that they may make men and women worthy of the name, and not vagabonds and criminals.

10. It will remove vice and supplant virtue. Many baby hearts are longing for a home, kindness, love and protection. With uplifted hands, they plead, 'Give us a chance, give us a chance!'

That is so true.

House Bill 112, establishing the State Home for Dependent and Neglected Children in Waco, Texas, was passed by both houses of the Thirty-sixth Texas Legislature, and the first children were admitted to the Home on January 1, 1923. Mrs. Smith and legislators did their job well in 1919, and today it is our responsibility to preserve their memory and their record of accomplishment.

All good things come from God. At age eleven, in 1947, I walked down the aisle and took Pastor Grady's hand and asked God to forgive my sins and take me to Heaven one day to be with a loving Heavenly Father forever. From that moment on, God has provided, guided, and protected my life all these many years. He used these wonderful citizens of Texas to provide shelter, education, and a better chance in life for these children.

As to the circumstances that brought me to the Home, I do not think that going into detail would be of any positive benefit, other than stating that there was a trial and my father went to prison. My mother was uneducated and unable to work or care for my brother and me. Child Protective Services looked into the situation, and the court took custody of us.

To go into the abuse and neglect we children experienced would require an entire book, but I would rather share the positive turn of events in our lives.

Some of my favorite memories of the Home are Saturday-night movies on the slab under the stars and Sunday-evening church services outside with the Baylor University students. We sang and listened to happy Bible stories.

One Wednesday afternoon, Brother Ewing from Grace Temple Baptist Church came out and presented a felt-character version of *Pilgrim's Progress*. It made it more alive.

Early-morning devotionals were also a favorite.

Another happy memory is going to the sewing room to try on our new, homemade dresses.

We were quite thrilled when an ex-student donated a new black-and-white television. He also had a chain of movie theaters in Waco and would let us come see movies.

Everyone loved Mrs. Parker, who taught us choral singing. Her husband was the star quarterback of the Baylor Bears. Mrs. Johnson, our voice teacher, also gave us girls lots of mother-daughter advice.

Precious Mrs. Stipes taught piano and devoted many extra hours to teaching me a repertoire of solo music. I was invited to sing for the Waco Lions Club and other civic clubs in Waco. On one occasion, the Light Crust Doughboys came to Waco, and they invited me to sing on TV. I dressed like a cowgirl and sang "Home on the Range." That was quite an experience.

I was also invited to sing at the Veterans Administration. That has a bittersweet memory. The auditorium was full of young men who had been wounded in

Korea, with casts on their legs and that sort of thing. I remember one man in particular who was sitting down right in front. When I started singing "Your Cheatin' Heart," that guy just started boo-hooing.

Mrs. Balch, our square-dancing teacher, was wonderful. We came up with a unique square dance called the Crawdad. We traveled to several major cities in Texas as a special guest to dance at square-dance festivals. Square dancing taught us discipline, loyalty, and teamwork and was an excellent emotional and physical outlet as well as wonderful mental stimulation.

> I dressed like a cowgirl and sang, "Home on the Range." That was quite an experience.

Another great memory is camping for two weeks at Camp Longhorn. On Sundays, we would get to go up front and eat ice-cold watermelon. We could sit on the curb with our favorite friends, including boys. Normally, we didn't get to mingle with the boys that much.

I have many fond memories of going to Lovers' Leap, which overlooked the Bosque River. It is a good five to six hundred feet down to the river. I once got the idea that I could climb that steep cliff. I got halfway up when I decided I would never make it. I said, "Oh Lord, if you'll help me out of this dilemma, I won't climb any more steep cliffs." I got my second wind and made it to the top, but it could have been a disaster.

My least favorite memory is working on the steam presses in the laundry room. An embarrassing thing happened to me there, so the laundry room will always have a negative memory for me. Because of the prior abuse before I came to the Home, I had a nervous disorder. Well, I peed on the bed. So my housemother said, "All right, young lady, you take that sheet, and you hand-carry it to the laundry." I had to carry this white sheet for the whole world to see and know that Sudie peed on her bed. It was emotional cruelty. I was so hopeful that my boyfriend would not see.

Ms. Eichelberger worked in the kitchen. She was an unhappy person and short-tempered. Eventually, I learned the reason. Before she came to the Home, her husband was deep-sea fishing when a swordfish jumped in the boat and that sword went through his heart and killed him.

My fiancé got leukemia and died there in the Waco State Home hospital. His twin brother and my brother kept running away. I prayed to God that we would get an adopted home and my brother would stop running away. It was so dangerous.

Then, my brother and I were adopted by a couple out in Ranger, Texas. They had a 200-acre ranch with cattle. I got to watch my brother participate in a roundup, roping and branding. My brother was in heaven, but I didn't like it that well. I was not much of a cowgirl. I preferred to sing and play the piano. So I came back to the Home in 1953 and graduated in 1954.

My huge graduating class consisted of twelve students. Our class colors were maroon and white, and our class flower was the white carnation. The class motto: "Learn to labor and to wait." That was taken from Henry Wadsworth Longfellow.

Our precious English teacher, Mrs. Vernon Legg, is the one who organized our graduation program, and it was excellent quality. The song she picked out for us was "My God and I." I really appreciated that dear lady. The last time I saw her, at age 101, she was still sharp as a tack. She was such a guiding light in all our lives.

I was a cheerleader for our football team. Our fight song, "Hurrah for the Gold and the Blue," sung to the tune of John Phillip Sousa's "Stars and Stripes Forever," went something like this:

> Hurrah for the gold and the blue,
> To its colors we'll ever be true.
> The emblem of our State Home School,
> We will pledge our love to you.
> We'll fight for the school that we love

As our colors fly proudly above.
In all that we say or do,
We will pledge our love to you,
For you are a grand old school.

After graduation, I attended Ranger Junior College, where I earned an associate's degree, then transferred to Stephen F. Austin State University and earned a degree in business administration with a minor in voice.

I worked for thirty-seven years in a business-secretarial capacity. I had a most satisfying career in the business world, working with lawyers and company CEOs—wonderful people. And I owe it all to these wonderful people at Waco and a lot of other good friends.

Martha Willeford Burns

1948–1955

If you look at the roster for the Waco State Home, you will see a lot of Willefords. Seven of us were there, although not all at the same time. I was eleven years old when I arrived.

Our parents divorced, and our father could not take care of us. The relatives could not do it either. My daddy got us out in 1955, but my oldest brother had to go back because my stepmother was mean to him. The court almost took their daughter away, too. Then my grandmother and grandfather died, so my two youngest brothers had to go to the Home. They were there only a couple of years. One of them graduated, and the other went with my aunt and uncle.

Mother had three more kids after she left us, and one before me. We have a lot of children in our family—eleven in all. I always refer to the first seven siblings as "the original seven." Mother wanted us to love and stay in touch with each other, and we do.

When we left the Home in 1955 to live with my dad and stepmother, it was bittersweet. We were all out of the Home until the two little brothers

Martha Willeford Burns posing with her new camera at the
Waco State Home. Photo courtesy of Martha Willeford Burns.

had to go. One of them graduated and went on to Texarkana Junior College.

I realize some people have said horrible things about the Waco State Home, but the only time I got in trouble there was when a boy kissed me. The matron was not there when it happened, but when she found out about it, I had to stand on the stairs for several days. That was the only bad thing I experienced out there. Was it worth it? Of course it was.

I had two or three boyfriends. You would find a boy out there you liked, but then you would find something wrong with him. I had one more or less steady boyfriend. I sat on the steps a lot and watched him play ball, because of the rule that boys and girls could not interact.

We had arguments with each other, of course. There were about 300 kids when I got out there, so there was always someone to get into an argument with.

When you first went there, you had to stay in the hospital for two weeks. You could not see any visitors for two months, not even your parents. When I first got there, I had a calcium deficiency. I had to walk to the hospital every day for a year or so to take a calcium pill.

I got childhood diseases like chicken pox and mumps. Whenever you got something like that, you would go to the hospital, and there would be a lot of other kids in there with the same thing.

After our little skirts were too worn to wear, we made shine rags out of them. We would get down on our knees and clean the floor in the little kids' dorm. It was a game to us. We had fun, or we thought we were having fun.

We learned to work at the Home. They taught us how to make a pretty bed. We shelled peas, canned pineapple, and worked at the laundry. It was hot, but we had to do it.

> I realize some people have said horrible things about the Waco State Home, but the only time I got in trouble there was when a boy kissed me.

When I got older, I worked in the hospital. I helped the doctor and the dentist. I think the dentist only came once a week, but I learned a little bit about dental work. I have had only two fillings in my entire life.

I served the tables in the big dining room. On Saturday, we scrubbed the dining room with lots of soap and water and then mopped it dry.

On Sunday, we had hot rolls and enjoyed making a "hole in the roll." We'd make a hole in the hot roll and put ice cream in it. Those rolls made good ice cream cones. I still do that now. I taught my kids how to do it.

We had pinto beans and cornbread on Saturday. Sunday night we fixed sandwiches and took them to the dormitory.

We had Sunday church services in the auditorium. Students from Baylor University taught us church and Sunday school. A missionary taught us *Pilgrim's Progress*. He had a felt board and felt characters to illustrate the story, and he was good. That taught you a lot about the Lord. The missionary came each week to teach us a new chapter of the story.

Later we got to go to church outside the Home. Some people from the Methodist church came out and spoke to us. They were having a revival. I went to this Methodist church near the Home and accepted Jesus as my savior. I was about fifteen years old. I had been brought up as a Baptist. The church at the Home was nondenominational because the kids were from everywhere.

I was not a terrific student, but I did okay.

Mrs. Legg was our English teacher, and she was wonderful. She was hard, but she was teaching us something.

I enjoyed square dancing. We went to Dallas to do an exhibition at some big commemorative event for the city. Tommy was my square-dancing partner. I saw him not long ago and asked him where he'd been all these years—had he been in prison or something?

He said, "Yeah, I have. I really have." I thought he was joking, but it turned out that he had a job at the penitentiary in Huntsville. I love to laugh at corny stuff like that.

I had a lot of jobs after I left the Home. I worked in a drugstore, a hat factory, and a nasty pickle factory. I still cannot stand some kinds of pickles. They stink. Then I went to work at A&P Grocery. I worked in the meat market for a long time. When Robert and I got married, I quit the grocery.

My husband and I started this business, and my son and I keep it up. We have eight greenhouses and grow vegetable plants, flowering plants, bedding plants, and hanging baskets. We don't do trees or shrubs. I haul them everywhere in a one-ton truck and sell them. In the spring, we get so busy we hardly have time to breathe.

We have two daughters, a son, eight grandchildren, and six great-grandchildren. I tell my kids and grandkids they just do not know how blessed I am. My parents are gone, and I lost my husband, but all my brothers and sisters are still alive. The "original seven" are really a clan. They look on me as the mother—they really do.

Raising my own children, I think that my trouble at first was that you learn to be strict because they were strict at the Home. And then you figure out that you are too strict. I have had no trouble with my children, so I must have learned something.

The kids from the Home still crack up about what they used to tell us about holding hands. They never explained why, but they wanted us to think if you held hands, you would get pregnant. We laugh about that now.

I still visit Brownie whenever I go to Waco. Her husband died a few years ago, and mine died in 2006. All these years, we have always been in touch.

I love going to the reunions. My brother Leroy is the president of the association. I love to see and visit with everyone I can. At one reunion, I had not seen Mary and her sister Yvonne in forty years. We're old kids now! It was really good to see them!

I am seventy-one, and that's getting on up there. But you're only as old as you feel, they say. I try to have a good attitude and have fun.

Of the "original seven," the four girls were born first, then the three boys. One of my sisters was a nurse, and she's retired now. One brother was a postman, and he's now retired, too. One of my other brothers is in construction. He builds and remodels houses.

Leroy is the one who went to college. He has been in the polyethylene industry for many years. I answer the phone, "Martha Burns, Plant Lady," so he says he is calling himself "the Polyethylene Salesperson."

I am the nosy sister. I believe in keeping in touch, so I know what's going on with everyone in the family. I guess it's just the mama in me. I have a closeness with my family, my kids, my grandkids, and my great-grandkids. God has been good to us. We all worked hard and we survived.

Ernest Whitener

1948–1959

W e were living over near Dawson, Texas, in 1948 when my father decided he had to get some help taking care of the family. I was eight years old with three younger brothers and a sister.

My mother had had a nervous breakdown and was in the state hospital. My daddy was a day laborer on the farm. He had been injured and wasn't able to work for a while. My mother's family lived in the country near Mexia. To get a little bit of assistance, my daddy took us to my aunt and uncle's place there and left us with them, hoping that he'd get straightened out and be able to get back to work.

My aunt and uncle were already on welfare and had younger children of

Ernest Whitener, center, and his two brothers in front of the administration building of the Waco State Home, 1951. Photo courtesy of Ernest Whitener.

their own, but they took us in the summer and kept us until October. When the state welfare people found out what was going on, they made arrangements to come down and pick up the four of us. An uncle on my mother's side, who lived in Borger up in the Panhandle, came and got the baby and took him back to live with them. The state took him from them sometime in 1949, and he was adopted. We never saw him again.

So there were still four of us at my aunt and uncle's when they came and took us to the Waco State Home.

One of the welfare caseworkers ended up taking my baby sister as a foster child.

I have many recollections of my life before the Home. My two younger brothers don't really recall anything about being with our mom and daddy. They were too young when they left home. As was typical back in those years, especially where the father was a day laborer on a farm, the kids were expected to pitch in as soon as they got old enough to help out.

> The way I remember it, some of the kids had a pretty rough time.

During the summers, when I wasn't in school, I had to go out and help my daddy bale hay. I was only seven or eight years old, so there wasn't a whole lot I could do. Even after I started school, during cotton-picking season the school bus would let me off next to the cotton patch where Mom and Dad were picking cotton. Mom would have some old overalls over there for me to change into, and I had to pick a little cotton before we went home that evening.

Life wasn't easy for us. It was pretty much hand-to-mouth. It wasn't the best of all worlds, that's for sure.

When we first got to the Home, they put us in what they called the hospital for the first week or two, then they released us to different dormitories, where we were separated.

The way I remember it, some of the kids had a pretty rough time. Of course, some of them got into lots of trouble, too. Some of the trouble was bad enough to justify the punishments they got, but not always. My brothers and I were pretty good boys, and the matrons didn't seem to have too much trouble with us. I had a good relationship with the people up there. They all treated me well and did lots of good things for me.

We still had school at the Home at that time, so we had all of our grades through the twelfth grade there. My sixth-grade teacher, Mrs. Speece, took me under her wing. She found out I was musically inclined and got me into playing the piano. She taught me a little about playing the fiddle and the guitar, too. I stayed with my music and played with some little bands during the years I was at the Home. Mr. and Mrs. Speece were real good to me.

They lived about a half mile from the Home. Later on, when I got into my teens, they would let us out of the Home after dinner on the weekends. We'd go to the park or downtown to the movie if we had the money, things like that. I would spend a lot of my time at Mrs. Speece's house because her husband had a woodworking shop and I was interested in woodworking, too. He let me piddle around in his shop, making things.

But I still wanted to be at home with my parents. After my mother got out of the state hospital, around 1950, she and my dad would come up to the Home on weekends and visit with us whenever they could arrange it, maybe a couple of times a year.

Kids who weren't from the Home, the ones who lived with their own parents, seemed to be in another world, so I pretty much stayed with my own little group from the Home. They were the ones I was raised with, so I felt comfortable with them.

A lot of the boys didn't like Mr. Whigham. He was a pretty rough individual. He had been a guard, I guess, at the old Gatesville State School for Boys, which was a reform school. He brought a lot of his habits with him and was rough on some of the older boys.

He was a houseparent for a year or two, but I never really had any trouble with him. Of course, I wasn't prone to getting into any real meanness or anything.

I was a calm individual, so I had a good relationship with all the matrons.

Over the years, I'd say there were several defining moments that probably affected my upbringing. When I was about nine or ten years old, I started square dancing out there. Our teacher, Mrs. Mabel Balch, was well known for her square-dancing expertise and had won national championships.

Mrs. Balch formed two squares out there called the Crawdads. Our square was called the Junior Crawdads. The other one was the Senior Crawdads. Our entry and exit number was to "The Crawdad Song." This was done by two-stepping backward in a single-file line. We left the Home grounds quite often to do exhibition dances. We danced at Lions Club meetings, too. I think it was in 1950 or 1951 when we went to a state competition and our square won second place in the junior division. We got quite a bit of notoriety from that.

In 1954, when I was about fourteen years old, they started letting kids go home for Christmas. Previously, the kids hadn't been allowed off the grounds to go home and visit parents. Now, they would let them stay with parents for Christmas, and then in the summer when you were old enough. I got to actually go home during the summer and spend time with my parents, maybe for a month or so. I always looked forward to spending time with my folks.

My cousin and her husband who lived in Waco occasionally would take us home on the weekend, so I was able to maintain my family ties. I never felt like an orphan. Our family is still a pretty tight-knit group. We have a family reunion in May every year.

I stayed at the Home from 1948 until I graduated high school in 1959. My brothers stayed until 1960, when the state decided to go ahead and let them go home. One of them was having problems anyway. My parents were just never in a financial situation to get us back home before we were all practically grown and able to leave on our own.

My sister, who went into foster care, studied music at the State School for the Blind and became a very accomplished pianist. Later on, after her foster parent passed away, she came to the Waco State Home during summers and holidays and stayed in the girls' dormitory. We were able to visit with each other then.

She ended up going to Navarro Junior College for two years and was the first blind student to attend college there. After that, she attended the University of Texas and graduated with a degree in sociology, but she ended up making her living as a musician. She married a guy she'd met in college, who was legally blind but who could see well enough to get them around. He's a very accomplished musician himself, a guitar player and a singer. He and my sister have been playing music together for the past thirty-five years or so.

I felt vindictive in my earlier years about being separated from my parents and all that, but in later years I realized it really was the best thing for us. I don't think I would have ever finished school if I hadn't been at the Home. My mother's folks had been working as day laborers on the farm. None of my aunts' and uncles' kids finished school. They all quit as soon as they could so they could work full-time. So there were a lot of benefits to being at the Home.

Fred Lamb

1949–1959

My dad was in the service, and both parents were alcoholics. We were put in a foster home for a while. We lived on a farm. We were expected to work hard, but we had a lot of fun, too. We started getting into trouble, and after a while we were moved to the Waco State Home.

I was sent there when I was nine years old with two brothers and a sister, all younger. Two people, a woman and a man, took us there in what I call a paddy wagon, a van with restrictive wire in the front and back. When we got there, they took us into a room where we talked to a counselor for a little bit.

Fred Lamb's brother Bobby Lamb, top row, number 10, *in 1955, when children from the Home attended public schools. Harold Larson's private collection.*

Then I went to one dormitory, one brother went to another dormitory, the other brother and sister ended up in the baby cottage, which had both girls and boys. It was a grueling experience for children our age to be treated as we were then. By today's standards, you would probably consider it being mistreated.

It was a very busy atmosphere. We were given chores to do based on our ages. I ended up milking cows in the morning when I was very young, nine or ten. My other brother also had chores to do. The baby cottage was more like a day-care center. They kept them busy, but they were not working.

We went to school at the Home. I started playing football very early. For me, it was a chance to succeed and get a little recognition. Mr. Whigham was always a big part of that. He was what you called dean of boys. He kept us busy. He would organize work crews to go to the farm and play ball in the evening. When I was fourteen or fifteen, we got a swimming pool at the Home. We would go out and work in the hay fields all day and come in and play ball. It was pretty similar to what kids do now.

At first, I was not a very good student. I failed the third grade the first year I was at the Home. Later on, I made the seventh and eighth grade in one year. By then, I had matured a little.

Mr. Speece, he was a good teacher. He had done pretty well in his life, but he liked kids, and he worked out there. He probably had some influence in my life, teaching me to save money and to take care of myself. He taught everything in the eighth grade—math, history, everything.

In tenth, eleventh, and twelfth grade, we had the opportunity to attend the public schools in Waco. I went to Waco High for three years and excelled in football and track. I earned a football scholarship to North Texas State University.

> By today's standards, you would probably consider it being mistreated.

In high school, I worked at 7-Eleven. I would get up and milk cows at four thirty in the morning, and then I had what we called the garbage route. We picked up garbage and fed it to the hogs. Then I would get ready to go to school. During the week, I probably worked three days, and on the weekends I worked the whole weekend and got a lot of hours. Work has always been fun for me.

I was the first kid in high school at the State Home to have my own car, which I bought. I had insurance and everything.

I met my wife in high school, and we are still married. We had three children and now have six grandchildren and one great-grandchild. High school was a lot of fun for me. For one thing, I got out into the general public and made friends. I was accepted into their homes and treated very well by some of them.

I guess I was about twelve years old when another boy and I ran away from the Home one night. We hitchhiked and made it to Albuquerque. One guy made us uncomfortable, and we were quick to get out of his car. Most people would pick you up, and they were not abusive at all. After five or six days, we got picked up and put in jail, in the drunk tank. They left us in jail up there for a week.

There was an old rancher in there who told us to stay with him and he would look after us. He was an older man, probably a pretty wise man. We stayed in there a day and half, and then they put us in a holding cell down by the courtroom, but even that was a good experience. It is hard to imagine a twelve-year-old doing that now.

I did not have a lot of dealings with Mr. Peek, the superintendent, but I do remember him busting my butt real good that one time when we got back to the Home. Kids would get the idea that they wanted to see their parents. That busting was what did it for me.

Carolyn Jean Gafford Lewallen

1949–1962

I was just five years old when I came from Madisonville with my two younger brothers to live at the Home. My daddy worked for the Huntsville prison system. He was gone a lot, and my mom couldn't find work except washing and ironing and odds and ends, so we didn't have much money. My dad went to a caseworker and arranged for us to go to the Home.

My half sister from a previous marriage got to stay with my mother. My youngest brother was only one year old, so he stayed with Mom until he was thirteen, and then he came to the Home, too.

We did get three meals a day, clothes on our backs, a roof over our heads, and medical care, but I didn't think the Waco State Home was a very happy experience.

Carolyn Jean Gafford Lewallen, at the Waco State Home Ex-Students'
reunion in Waco, June 2010. Photo Barking Pen.

I got a whipping every day, starting with my first day there. One girl was always falling down and blaming me for it.

I did like Mrs. Garner and Mrs. Story, but when I got to Mr. and Mrs. Gay's dorm, all hell broke loose.

The smallest infraction of rules could get you in trouble. When my little brother had appendicitis and was taken to the hospital on campus, I went with him because I thought he was about to die. When Mrs. Gay found out, she called me in and told me I didn't get permission and I would have to be punished.

I told her, "I don't need permission from anybody here if my brother is about to go live with the Lord."

She said, "You're grounded."

That didn't mean anything to me, though, because I was grounded the minute I landed at the Home.

We had to wear those horrible uniforms. Girls were dressed in jumper suits and blouses, and boys had pinstriped coveralls. If that wasn't prison garb, I don't know what you would call it. Remember, I know what I'm talking about because my daddy worked at the prison in Huntsville.

There was barbed wire around the whole place. Of course, we managed to get over it when we really wanted to.

We had to get up at the crack of dawn to clean the dorm, make beds, sometimes even take a razor blade and scrape the old wax off those floors with the octagonal tile. Then we had to wax them again.

In the summers we weren't in school, but the girls had to work in that hot cannery to put up vegetables and fruit. The boys planted and harvested the crops on the farms.

Sometimes we'd meet the boys in the middle of the campus, just to get a chance to see and talk with each other.

My worst whipping came when I was seventeen. I was canning peaches when one of the girls claimed I said something ugly. Mr. Gay came down and told me to put on the tightest jeans I could find and report back to him. He whipped me with a split baseball bat with holes in it, and I couldn't sit down for a month.

All the dorms had equipment to punish you.

I was talking the other day to David Tucker, one of my best friends from the Home, who is still just like family to me. We talked about things we used to do to staff members who were mean to us. The boys would vandalize their cars—smash the windows, cut their tires, put sand in their gas tanks. That's why they kept their cars locked. Sometimes when they went to check their mailboxes at night, a brick or a handful of gravel landed on them.

We knew not to tell anybody if we were abused. You couldn't trust anyone on staff.

Pop Taylor was weird. He'd pop your bra strap whenever he could. Mr. Gay would come over to our rooms and watch us while we were getting dressed.

I felt sorry for Mrs. Gay because she was young and didn't know what she was doing all the time. Later on, after leaving the Home, I used to see the Gays in Waco. They ended up moving away to work for the state prison system.

I quit school in the middle of tenth grade to attend a beauty school off campus, and I finally left the Home when I was eighteen. I got married right after I left. That marriage lasted two years, and the second ended in divorce, too, but I have two daughters who are very sweet kids.

We never ever fail to say "I love you" any time we come in contact with each other. My daughters and I are a very close-knit family, and we're always helping one another.

I am Pentecostal, but I attend the Baptist Church here in Waco. I believe in forgiveness because I have a big heart, but I don't forget. I remember what everybody did to me.

I am glad I was put out at the Home. I needed somebody to take care of me.

> I believe in forgiveness because I have a big heart, but I don't forget.

Sewing and doing needlepoint in the living room of the big girls' dorm, which was highly valued for its larger, semiprivate bedrooms and baths. Harold Larson's private collection.

CHAPTER THREE

The Fifties

Memories of the Depression and the sacrifices of World War II made for a determined America in the fifties. The new age of prosperity was symbolized by the burgeoning middle class, which, by the end of the decade, represented 60 percent of the U.S. population. With most suburban households claiming a washing machine, a television set, and two cars in every garage, the future looked bright as the baby boom continued.

Television brought Elvis Presley and other rock 'n' roll icons to the living room. African American, Jewish, and Southern writers, as well as Beat poets, took their rightful places on the literary scene.

Despite the rosy picture, the ominous took its place on the stage, too. Fears of communist expansion, which provided the impetus for the brief Korean conflict, were amplified by the Soviet Union's acquisition of the H-bomb, its launch of *Sputnik*, and its relationship with Fidel Castro in Cuba. Senator Joseph McCarthy's shameful hearings on supposed communist infiltration of the government and the army turned into witch hunts before he was finally censured.

The civil rights movement, encouraged by the integration of the U.S. military after the war, won a major victory with the 1954 Supreme Court ruling that ordered the integration of public schools.

The U.S. Department of Health, Education and Welfare took over the task of improving aid to families, and states were required to match federal child welfare funds if they chose to participate. Again, the programs to help families rested greatly on the goodwill of local officials, and mothers were usually the ones required to prove a "fit home."

Children who came to the Waco State Home during the fifties often blamed family tragedies, divorce, poverty, or abuse for their separation from their parents.

Edward Kainer

1950–1961

Before being taken to the Home, I remember standing at the screen door with my brother, Jerome, crying and wondering where our mother and father were. We lived in the Wharton—El Campo area just southwest of Houston, and my mother was always gone working, trying to support us. My father was in the army during the Korean War and had deserted the family for reasons unknown. I never knew my father and have no memories of him.

Jerome and I became wards of the State of Texas and were sent to the Waco State Home in 1950. I was seven; Jerome was five. My eighteen-month-old sister was put up for adoption at the Faith Home in Houston, which is now the DePelchin Family Center.

My mother moved to Mississippi, married a sharecropper, and started another family. We corresponded by mail once in a while, but she never

Lieutenant Commander Ed Kainer, a navy pilot, preparing for a flight while stationed in Brunswick, Maine, 1979. Photo courtesy of Ed Kainer.

visited until my high school graduation. When she came, she suggested that Jerome and I go with her to visit our relatives in El Campo. My mother wanted me to drop everything to spend time with people who had never come to visit me in the eleven years I had lived at the Home. I refused, but Jerome went with her, and he never forgave me for not wanting to forgive my mother. I have since forgiven my mother, but at the time I was just unable to do so.

My father once sent me a letter, but only one. I recently learned that he had deserted us because he found out that my mother had had a baby while he was gone and the child was not his. That baby was my half sister, who was put up for adoption. I have never tried to locate my half sister and really do not know why.

Because of the differences in our ages, Jerome and I were together at the Home for only a short while, each progressing to different dorms as we grew older.

I remember telling the caseworkers at the Home not to worry, that my mother would be there "any day now" to take me home. Although I have a transcript of every meeting I had with the caseworkers, I have not read them yet. In 2002, I secured all the records of my stay at the Home from the state and started to read them, but it was too emotional. My wife suggested that I put them up and only read them when I am ready. I think it will confirm what I already know—that my mother did the best she could at the time and that there were other circumstances at work that I was not aware of. One day I will take them out and read them, have a good cry, and put it all behind me.

There were some bullies and other characters at the Home who would try to beat you up or try to take sexual advantage of you if you let them. If you did not stand up for your rights, you were going to be a victim. I stood up for my rights, and it strengthened me. Peers and friends would band together and protect one another. This kind of thing did not happen all the time, but when you have a big group of boys, there are going to be disagreements. Most of the kids in the Home were basically good kids, but some were constantly in trouble and later ended up in Gatesville reform school or prison.

I attended East Waco Junior High School, in the rougher part of town. I attended University High School, and was elected vice president of the senior class. I was popular, but quiet and shy. I was always on the honor roll and in the National Honor Society.

At the Home, we were constantly involved in baseball, basketball, or football. We were always one of the top teams in the region in all sports. I was active in all sports, but really only an average athlete.

I remember Mr. Whigham coached us in baseball and basketball at the Home. He was a big guy, a little overweight, robust, assertive, and very strict. I remember him vividly. You did not want to question him, and I never did. His wife, who was a dorm matron, was a large woman, but very caring.

Most of us attended the First Baptist Church in Waco. I remember being baptized there.

We always had chores, slopping the hogs or working on the farm. I remember milking cows early in the morning and again after school. They put me in charge of the creamery, where we pasteurized and homogenized all the milk. I also drove tractors and trucks on the farm, as I was considered one of the more trusted individuals.

We would smoke cigarettes if we could get them, or we would smoke grapevines. We would also try to get some beer if we could, but that was rare. During the summer, we would occasionally get a bushel of peaches to peel for preserves, and we would save the peach peelings and bury them in a jar, trying to make peach brandy.

I remember a couple of summers going to camp at Marble Falls for a week and sleeping in cabins. I also remember Christmas, when the Kiwanis Club or the

> I remember telling the caseworkers at the Home not to worry, that my mother would be there "any day now" to take me home.

Jaycees would take a few of the boys shopping. They would give us five bucks to buy a football or some gift for ourselves. During my last years at the Home, I remember receiving a small weekly allowance.

In my early teens, I participated in the soapbox derby, which was held in Waco. Servicemen from James Connally Air Force Base would sponsor us and help us build our cars. I never won anything, but it was a lot of fun.

During my stay, some of the kids would leave the Home early to live with a parent in Waco, and we would visit them once in a while. One or two of them had access to a car, and we would drive around town trying to buy beer, but staying out of trouble.

You could find a way to get in trouble if you wanted. Sometimes boys and girls got together and got caught. I never took chances like that. I just worked, went to school, and stayed out of trouble.

After milking the cows in the afternoon, I had an evening job at a drive-in grocery called Cabell's, right outside the front gate of the Home. Once in a while, the owners, who had no children of their own, would invite me to their house. By the time I graduated in 1961 I had saved about $1,100. Halfway through my last year of high school, I had another job, at an appliance store.

A man named Robert Kennelley, who owned a tire retread shop in Waco, was a regular customer at the drive-in store. He was always asking me, "What are you going to do with your life?"

At the time, I had no real plans. When you graduated from high school, you were no longer a ward of the state. If you wanted to attend college, the state would pay your tuition and books until you reached the age of twenty-one. Most of the people who left either got a job or went into the military. There was no career counseling, so to speak. You just had a houseparent. That was probably where a lot of people failed—they had no assistance for the transition into the next stage of their lives.

By the end of my senior year, I told Mr. Kennelley I wanted to attend college. He was a graduate of Texas A&M and helped me make arrangements to enroll there. He had been taking me down there on weekends to visit the school and attend football games.

So at the end of summer 1961, the same weekend Hurricane Carla came ashore and devastated the Texas coast, we got in his little Volkswagen Beetle and drove to College Station with everything I owned. He took me to the placement office, got me a job waiting tables in the mess hall, and then I was on my own.

I got a job at the Owens-Illinois glass plant in Waco for the summer from college. Mr. Al Mercer, my former employer at the appliance store, told me I was always welcome to stay at his house, because, of course, we couldn't go back to the Waco State Home once we left. Every summer in college, I worked a summer job and lived at Mr. Mercer's house.

While I was in college, my brother, Jerome, ran away from the Home. One day he just disappeared, and I had no way of finding him. Later I found out he had gone to New York City.

When I graduated from A&M, I went to work for a consulting engineering firm, then joined the navy and enrolled in Officer Candidate School. I spent twenty years as a navy pilot, flying the Lockheed P-3 Orion, a submarine-surveillance aircraft. I also earned advanced degrees in computer systems, retiring after twenty years in 1986 with the rank of commander.

When I left the military, I worked for companies in Washington, D.C. Then I moved to Houston in 1992, where I married my lovely wife, Ginger, and started a consulting business. Later, along with two engineers, I started an engineering software company in Houston for oil and gas pipelines. I still work there today.

My first wife and I had four sons. Our son Michael was murdered in Washington, D.C., in 2003. My eldest son, John, died of a brain tumor in January 2009. Our twin sons, James and Paul, live in Lafayette, Louisiana, near their mother and her family. My current wife, Ginger, has one daughter, and we are blessed with five grandkids.

Finally, in 2003, I found my brother, Jerome. I got a call from the police in Lufkin. He had shown up there after living on the streets for thirty-five years.

The message said, "We've got this fellow who claims to be your brother. He's located at this shelter here. If you want to contact him, please call him at this number, or if you want to ignore it, then that's fine, too." I called and contacted him, verified some information, then got in my car and drove up there to meet him.

The last time I had seen Jerome, he was chubby. This man was so gaunt I did not recognize him at all, but I asked a few questions, and I was able to confirm that he was indeed my brother.

I set him up with a place to live in Beaumont at a motel where the manager was someone we both knew and trusted, and I made arrangements for financial support. All those years of living on the streets, however, had taken their toll. On December 15, 2008, Jerome died of a heart attack. He was sixty-three years old.

When I found my brother, he told me that our mother died in 1992 in Vicksburg, Mississippi, when she was seventy-five years old. The last time we ever spoke or communicated was at my high school graduation in 1961. Just a few years ago, I met my first cousin on my mother's side. The family name was Trojcak, and her family was Czech. My cousin had traced the family genealogy all the way back to Moravia [in Czechoslovakia].

My father died in Syracuse, New York. He was also seventy-five. Recently, my first cousin on his side of the family gave me pictures of my father. I had never seen pictures of him before.

My mentors, Robert Kennelley and Al Mercer, have also passed away. After Bob Kennelley died, his wife told me that he had always wanted to adopt me but just never did. She lives comfortably in Fort Worth, and I maintain contact with her and visit from time to time.

Every once in a while, somebody I knew at the Waco State Home will surface out of nowhere. In 1991, I was going to attend my thirtieth high school reunion when James Emfinger contacted me out of the blue and talked me into attending a reunion of the Waco State Home alumni, too. That was the first one I attended. When my wife and I drove through the grounds of the old State Home, everything seemed so much smaller than I remembered.

A few years ago, I was sitting down to eat Thanksgiving dinner with my wife when I got a call from Ann Edwards, my first girlfriend at the Home. It felt a little unusual to have this conversation while having dinner with my wife, but she said, "Don't worry about it; just talk." So we talked for a while.

As I view my history, I know that I was blessed. The Home gave me structure and a caring environment. The houseparents were strict, but they cared for us. More important, there were people in my life, mentors, who were there for me at critical times and who watched over me. I call them my angels, and I strongly believe that God has had his hand on me throughout my life.

A lot of the kids who were at the Home had no family or mentor that was there for them. So I try to mentor young folks, to return the favor for those who just need a little hand every once in a while.

Linda Cooey Weeks

1950–1966

I was born in Firebaugh, California, in 1948. My parents had moved there to obtain work. They had the whole family picking cotton. Shortly after I was born, they moved back to Texas, where their other children were born.

In the early fifties, my parents went through a divorce, and my mother abandoned the entire family. My father had to make the difficult decision to put us in the Waco State Home. I think this was his only choice. He knew we would be fed, clothed, and educated and would attend church.

He moved to Dallas, but he made it a habit to visit us the second Sunday of every month, rain or shine. Our mother later remarried and had a son by her second husband when I was five years old. When that brother was about eleven years old, our mother put him in the Home as well.

Most of the children there had parents or one parent. It wasn't like they were orphans. The parents just weren't able to support them or be with

Linda Cooey Weeks, right, age five, with sister Loretta, standing on the lawn of the Home, 1953. Photo courtesy of Linda Cooey Weeks.

them all the time. I cannot remember any child ever being adopted after being placed there. From what I understand, our mother would not sign papers for us to be adopted because she didn't want to split the family, even though she had abandoned us.

For the first five or six years of my residence at the Home, we were not allowed to leave the campus at any time for any reason. They finally changed the rules so we were able to leave the campus with a family member. Of course there was paperwork involved. The matron had to have a release slip, giving specific dates and times, written in his/her hand before we were allowed to leave. Thank God for older sisters who were able to come get us on holidays and summer break. What a blessing that was.

My first education started with kindergarten, which was on campus by teachers from outside the Home. By the time I had reached fourth grade, they were busing us to different public schools in Waco. I always tried to stay out of trouble and be a good student. As a result, I almost always made the honor roll. I learned early to try and do the right thing and that nothing was impossible for God, as long as you give him the glory.

The Home was just immaculate. We were all given chores to do each day that kept it that way. When I was old enough to hold a broom—about the age of three—I was sweeping the front porch every morning. We slept in little iron beds lined up in one big bedroom. Every day, all the beds were moved from one end of the room and the floors were swept and then moved back to the other end until the whole room had been swept. All the toilets, tubs, showers, and sinks were cleaned daily with Bon Ami.

Before we got dressed to go to the dining hall, we all lined up with our fists out to be measured for the socks given us to wear for the day. If the heel of the sock met with the toe of the sock wrapped around a closed fist, it was determined that the sock would fit.

We had a farm where we raised vegetables and shelled the peas and shucked the corn.

We were also assigned to work in the dining hall. Our duties included serving, scraping plates, running the commercial dishwasher, and sorting and wrapping silverware. The Home hired cooks to do all the cooking. Sometimes you were assigned to work in the kitchen with the cooks. We really didn't learn how to cook, because everything was prepared in large quantities. The only thing I learned in the kitchen was how to flip pancakes and fry eggs on a commercial grill. I did love the ladies in the kitchen, especially Mary Lou.

The food was probably one of the best memories I have of the Home. It was simply delicious. Every Sunday for lunch we had fried chicken, mashed potatoes with gravy, green beans, and rolls, and for dessert, ice cream. All of it was homemade. It's a good thing we didn't have access to snacks and we got a lot of exercise, or we could have been overweight.

From time to time, we were also assigned to work in the laundry room. I volunteered a couple of times and ended up ironing. It really didn't bother me, but it was extremely hot there, especially in the summer. We did not have the luxury of air-conditioning in any of the buildings on campus. The main office was the only building that had air-conditioning.

We had a sewing room on campus. Seamstresses were hired to come in and make our clothes. Our clothes were all made from the same fabric, even house shoes. Eventually, they phased out the sewing room, but they kept a seamstress on staff for repairs and special clothing. I remember how excited I was the first time they took us to Sears to buy clothes. They also purchased our shoes from the Lewis Shoe Store, which was downtown on Austin Avenue. It was such a treat to be able to wear store-bought clothes and shoes.

There was also a barbershop on campus. The barber, Mr. Concillo, cut my hair in a bowl cut until I was old enough to style it myself. One thing for sure, it was easy to take care of.

We had bikes, but we had to take turns riding

them, fifteen minutes at a time. We played softball almost daily, since we had plenty of people to make up two teams. We were allowed to participate in softball tournaments with church groups and the Methodist Home [another children's home in Waco]. The championship always came down to us and the Methodist Home children. We kind of had an advantage because we played together every day. We also were taken bowling every Wednesday in the summer. We had a swimming pool on campus and swam daily during the week at a specified time. I learned to swim by myself at an early age and absolutely fell in love with the water. Later, when an instructor at the YWCA spotted me swimming, I was asked to join the Little Dolphins swim team.

In my late twenties, when I was married with two daughters, I took lifeguard training and, after receiving my certification, taught swimming lessons at a local swimming pool. I still try to stay active today by walking and jogging on a regular basis with my husband.

We were disciplined regularly. You would be "campused," which was basically the same as being grounded, for certain offenses. If you left an item of clothing—all our clothing had our initials marked inside—you would have to stand and hold that piece of clothing with one arm for fifteen minutes without moving. That may not seem like a long time, but it's not as easy as it sounds. On the second infraction, your time was increased to thirty minutes, then forty-five minutes, etc.

For more serious offenses, you were given licks with a paddle made from a baseball bat. You were made to bend over a bed while the person administering the punishment hit your bottom as if swinging at a baseball. I did see a few girls get licks. I got licks on only one occasion. One of the boys my age had given me a knife to keep for him. I thought nothing of it because we had never had any kind of violence on campus among residents that went beyond a fistfight between boys. When the boy asked for the knife, I gave it back to him. Another boy in his dorm reported me, and I got ten licks.

I was lucky I wasn't one of those who got a lot of licks. One person really sticks out in my mind. She was very sweet, not very attractive, and today she would probably be classified as having intellectual disabilities. One day when a relief matron was on duty, the girl decided to run away. When they found her and brought her back, she was given licks by the relief matron.

I am not sure how many licks she received, but when she returned to the dorm, she was not able to sit down. It looked like every blood vessel in her buttocks was broken. We were all outraged, but there wasn't anyone to whom we could report the incident.

When my sister and I lived in the dorm supervised by Mr. and Mrs. Taylor, she had similar experiences that I had with Mr. Taylor. In fact, every little girl I talked to as an adult had something to say about him. Both of his hands were weird. One hand had only two fingers. I don't know if he had been in an accident or if he was born that way.

At several of the Waco State Home reunions, some of the women would sit around discussing the experiences we had while living there, and the subject of Mr. Taylor always came up. The conversation always led to one of us saying, "Oh, he did that to you, too?" The answer was nearly always, "Yeah, he did that to me, too." Even girls who were younger than me, who lived in the dorm after I had moved out, said that they had the same experiences with him. I think that this was probably an ongoing thing during all the years he was at the Home. He more or less made us fondle him when no one else was around.

I remember having nightmares about him. I remember one particular incident in which I woke up in the middle of the night being really, really scared. I think I kind of blacked out and woke up shaking and holding on to the sheets of my bed. To this day, I don't know if anything happened or if I was just having a really bad dream. In that day and time, if you tried to report these incidents to an adult, they didn't believe you, since they didn't take the word of a child over an adult. Thank God, things have changed.

In the 1970s, when I was an adult with two young daughters, I was going through a divorce and had moved to an apartment complex here in Waco. There was a young lady who lived there with her young child, whom she pushed around the complex in a stroller. We were visiting one day, and she made a comment about this real sweet couple that lived there who were always talking to her and the child. When she told me their names, I decided I would pay them a visit. As it turned out, it was Mr. and Mrs. Taylor, who were still alive and living in the same apartment complex. I immediately warned my neighbor to avoid talking to them and especially to keep her baby away from them.

Then there was Mr. Whigham, a house-parent in the boys' dorm. I was having a conversation with him when I was about fourteen. He told me that he liked to try and help certain worthy individuals at the Home. He said he had chosen me because I tried to follow the rules, made good grades, and was a cheerleader at North Junior High. Not knowing what his expectations were, I asked him one day to have some film developed for me, which he did.

Shortly afterward, we were at a church function where we were allowed to go back to the bus if we chose to. Several of us decided to go, as we were bored with the program. Mr. Whigham happened to be our bus driver that day. The next thing I knew, he was sitting next to me and told me, "I want the first time to be with me. It's gonna smart just a little bit the first time, then it will be okay."

I really didn't understand what he was talking about, because I was very naïve, but I knew enough to know that whatever he was telling me was wrong and something I didn't need to know, especially from him. I purposely avoided him from then on.

They didn't believe you, since they didn't take the word of a child over an adult.

Later on, when the Home had caseworkers, my counselor was Nina Alford. I would go to her office once a month or so. If I had something I needed, I could see her anytime. Once she took me to see the movie *Old Yeller*. She was of Norwegian descent and had always dreamed of going to Norway. She even taught me the Norwegian national anthem, which I still remember today. It is too bad she wasn't around in my earlier childhood. I think I would have been able to talk to her about all of those incidents without feeling she would betray my trust. We kept in touch until she passed away, maybe five or six years ago.

The person who inspired me most at the Home was Mrs. Marie Yarbrough. I was at the age, thirteen to fifteen, when I really needed a mentor. I truly believe God put her there for me. I think that all girls, especially at that age, need someone they can look up to. She was my saving grace. I learned so much from her. She was outgoing, funny, and lovable and had a great sense of humor, but most of all, she was fair. She also taught me that everyone needs to learn to be a good sport and be able to laugh at themselves.

Mrs. Yarbrough was a prankster. One night I had fallen asleep in the TV room, and when it was time to go to bed, she woke me up. She did her usual routine of standing by the light switch to turn out the lights once everyone was in bed. I was so sleepy, but for some reason I couldn't quite seem to get under my sheets. When I finally looked up at her through my sleepy eyes, wondering why she hadn't turned off the lights, she was laughing so hard she was almost crying. After I had fallen asleep in the TV room, she had gone to my bed and short-sheeted it. Through her laughter and tears, she came and helped me make by bed so that I could get in bed without my knees being up around my chin. Needless to say, by that time I was laughing with her.

The summer before my sophomore year, Mrs. Yarbrough commissioned one of the male houseparents, Mr. Burns, to take us on a trip to the beach. We drove to Freeport, Texas, and camped out on the beach for four or five days. The adults slept in tents, and we slept on the bus seats. We cooked our meals over a campfire. I cannot begin to tell you how much fun we had.

When I was a cheerleader at North Junior High, Mrs. Yarbrough would let me go to one of the other cheerleaders' homes after the game without all the usual paperwork. On one occasion, she even let me spend the night. She would do the same thing if I was attending a swim meet with the Little Dolphins. She was such a blessing for me and probably for a lot of other girls as well. She passed away in 2006, and I was fortunate to be able to attend her funeral and visit with her daughter, Diane.

My older sister, who was married and had four children, was able to get me out of the Home when I was sixteen years old. I lived with her my junior year of high school. When I was enrolled at Connally High School, I did not know a single person at school. I made up my mind I was going to meet a new person every day until I knew everybody.

The following summer, my sister was divorced from her husband, so the four children and I moved in with her mother-in-law, whom everyone called Grandma Gregory, even people who were not related. This made ten people living in a two-bedroom, one-bath house. Grandma was the manager of the high school cafeteria. It was a good thing, because trying to cook for and feed ten people while working full time was almost impossible. We ate a lot of leftovers from the school lunches.

My senior year I was elected homecoming queen. It was such a surprise. Again, God was watching over me.

After graduating high school, I attended Durham Business School in Waco and received a degree in keypunch. I went to business school until noon each day and then drove straight to K-Mart, my first job, to work an eight-hour shift. This job paid for my schooling. I have held several jobs since that first one. One of the last positions I had was office supervisor at Hillcrest Medical Clinic.

In 2000, I retired from work, but not from life. I take care of my grandbabies, and I have become an avid quilter, doing both machine and hand quilting.

When people find out you came from a place like the Waco State Home, they want to know your story. As you can tell by this story, we had some really fun and memorable times, but we also had some really horrible times. I have forgiven the people who committed these atrocities against us, because the Bible in Matthew 6:14–15 states: "If you forgive those who sin against you, your heavenly Father will forgive you. But if you refuse to forgive others, your Father will not forgive your sins."

I have one more story to tell that happened several years ago. My husband and I attended the Starburst basketball tournament, which is held at the Ferrell Center in Waco, where the Baylor basketball team plays. I noticed a group of young boys who told me they were from the Waco Center for Youth, which was formerly the Waco State Home. I knew what it was like to go to events like that and only be able to sit there, having to ask permission to go to the bathroom, not have any money for snacks or drinks.

After taking a head count, my husband and I went to the hospitality room and stuffed a sack with all different kinds of candy for each of the boys. One of the boys cried and hugged me as he thanked us. I remember telling him, "I know what it's like." It was so special to be able to give back.

Lillian Cooey Johnson

1951–1955

Our parents were married twenty-three years before they got divorced, and neither one could afford to take care of all of the children, so the six youngest ones were taken to the Waco State Home. There were eight of us in all. By the time we went to Waco, I was almost eleven. The youngest, Linda, was about three years old.

My parents came to see us every month. They were only allowed to come one weekend a month. So one weekend my mom would show up, and the next my dad would come. Someone came to visit us at least three times a month.

Linda was put in Mr. Taylor's dormitory. Pop Taylor, they called him. I can remember him now. He was the dirty old man who bothered all the girls.

We were just put out there, and it kept us off the streets. Being out there had its advantages and disadvantages, but it was probably good for us.

You had to work. The boys raised the

Lillian Cooey Johnson at the Home, where she lived in the fifties, c. 1954. Photo courtesy of Lillian Cooey Johnson.

farming products, and the girls canned them. At different times, I worked in the cannery, I worked in the laundry, and I worked in the dining room.

Mrs. Eichelberger was the dining room matron. She was a witch. She slapped my sister in the face one time.

My brother said he was never beaten, but there was evidently one person out there who liked to do that to the boys. I don't know who it was. I just heard the rumors. I do know that they had a baseball bat that they sliced and drilled holes in and used on the boys. But my brother said he was never treated to that.

The dorm matrons were strict, but they had their good points. They weren't all bad.

When we moved into the big girls' dormitory, we were given a bedroom together—you didn't sleep in a big common room like in the other dormitory. You had individual rooms. It was pretty nice when you got to the big girls' dormitory.

Your locker had to be clean and in order. What they called your locker was actually a space about eighteen inches wide next to the wall with a little shelf. If you didn't keep your dirty laundry picked up, you'd get to stand in the corner holding it for fifteen minutes or so. I remember that. They wanted you to learn how to keep house.

They had good teachers out there. Our English teacher, Mrs. Legg, was really good. We were studying college-level English after the eighth grade. Our art teacher was good, too, but I guess they were all good, because we excelled when we transferred to the public schools. Some went to University High, some to Waco High. I went to East Junior High in the eighth grade.

Going to public school from the Home was different because we were exposed to the outside world. Unless people came to visit you, you really didn't have much exposure except when they loaded us all on a bus and drove us to the drive-in movie in the summertime.

> Kids would run away, and then they'd bring them back and beat them.

The Home had playgrounds and benches and things out there. They also had what we called "the slab." We'd go to the slab and roller-skate. Movies, roller-skating, and swimming were basically our main sources of entertainment until television came along. They didn't have television when I first got there but got TVs later on. At night, we listened to the radio.

We didn't just sit in the dormitory all day. They had activities for us. The Home had a square-dance club. I remember our square-dance dresses were pink and brown, with big full skirts. That was fun. And you could get in the choir if you wanted to, and you learned embroidery, too. We embroidered little scarves to line the shelves in our lockers.

Kids would run away, and then they'd bring them back and beat them. Or if they ran away too many times, they'd get sent to the reform school. The boys went to Gatesville, and the girls went to Gainesville.

I never ran away, but I did get in trouble for going to a movie one night without permission. They sent me home for that. Instead of going to church, another girl and I walked up to the movie theater and met a couple of young boys. When we got back, we were in trouble because they had found out. They sent me to my mother. That was all it took.

I think I was glad. Everyone wanted to get out of there anyway.

I was still pretty close to my parents. One sister and I left at the same time and went to live with my mother. I kept going to East Junior High because she lived near there.

Another sister graduated from Waco High, and then they paid for her to go to Navarro Junior College in Corsicana. When my brother graduated, he went to work for ARMCO National Supply in Houston until he retired. He married a girl who had been at the Home. They're not married anymore, but she's still around.

My sister Linda graduated from Connally High School. I don't remember the reason, but she left the Home her senior year and lived with my husband

and me. Linda lives in Waco now. She's married and retired. Her husband makes enough money that she doesn't work any more, and that's nice.

As for myself, here's a little history. I quit school after the ninth grade, got married, had four kids, separated, married the man I'm married to now, and went back and got my GED. Then I went to commercial college and got my secretarial degree. I was a bookkeeper–payroll secretary until about 1993, and then went to work for the State of Texas as an environmental investigator. I retired from there, and during tax season, I do taxes for H&R Block.

Right now, I'm working for a man who used to own a grocery store chain here in Abilene, and I also do the bookkeeping for twelve companies up there. But I'm giving my notice to go back to work at H&R Block. It's seasonal, but that's okay. I don't want to work forty a week anymore.

My husband and I have made investments, and we've done very well. We carry real estate notes for people and finance houses—things like that. We've always saved our money, so we have quite a bit in the bank and in investments. We're comfortable.

Growing up at the Home was beneficial to me. It probably taught me to be a better person. The teachers out there always taught the Golden Rule, and we've always tried to live by that. I don't regret having been out there at all. It was good for me.

Ann Edwards Gilbert-Pulliam

1951–1961

My family lived in Winnsboro in East Texas, an almost primitive area back then. I was born in 1942, so I would have been six or seven when it all kind of started. My dad was a farmer, and in the off-season, he would work as a logger or in the sugarcane mills. He was working as a logger one day, and a tree fell on him. His body was crushed all over. He more or less recovered, but he could never get any kind of meaningful job, so my parents had a very meager life.

There were four kids, and I was the youngest. We'd always lived out in the country on the farm. The two older kids had been working for a lot of the farmers around there during planting and harvest, so they were taken in by people. My oldest sister went to work for some people up the road who had a big dairy.

I went to a foster home, then another one. I ran away and went all around the country for a couple of years, between the ages of seven and nine. I look back at it now, and it scares me half to death. That's when you know the good Lord was looking over you, had his hand on you.

Ann Edwards Gilbert-Pulliam's senior portrait, taken in 1961 at Michael's Studio, Waco, where she was often asked to model. Photo courtesy of Ann Edwards Gilbert-Pulliam.

I finally ended up in the courthouse, became a ward of the state, and they delivered me to the Waco State Home.

The Home was a pretty scary thing at first. It was hard to realize that everybody out there was just like me, because a lot of them had these big, grandiose stories, every one of which ended with "And my mother's coming to pick me up real soon." We were all eight, nine, and ten years old and scared to death.

I knew my mother wasn't coming to pick me up, so I just kept my mouth shut. She came to visit me one time. The only reason she came was to get me to sign over some money to her. She didn't really come to see me.

For a while, I had lived with a couple on a farm, and when one of their cows died after giving birth, I slept out in the barn and fed that calf and kept it alive. That little calf was just like me. She didn't have anybody, either.

Those folks told my mother that that was my calf, so after I went into the Home, my mother went to see them. She wanted to make a little money by getting that calf and selling it. She wanted me to write the people a letter getting them to give her that calf.

I asked her to never come back again.

We were just kids. There were a lot of wonderful, good kids who had a lot of pain, a lot of baggage. Some of them had been living with their mom and dad, and being put in the Home was an all-of-a-sudden thing. Some of them, like me, had been running all around the country, up and down and everywhere.

Rejection is really hard on young kids. They don't know what to make of it, what to do with their pain.

You still love your parents. You might not be able to admit that they rejected you, but in your heart, you know the truth. We had kids who'd been sleeping on newspapers on riverbanks, hiding under bridges— just all kinds of things. It was pretty sad, but that was just the way it was.

When I was twelve or thirteen, I worked in the hospital at the Home and took care of a lot of the new kiddos. It just broke my heart all over again because I was seeing myself coming in one more time, scared to death, just scared to death.

A doctor came in to give every new kid a complete physical. He decided how many shots they needed. Some shots you can't give all at once, which was one reason that the length of the quarantine varied for each kid. We'd keep them two or three weeks, giving them shots and doing the hair treatments for lice and other things that needed to be done.

The head nurse was Della. She was of Czech descent and had been in the war. When she marched down the hall in those clickety-clackety shoes and in that fresh-starched uniform, everybody at the end of the halls in the wards straightened up. She weighed all of seventy-five pounds, and she really walked it like she talked it, but underneath was a heart of gold. She took care of those kiddos and she loved them.

She didn't beat around the bush. When kids came in and they were sick, she checked them out, and if they were running a temperature, they were generally put in the ward for her to watch overnight. We couldn't take a chance of something spreading. Every two or three days, a doctor would come out. We didn't actually have a doctor living on campus, but Della lived there in the hospital.

I did what Della told me, and she liked that, so we became close friends.

Later on, when I was in about seventh grade, they started busing us to the public schools. We had been going to a school on campus and had our own football team, square-dance club, swim teams, acrobatics, and all kinds of things. A lot of us were lifeguards, and the Red Cross came out and taught us. That was a lot of fun. I loved the water and it was a good stress buster.

Junior high was a pretty good time, and I made a lot of friends. I had privileges at East Junior High that

There were a lot of wonderful, good kids who had a lot of pain, a lot of baggage.

I hadn't ever really enjoyed before. I got to ride on the Christmas float in the ninth grade, and I was elected class president. We went to University Interscholastic League with a play, and we won second place. We got to do a lot of interesting things that year.

Then I went to a big high school with so many kids and so much competition. It wasn't a good, healthy competition. A lot of girls had daddies who were doctors or lawyers or the mayor. It was a whole different ball game. I just managed to survive.

The high school years turned out to be hard for me, and I really had to study a lot. I did have one good streak of luck—I got a wonderful new roommate, Phyllis. She saved my life. We laughed and talked into the nights and told our secrets.

We would wear each other's clothes, and that was great because we had precious few. She was a trusted, true friend, and this was good for me.

My first husband, Bobby, and I had two sons, grown and gone now. Bobby died, and I sold our company back to State Farm. I retired and traveled and seven years later I married a wonderful man who had been our neighbor and friend for years. My boys are very happy for us. They love Henry, too.

Buddy Tucker

1952–1961

I was nine when I went out there, the last day of April 1952. We were born and raised on the Brazos River in Freeport, Texas, five boys and two girls. My sister went to school, but I never did. My dad was a shrimper. I was kind of on my own.

I'd go to the shrimp boats and clean them. The shrimpers would give me their money to hold when they got drunk so they wouldn't spend it all. Sometimes they'd get so drunk they'd forget to ask for it back. I took care of myself, but I would steal, do whatever it took to get by. That's how poor we were. It was rough. We were just poor, and the state took us away.

Two of my brothers were adopted, and the other one stayed out there

Buddy Tucker, left, and his lifelong best friend, Gary Dempsey, at the Waco State Home, 1957. The two still get together to play dominoes and go fishing. Harold Larson's private collection.

until we left the Home. About forty-eight years later, we finally located my brothers. They're doing well. One lives in Fort Worth and the other in Illinois. But we're all close again, back together. Mom and Dad felt sad the way things went, but that's just part of life, I guess.

My mother came to visit a couple of times. Later on, they divorced. My dad was still shrimping. He came and got a couple of us, and we went to visit him a while in Port Isabel.

It was hard to adjust because I was on my own for so long. Finally, they told me they wouldn't let me see my brothers and sisters unless I started behaving, so I did. You have no friends when you get there, so you've got to find your place in the food chain, show how tough you are—or not—and that worked out well for me.

Of course, we had duties. You'd get up in the morning and feed the cows and clean up the mess after them. They'd teach you how to homogenize and pasteurize the milk, too.

I have good memories of school. I had a foul mouth, so I had to take my punishment for that. My third-grade teacher was the prettiest redhead you've ever seen in your life. We were in class, and I was talking, and she told me to be quiet, but I kept talking and snickering. She said, "Buddy Tucker, if you don't shut up, I'm gonna jump right in the middle of you." I threw my arms back and said, "Please!"

I went to the principal's office and got my licks, but she remembered that when I saw her again, many years later.

Sports and competition were the things that helped me the most. Mr. Whigham, our coach, knew I wasn't scared of anything. I weighed about 75 pounds, and these other boys weighed 150 or so. He put me as a middle linebacker and said, "When this guy comes through, you tackle him." Here came a guy named Charlie, a bulldog, and I had no fear. I hit

After my kids were born, I decided nothing is worse than holding a grudge. Friends are better than enemies.

him, and when I woke up, Whigham was in my face, laughing.

He told me, "Well, learn to tackle." There it was, I learned fear.

My best memory is finding the underground tunnels. I found one that was unlocked, and a buddy of mine and I decided to see where it went. We found out this tunnel came up underneath the girls' dormitory. I knew they'd be taking their baths, so I climbed up that brick wall like a spider and reached up underneath the shades, and next thing I knew I was eyeball to eyeball with one of the girls' matrons, Mrs. Yarbrough. She said, "What are you doing?"

"I'm trying to look at the girls," I said.

"I'm giving you about five minutes to get back into your dormitory or you're in trouble," she said.

I cleared that second story to the ground and got back in bed. She never did tell on me.

Later on, as the girls got bigger and moved into the big girls' dorm, we tried sneaking in that dorm, too. We started out in the tunnels, but the passage kept getting smaller and smaller. We finally hit a dead end. It was too little to crawl, and we got stuck. We barely got our tails out of there, and so that was enough of that.

It didn't take much to get a whipping back in the old times.

If you talked or did something out of place, Ms. Belcher would grab you by the hair right by your ear, where the sideburns were, and she'd pull on that. She had something else she'd pop you on the head with, too. She'd pop you a good one.

Mr. Whigham could be pretty rough on you. He broke my wrist with a board.

It was my fault, I guess. I hated Sunday evenings because you ate sandwiches and stuff like that out on the outside, and I hated sandwiches. I was pitching grapes and catching them in my mouth. Ms. Wallace, my houseparent, told me to stop, and I smarted off to her. Mr. Whigham took me upstairs and gave me ten licks. I was pulling up my pants afterward, and he said, "You're not going to cry?"

I said, "No, sir."

He said, "I'll make you cry," and swung at my head with that board. I threw my arm up, and—pop—that was it. They took me to the hospital on campus and patched me up.

Years later, after Whigham retired, I saw him downtown. He was having car trouble, so I stopped and fixed his car for him. We talked about old times for about three hours.

I remember he had a rule. If you had a bully in the room and nobody could whip him, he would take that bully and put him in the equipment closet and put as many boys in there as he could and let them give him a whipping. So you had to be careful about being the bully.

They told me that I could go into the military to learn a trade after graduation. I didn't want military, because I felt like I had already been in the military at the Home.

I was washing buses one day, and one of the guys who maintained them was working on an old Chevrolet six-cylinder. He showed me the parts. "There's your motor," he said, "the sparkplugs, the wires . . ." Then he said, "A mechanic can do pretty well for himself, you know."

Al Burns, my houseparent, took me to Crankshaft & Valve in Waco. I walked in there and said I needed a summer job. The owner, Shorty Kinnet, said he couldn't hire me because I was only seventeen, and he wouldn't be able to insure me.

I lied to Mr. Burns. I said I got the job and would start the next day. He dropped me off the next morning. I'd been there about an hour, cleaning the grease off the floor, when Shorty came in and asked what I was doing.

"I'm working," I said.

"I can't hire you," he said.

"I don't care," I said. "You don't have to pay me anything. I've got to learn."

He looked at me and said, "Well, I'm gonna hire you. I'll just have to take a chance you don't hurt yourself."

I stayed with him about four years until after I got married. I'm still a mechanic, enjoyed every minute of it.

The Home, overall, was a good experience. I met my wife, Bess, out there. She was only there a year and a half or so. That was the best thing that ever happened to me. I ran away in 1961, when I was seventeen. I had a little run-in with Mr. Gay, Bess's houseparent, and I thought I was going to get in big trouble. They tried to kick me out of high school and get me into the military. I got the justice of the peace to certify me as an adult so Bess and I could get married after I graduated.

The state sent a guy from the youth council in Austin. He wanted me to go back. "I'm about to turn eighteen," I said. "I won't go back. No matter what you're going to do, I won't go back."

He said he understood. "You got a clothes allowance coming to you," he said. "Take advantage of it, and if you have any problems, call me." In the end, they treated me right.

After my kids were born, I decided nothing is worse than holding a grudge. Friends are better than enemies. If you can make yourself and the people around you happy, then life is good. We're not rich, but we're rich in that we have good families.

Dorothy Nash Roach

1955–1959

W e lived in Conroe. The court sent us to the Waco State Home because there were nine kids and my mother couldn't afford to feed us. My dad was a truck driver and had TB on and off all his life. He just came home to have kids, I guess.

Three of my brothers went to Boys Harbor near Houston, and my mother kept the other four. Another girl was born when my sister and I were at the Home. My mother came to see us twice, once when the baby was born and the other to take us home again.

My sister and I came to Waco on April 11, 1955. I was eleven; she was thirteen. We had to stay in the hospital five weeks before they released us to the dormitories.

They also cut my hair very short. I got up in the barber's chair, he put a bowl on my head and cut it all off. Certain girls got to keep their hair longer, but they kept mine short for a long time, and I don't know why. They didn't

Dorothy Nash Roach, right, *with her sister at Cameron Park.*
Photo courtesy of Dorothy Nash Roach.

let me grow my hair out until I moved up to another dormitory. I think they cut my hair like that because they just didn't want to fool with it.

I wasn't very nice out there, but they weren't nice either. I wasn't a troublemaker, but I was eleven and I just didn't want to leave my mother. I got a lot of whippings. If they didn't whip me at least once a day, I had a problem with it. I had to figure out what I had done right that day.

If I ever get to heaven, I hope Mrs. Garner is up there. She whipped me so hard one time I couldn't sit down for weeks. And I didn't even do the thing she said I did. Something like that stays with you all your life. What happened was that someone had written something in the bathroom, so they took us all into this room and had us each print different letters. Mine matched, so Mrs. Garner whipped me. She was the matron in my dorm.

The other big whipping I got was by Mr. Wilson, the superintendent. The reason he whipped me, he said, was that I made an F in attitude and an A in the subject. He made me pull my pants down and whipped me real hard. I couldn't sit down for a long time.

That's pretty sick. It's bad for a man to pull some little girl's pants down. They didn't try to touch me or molest me, but Mr. Wilson shouldn't have disciplined me that way.

Sometimes they'd make you pull weeds from the area in front of the auditorium. That was the most weed-free place you've ever seen.

I don't remember her name, but the matron for the first dorm upstairs was the best one I had out there. They didn't keep her very long, probably because she was nice to me.

Mrs. Powell was my caseworker. I liked her a lot. She took me to town and got me prescription glasses.

We got to go to camp every year, and that was the only time I wasn't grounded. Maybe it was so some of them could take a vacation or something. I always got to go to camp. Also, one year we went to the state fair in Dallas.

My first year out there, school was still at the Home, but in the middle of my second year, we attended public schools in Waco. I went to East Elementary, then North Junior High.

Some of the regular kids in Waco would make fun of us, but things like that happen in all schools. When they took us to town to a department store to get clothes, we would be in a group, so when we got off the bus and went in some place, everybody would stare and point. We loved getting our clothes, but that was embarrassing.

They never let me work out anywhere but always made me work in the dormitory. I had to shell peas, of course, but you never missed that, even when you were being punished.

My sister got along fine at the Waco State Home. Since she was thirteen, she was more adjusted to the idea of leaving home. I didn't want to leave my mother. I didn't like it at all. The whole time I was out there, I never would say I liked it.

I had several little boyfriends off and on.

I left the Home the summer after I finished ninth grade, just before my sixteenth birthday. I went back home and attended school half a year and got married. I met my husband at church. He was a good friend of my cousin. I was almost eighteen then.

Things worked out all right after that. I was married for twenty-one years. We had two daughters. We did great. Starting out the way I did didn't bother me at all when we were raising our own kids.

Now I live at Cedar Creek Lake, which is near Athens, about ninety miles east of Waco. My sister and I have been attending the homecomings since 1978. That was my home and my family for four years. I like going back and visiting with my old friends. They are like sisters and brothers.

For the most part, my own sisters and brothers

She whipped me so hard one time I couldn't sit down for weeks.

turned out pretty well. One of my brothers turned out real well. One brother was in and out of prison all his life, and he died young, about two years ago. Another brother went to prison for a little while, but he straightened out. He has since passed away, too.

One of my youngest sisters took off in 1975. She had her son when she was fifteen. One day, she said she was going to see about a job and left her son with my mom. We haven't seen her since, and we don't know if she's still alive or not. The boy was raised by my mother.

All in all, I guess the reason I've had a better life is that the Home gave me discipline. When I lived there, however, I didn't think I was so lucky. I just wanted to go back to my mother.

I hope we get our records from the Home. I just sent off for them about a week ago. I'd like to know more about things, like what they said about me. I tell people that those records may never get here because they may have burned up in transit.

Billie Jean Folkner Baumann

1956–1966

O ur parents divorced, and my mother got custody of all five children, but she was financially unable to care for us. My oldest brother, Charles, and I were put in the Sunshine Home in Dallas, but then the state removed us because my father, who was not supposed to see us, found out where we were. They put us in a foster home where they tried to sexually molest us.

The three younger boys had gone to a foster home. It was also a bad place where kids were being mistreated. Finally, all five of us were admitted to the Waco State Home in 1956. I was eight years old, and the youngest, Paul, was a two-year-old.

Billie Jean Folkner Baumann at the flagpole on campus, with, left to right, brothers Billy and Steve Folkner. Photo courtesy of Billie Jean Folkner Baumann.

It was scary at first. I couldn't see my brothers, because the boys were on one side of the orphanage and girls were on the other. It was exciting whenever I got a chance to be near my brothers or even catch a glimpse of them. It was hard getting adjusted.

The last time I saw my mother, I was fourteen. She remarried before I graduated and left the Home. She had more children, too.

It was only later, as I grew older, that I began to realize what I was missing. I would watch movies on television in which there was a mother, a father, and a child, and it would make me cry.

> It was exciting whenever I got a chance to be near my brothers or even catch a glimpse of them.

When anything went wrong at the Home, the houseparents always assumed you were guilty. For example, once a month we had to strip the wax from the wood floors, then wax them and shine them with big commercial buffers. One time I was using the buffer, and the electrical plug had somehow gotten bent and would no longer fit in the wall socket. When I told the matron, Mrs. Yarbrough, she got everyone's attention and said, "I want all of you to see this. Jean didn't bend this, of course; it wasn't her fault, but she just ruined it." Then she started beating me over the head.

One time I was planning to visit a couple that lived outside the Home, but Mrs. Douglas refused to give me permission. When these people found out, they called the Home and let Mrs. Douglas know they had friends in high places. Mrs. Douglas yelled and screamed at me, demanding to know what I had told them about the Home, but I had not told them anything. Then Mr. Pharr came down and threatened me within an inch of my life. They were going to take me to the police station for a lie detector test. I said, "You can take me down there and do anything you want, because I am innocent, and I did not do anything."

Mr. and Mrs. Gay had a bad reputation, but I never had any run-ins with them. I know they had worked in a lot of different places before they came to the Waco State Home, including a penitentiary. They were Christians and were always talking about the Lord.

I learned how to get along by becoming friends with all the houseparents. Call it brownnosing, but I knew it was the smart thing to do. When my friends wanted to go to the store or something, they came to me to ask the matron for permission. If the matron was in a good mood, usually we were able to do it. If they were in a bad mood, I'd tell them, "Not now. It's not a good time."

You had to figure out how to get along with them, for fear of being beaten to death. They would take a baseball bat, trim it down, and drill holes in it, and that's what they would whip you with. It would make huge, bloody welts on your body.

I never got a whipping. I know my brother Steve did, but my brothers never talked to me much about it. Once in a while they will say something, but still they come back for the reunion. That was a bad time in their lives—literally, a nightmare. These orphanages are supposed to be something that helps kids find a better life, but it is just torture. I can't put into words what a lot of the kids had to go through.

A lot of them were being molested by houseparents. I was very fortunate, however, because I could always duck out of sight. The boys had it much worse than the girls.

There was one kid the houseparents didn't like for some reason. A houseparent fought with him at the pool during a water show the kids were putting on. In the dining room the next morning, the fight picked up again. There was a sickly sweet smell in the dining room, and I still associate that smell with what went on that morning. We never saw that boy again. I don't know if they transferred him somewhere else or what, but we never saw him again.

I ran away from the orphanage once, when I was ten or twelve years old. A girl from Austin convinced several of us to go with her. So over the fence we went, and when I was going over, I ripped my dress. I was scared to death. We started running. We ended up in a cabin in a summer camp. We found some nail polish and painted our nails. We weren't allowed to do that at the Home. I think you had to be in junior high before you were allowed to wear makeup and nail polish.

Someone called the police, and they called the orphanage. The houseparent put us on restriction for two weeks. We weren't allowed to go swimming or anything fun. We had to go down to the swimming pool and sit there and watch all the other kids play and have a good time. Before two weeks were up, though, our houseparent saw how miserable we were. She came up behind us and pushed us into the water, which meant we were off restriction.

There were times that we had fun. We would set all these rocks in a square to build a house and we'd mark off the rooms. We'd get dishes and put water in them, and then we'd find the darkest leaves that had fallen from the trees and put them in the water to make tea. We actually would drink the tea.

Certain times of the year we had to get up at the crack of dawn and go out to the farm to pick corn or peas or beans. It was hard work, and we were not allowed to sit. Then we'd have to take it all back to the Home and clean everything.

The food was great. We had dieticians. They made fresh bread. I had never tasted chocolate milk until they started getting rid of our cows and they brought in chocolate milk.

I went to beauty school when I lived at the Home, and I got married there, too. The school was outside the Home. Starting when I was fourteen, I attended beauty school all summer and on Saturdays in winter until I graduated. I didn't have any money to pay for the school, so they gave me a job after school. I carried out the trash, scrubbed the floors, and cleaned the bathrooms.

I was able to pay for my wedding and have my wedding dress made. Some of the girls there were my bridal attendants, and my brothers were the ushers and lit the candles and everything. A lot of the kids had never seen a wedding, never seen a girl in a white dress, and I can tell you I was more than qualified to wear that white dress. One girl told me she had never seen anything as beautiful as that wedding.

We had the reception at the big girls' dormitory. That was a happy time. I probably should have taken advantage of the two years of free college that I was entitled to, but I wanted to get out of the Home so badly that I got married.

When I was halfway through working off my tuition, the state decided they would pay for it, but I turned down the offer. I wanted to pay for it myself. I wanted to be proud of something.

My husband and I had two daughters, but after seven years we got a divorce.

I got married again, and I have two stepchildren. I treat them as if they're my own.

My brother Billy and I were very, very close. He died of hepatitis in 2006, and I miss him. Charles, my oldest brother, recently passed away of cancer, and I miss him as well.

Paul, being the youngest, is the type who knows everything. You don't ever want to try and argue with him. My brothers used to come stay with me sometimes, and I always tried to make sure there was food for them to eat. Once, I left a whole batch of milk cakes for them, and when I came home, they had eaten every last one.

Paul would say, "I got dirty clothes in there. When are you going to wash?"

I would just let him have it. I'd tell him, "Tell you what, buddy boy . . ."

It's sad we don't have more stories to tell about our family, because we just didn't see each other that much. There were four boys there and then me. They saw each other all the time, but I didn't see them that often.

In high school, I remember being at football games and Billy trying to hang out with me. I'd say,

"Bill, you've got to go hang out with your friends. My friends are going to think you're my boyfriend." That would make him so mad.

I don't know what our life would have been had we not grown up in the Home. At least we had the best food, we had medical care, and we had new clothes and shoes for school. Every summer we went to camp in Marble Falls. It was so good to get away and go swimming and just be away from the Home.

Overall, I think we have to say it was the best thing that happened to us. If not, we would have ended up on the streets, dead, prostituting ourselves, doing anything to stay alive.

Many of the kids who grew up in the Home still live in Waco because it's the only place they know. Billy never left Waco. He grew up, married, and never left except when he was in Vietnam.

I stayed in Waco for a while, then moved to Houston, then moved to Round Rock three years ago. I have a beauty salon here called Shimmering Lights.

We moved here before selling our house back in Katy. All of our money was going to support that house, and we still had not found a place to live here. So for a couple of nights, we were virtually homeless. We slept on the floor of the beauty shop. My husband and I lay on the floor talking half the night, laughing, saying, "Who thought at this point in our lives we would be homeless?" We now have a home and are very happy.

Paul Folkner

1956–1970

There were five of us kids. I'm not exactly sure about the reasons, but I think my parents divorced. We were living in Dallas, and the judge told my father he could never see us again. I was two years old.

They originally sent us to the Sunshine Home in Dallas, but for some reason, we were taken out of there and brought to Waco. My mother would make frequent stops, once a week or once a month, to see us. I remember she brought my brother Steve and me a tricycle, and she brought my brother Billy a wagon. But they didn't last long. The other kids didn't have toys, so they got torn up. I was nine years old the last time I saw my mother. She moved to California.

Paul Folkner, left, in hat, with classmates on a bus trip to camp at Marble Falls. Photo courtesy of Paul Folkner.

I've got my signature at the baby cottage. The cement was wet there, and I stepped in it, and my footprints are still there. I was the youngest person to ever go out to the school. Later, they moved me and several other younger kids to what used to be the hospital.

My brother Steve and I were in kindergarten when we went there. When they quit having school at the Home, they sent me to Baylor. I tell everybody I went to Baylor because I had to go to kindergarten there.

They had cows for milking, chickens for eggs, pigs for slaughter, and their own vegetable garden. I even worked in the butcher shop. I had to work the kitchen when I got older. Sometimes I had to serve on the line, but I always seemed to have to wash the damn pots and pans. Ms. Gropel would make you wash the pots and pans in nothing but hot water. I bet she weighed every bit as much as 300 pounds, and she was tall enough to be a basketball player. Her husband was a little skinny guy. We used to laugh and make jokes about it. How in the world did they have sex?

The food was great. They hired outside people to come in and cook.

We planted the garden in front of the administration building. We arranged the flowers so they spelled out "Waco State Home." When a visitor stopped to admire it, Mr. Whigham would say, "Yes, I did that." As if a person as big and fat as he was could really get down and work like that. Big, fat, and bald-headed.

Steve and I got out of the Home when I was nine and lived with a couple on a farm for about a year, then we had to go back. When we were out there, we had to clean the manure out of the barn. They paid us twenty-five dollars for it, but they had to give the money to the Home to put in our account. We never got it. Our caseworker put it in his pocket.

Roy Rogers, the cowboy star, came out there and had his picture taken with me. It was in the paper. He wanted to adopt me. But whoever was responsible told him no, he couldn't have me. That was interfering with my life. If I could find whoever was responsible, I'd sue them. They had no right to do that.

We liked Mr. Burns, and everybody loved Mom and Pop Collins.

Just about all the houseparents were rough people. Mr. Jordan was mean. He would whip us with a baseball bat, whittled down to about an inch wide, with holes in it. I was small, but I was fast and strong, and I could whip anybody who came up against me, so Mr. Jordan used me to punish the other kids. If somebody got in trouble during the day, that night he'd put me in this little room we called the "closet" with the other kid, and I was supposed to beat the snot out of him.

We were not allowed to wear shoes in the dorm, and he'd step on our bare feet with his hard shoes to see if we would holler. If we didn't say anything, we would be okay, but if we hollered, then he would get mad at us.

Mr. Valen was another hard-nosed dorm parent. He would beat us with bats, too. They would brag about how the holes in the bat made it catch the wind, and it would knock you up off the floor when it hit.

Mr. Valen asked to be in charge of a little girls' dormitory, and he got the baby dormitory. The way it started, he would go in and watch the children take a shower. Then he started taking off his clothes and going in there with them. Then he would kneel down and put the girls in his lap and play with them. The girls got smart and realized it wasn't right. They marched up to the office and told them what was going on. By the time they came down to find him, he'd packed his clothes and was gone.

The worst one was Mr. Chapman. He beat me so hard my ass bled, just because I told my teacher I didn't have a conscience. I did that because she was being a smart mouth to me.

> I stayed there for fifteen years and then ran away because I finally got tired of being a piece of trash.

I went on to Mr. Gay, then Mr. Whigham, and then Mr. Burns. I didn't have any trouble with Whigham, because he was getting old and he'd heard things about me. He'd heard that I'd rather fight than snitch, so he left me alone.

Mr. Reedy, a tall, slender, bald-headed man, caught one of the boys with an upper cut and knocked him down the stairs. The next day, Reedy was digging through a closet, and the boy came up behind him, bopped him in the head with a ball-peen hammer, knocked him out, shoved him inside, and locked the door.

In those days there was no such thing as child abuse. They could do virtually whatever they wanted to do to us. If anyone ever raised their hand to a dorm parent, they would call the cops. You would end up in Gatesville or someplace like that.

I enjoyed playing football. I played offensive end and defensive end. I loved playing defense because I got to hurt the quarterback. I was the fastest man on my team. I was pretty strong, and I didn't care who you were—if you came up against me, I was going to pop you.

We got to spend two weeks every summer at Lake Marble Falls. I won a couple of fishing tournaments for catching the largest fish. We used to go fishing and hunting all the time.

For deer hunting, we used .30-30 rifles, but they were not supposed to be loaded until you were ready to shoot a deer. One day, a couple of the boys were pretending to shoot at each other, and one boy's gun turned out to have a round in the chamber. When one boy pointed the rifle at the other boy, he said, "Bang, you're dead," pulled the trigger, and the gun went off

and killed him right there on the spot. After that, we never got to go hunting anymore.

Knowing what I do now, I'd rather be dead than have to go back and do that again. I stayed there for fifteen years and then ran away because I finally got tired of being a piece of trash.

I ran off to live with a friend and his family in Waco that I knew from school, and finished high school at University High. Then I went to live with my sister's husband's family and learned to be a carpenter. I went into the Air Force during Vietnam.

After the service, I went back to carpentering, got married, and had a daughter. I got into welding, started a welding business, got divorced, came back to Texas, and got into the refineries in Houston.

I rode bulls in the rodeo. One Saturday night, I drew a Black Angus that no one had ridden before. I lasted six seconds. He kept stepping on my foot every time I tried to get off the ground. Finally, I got up and started running for the gate. I ran so hard I didn't see the clown. I ran over him, and they had to get the ambulance to take him out of there.

I'm retired now. I have a wife and two children. I have a little girl, Hannah Kay, six years old. I call her the Scooter. I have a little boy who's about to turn eight. His name is Daniel, but I call him Pepper and my little cowboy because he likes country living and likes to go fishing. We live way out in the country. My daughter in Colorado is twenty-eight.

I stay in touch with Richard and Buddy and several other guys from the Home. I still have my brother Steve and my sister, Jean. I call up Mr. Burns now and then. I try to go to the reunions when I can, but it's a long way from Brownwood.

Steve Folkner

1956–1970

I was four years old when they brought us to the Waco State Home. I was too young to understand why, but I assume it was because our mother and father could not take care of the five of us. Surprisingly, I remember a lot that took place before we were taken to the Home.

I remember living in a trolley car in Dallas. They had taken all the old trolley cars out of service and set them up for people to live in. I remember not having a lot to eat. We got sick of eating rice. There was a big hill, and we would take turns rolling down the hill inside an old tire.

We lived in an Airstream trailer in Idaho. There was no toilet, and the snow was so deep outside it could have swallowed us when we went out to use the outhouse.

Left to right: Billy, Paul, and Steve Folkner on the grounds of the Waco State Home. Photo courtesy of Billie Jean Folkner Baumann.

I hate to say it, but my mother was mean. I told her I had to go to the bathroom, and she said, "You peed in your britches, didn't you?" She started chasing me with a broom. I hid under the table, and when she started poking me with the broom, I peed in my britches again.

She burned my brother Billy's hand on the space heater to teach him not to play with it.

I remember getting a box of animal crackers for Christmas once. I think we were living in California then. I remember one of us falling out of the car, too. I think that was Billy.

I still remember when our caseworker, Mrs. Greenwalt, took Billy and me to a foster home. Mrs. Greenwalt was talking to the lady at the house, and my mother was sitting in the car. I was playing with a toy six-shooter and a holster. When Mrs. Greenwalt started to leave, I took the holster off, but the lady grabbed me because we were going to stay there. I guess that was the last time I saw my mom.

The foster-home lady was mean. After that place, we went to a home for kids in Dallas for a while. Then one day they took us all to Waco.

Billy and I were separated from our sister, Jean, and my oldest brother, Charles, but we were more or less used to that.

I remember that after Kennedy became president, the Home became integrated. A lot of the Mexican kids could not speak any English when they got there, so we taught them, and as the years went by, they would forget how to speak Spanish.

One boy named Joe really did not like the school. He was the same age as Billy. Joe ran away a lot, and one time when they caught him, Pop Collins, our dorm parent, and two other men took him into the restroom in the dorm. You could hear Joe hollering and screaming while they held him down and beat him. Joe was screaming for his mother. The rest of us did not know what was going on. We were afraid. I remember hiding under the bed. Some of us hid in closets. We did not want to be next.

I do not know what happened to Joe. One day he just was not there anymore.

Pop Collins was a good old guy. I do not want to make him sound like a bad person. Mr. Collins and his wife were good people. They just wanted all the children to grow up and learn to be responsible.

Most of the people working in the dormitories had no education. When they were hired for the job, they were probably paid as little as possible.

There were some people at the Home, however, who were abusive. Mr. Pharr was a person who liked to flex his muscles. He wanted you to know who was boss.

When I was twelve or thirteen, my friend Kim and I ran away for a week. Kim was an outdoorsman, a Huckleberry Finn type. He wanted to get on the Brazos River and just live there. We took off, and we were getting ready to swim across the river. But it was cold, and we were trying to get up the courage to jump in when we looked up on the bank, and there was Mr. Pharr.

Mr. Whigham, our dorm parent, and Mr. Pharr took us up to the main office. Mr. Pharr said, "Which one of us do you want to whip you?"

I chose Mr. Whigham. He had a board about three feet long. They made us strip down to our underwear. We got over thirty licks apiece. He would rear back with his board like he was going to hit a baseball. A few times, he hit me over the handrail.

When I went to PE that day, the coach said, "Folkner, where's your excuse?" I told him I didn't have one. He said, "You know what that means. You get a lick for every day you were absent."

He told me to pull my gym shorts down, and when I did, he could see the blood on my rear end. He said, "I think you've already had enough. Pull your shorts back up and go to class."

When I was in Mr. and Mrs. Gay's dormitory, Mr.

> I tell people my parents were the richest parents in the state of Texas because my parents were the State of Texas.

Gay came into the locker room, upset about something. We had wooden lockers. There was a guy named Earl, and I do not know what Earl did to provoke Mr. Gay, but he slugged Earl so hard he knocked him through one of those wooden lockers. Earl ended up in Gatesville.

We received an allowance of fifty cents a month. We did quite a bit of work, but it taught us how to work. We raised vegetables; we had poultry, hogs, and cattle. We milked cows. We made our own ice cream. We had our own butcher shop. We had a barbershop. We had our own trash pickup, our own dump grounds. We were just a self-sufficient little community.

Mrs. Burt was the nurse at the clinic. She had been a nurse in World War II. She had an aide named Mrs. Bertram, whose nephew was Dan Blocker, the actor who played Hoss Cartwright on *Bonanza*. She had pictures of him and her on the wall in the office.

Mrs. Burt's daughter, Cynthia, was a buddy, but she would get you in trouble. One day in the old hospital, we were playing and she said, "Let's hide inside one of those lockers."

As soon as we climbed inside, the door locked on us, and we panicked. We were beating on the door, and Mrs. Burt came in, probably thinking it was all my idea. She was fit to be tied.

When we were in the big boys' dorm, Reuben was one of my best friends. He had a 1958 Fairlane that he kept over at the Texaco station across from the Home. The station was owned by a deputy U.S. marshal, and he knew we were not supposed to have cars at the Home, but he pretended not to notice.

We would go get girls from their dorm and take them cruising—drinking beer and having a good time until one or two in the morning.

Jesse, Richard, and Charles were friends of mine, too. My friend Charles went into the army and got killed in Vietnam. When they brought the Vietnam

Illustration by Steve Folkner, who often created drawings of staff and other children while living at the Home. Courtesy of Steve Folkner.

Memorial Wall to Mineral Wells, I found Charles's name on it.

When I finished school, they said I could go to any state or community college in the state of Texas. I worked on Pancho's car all the time, so I thought I would go to TSTI [Texas State Technical Institute, now Texas State Technical College] to learn to be a mechanic. I went there but only stayed a year or so.

My brother Paul was living in Kentucky, and Billy and I decided we would go there and bring him back. We became hobos—living in the woods, sleeping in barns, working odd jobs, staying at the Salvation Army, and drinking a lot of whisky. Finally, we got real jobs and bought a car. We went to Lexington and saw Paul crossing the street. We said we were thinking about going home, but he wanted to stay there a while. We were tired of being hobos, so we went home without him.

I spent twenty-three years in the oil field working for the Western Company of North America. Eddie Chiles was my boss. I work for myself now. I own a sheet-metal shop. I have one child from my first marriage and two from my second marriage. We adopted two babies right out of the hospital.

People look at me and tell me it must have been horrible, growing up in a place like the Home. I tell them it was not horrible at all. It was just reality. I tell people my parents were the richest parents in the state of Texas because my parents were the State of Texas.

We got to do things other kids did not get to do. We got to go to Six Flags. If we were sick, we had our own hospital. We had clothes, and we had shoes on our feet.

We did not have to worry about keeping warm in winter or cool in the summer. We always had food on our plates.

I always weigh the good, not the bad. Sure, there were bad parts, but where would I be today if I had not gone to the Home? If my mom and dad were as mean as I think they were, would they have accidentally beaten me to death?

I just look at it for what it was.

Neelee Thames Walker

1957–1964

My given name is Nelta Ruth Thames, but after my last parent died, I changed my name to "Neelee" and dropped "Ruth."

My parents were separated at the time the Harris County Probation Office took over custody of the seven of us siblings on December 20, 1955. A criminal complaint had been filed against my father for sexual abuse, but the grand jury declined to indict him.

Until the following spring, four of us lived at Burnett-Bayland Home in Pasadena. The court took custody of the three youngest siblings and put them up for adoption. My oldest sister and my oldest brother were placed in separate dorms. My other older sister and I were placed together in another dorm.

Left to right: *Neelee Thames Walker with her siblings Bonnie, Joe, and Rosemary, in their parents' living room before they came to the Home, c. 1953. Photo courtesy of Neelee Thames Walker.*

The campus was a beautiful place. The two front dorms were two-story Colonials with six big columns across the front porch. This was a temporary county home intended as a holding place until permanent housing could be arranged. Due to the temporary nature of the Home, the residents were allowed few personal possessions. Each evening we lined up at the central closet, where we were issued clean pajamas and clothes for the following day.

There was a pretty little redbrick chapel, where we had services each Sunday morning and evening. People in the community would take us to Sunday school, after which we would spend the day with them. There was a swimming pool and a gym. We took great pride in doing our chores and keeping our dorms looking nice.

It was about a year and a half before we moved up on the waiting list and were transferred to Waco. Kids were always talking about "going to Waco," and I did not know what that meant except that when you went, you never returned. It sounded scary.

At breakfast in the dining hall on April 9, 1957, an announcement was read, listing which students would not be going to school that day. I was on that list, along with one sister and one brother. Another sister stayed behind and was transferred to the Austin State School. We waited for several hours, and eventually social workers from CPS (Child Protective Services) came to get us.

We headed north and stopped in College Station for lunch. I guess they thought we were finally far enough away from Houston to tell us we were going to Waco. What did that mean? I felt like I was going down a big black hole, never to be seen or heard from again. We arrived at Waco State Home about midafternoon. I finally realized what "going to Waco" meant.

All new arrivals were taken to the campus hospital for vaccinations and overnight observation before being moved into a dorm. I was assigned to the Taylor dorm, and my sister to the Chrisman dorm. I had never been separated from my sister before, and it was very traumatic. I cried. My sister comforted me and made a joke about her being "over my head" and watching me because her dorm was on the second floor. We didn't see my brother again for a long time.

The saddest time in Waco was during my time in the Taylor dorm. Mama Taylor did not participate much in watching us, but Papa Taylor certainly did. Every Saturday morning, we had to strip naked and get on our hands and knees in the bathroom and scrub the floor. Papa Taylor seemed to think that this was the only method for cleaning the floor.

We never saw Mama Taylor during these cleanings, only Papa Taylor, who stood over our little naked bodies, directing our efforts.

As far as I knew, the superintendent was unaware of the situation. Most of us who came there had already been abused. I think we just thought that was the way it was. We assumed that was simply how men behaved and you just did what they told you to do.

Even when we were living with our father, we kept quiet about what he did to us. He never threatened or said anything to us about his activities. It was just understood that we should never say anything. We knew it was very, very wrong, and the fear of anyone knowing kept us silent. Daddy by day—monster by night.

Papa Taylor was like that, too. When someone was around, he was just a guy who had a job at Waco State Home. He worked over in the receiving area at the back of the campus, and he ran the furnace system with all the underground pipes that carried steam heat to the radiators in all the buildings. I remember him leaving the dorm early each morning in the winter and then, shortly thereafter, hearing the radiators clanging with heat.

His left hand had been amputated so that his

> We assumed that was simply how men behaved and you just did what they told you to do.

left arm just kind of came to a point at the wrist. He used that stub to wiggle around on us little girls. It didn't take long for us to keep out of his reach. As far as I know, he just liked looking at our naked bodies and feeling us. It was my impression that, unlike my father, he did not go farther than that.

As a child, all of my encounters with men were traumatic. I went to counseling once, about six years ago. It was the first time in my life that I had ever spoken about these things to anyone. If I could have continued, I might have learned how to deal with all the trauma. I live with all the memories every day of my life.

There was a girl at the Home who was an excellent singer. When I was in the fourth grade, I took her to school with me for show-and-tell, and she sang several songs for my class. I was proud of her. She left the Home shortly after that, and no one ever heard from her again.

About 1962, our mother started taking my sister and me out for holidays and summer vacations. It was the first time in my life that my mother showed any interest in me. Then I realized that having two pretty teenage girls to pal around with meant getting more attention for her from men.

My sister and I lived at the Home until June 1964. I wish I had stayed until I finished high school. When we left, I was sixteen, and Rosemary was seventeen, and we had just finished the tenth grade. When we started school that fall, we were both in the eleventh grade. Rosemary went one semester and quit, but I stayed in school and graduated in June 1966.

I was smart and made good grades, but I was so socially traumatized that I pretty much lived inside myself. I had one close friend in Waco, Linda, but when I left, we gradually lost touch. Linda lives just north of Houston now. I did get back in touch with her a few years ago at one of the reunions. I usually make a few close friends wherever I go, but when we go our separate ways, that is the end of the friendship. It is time to start a new one.

I have been that way my entire life. It is hard for me to stay in one place. During those first five or six years with my mother and father, we must have literally lived in a hundred different houses—a few months here, a few months there. I assume they could not pay the rent.

At the Waco State Home, we moved to a new dorm about every two years. In the two years after I went back to live with my mother, we lived in three different houses.

My brother had a rough time at the Home. He started running away at the age of twelve or thirteen, and he did it constantly. The last time he ran away, he ended up in Mexia. Our father lived there, and we had relatives there. My brother befriended a lady in Mexia who owned a hotel and cafe. She contacted the superintendent of WSH and made arrangements to allow him to stay there. She made sure he went to school and gave him chores to do for room and board plus some cash. Our father found out that my brother had a steady place to eat, sleep, and make a little cash. He started hanging around and kept trying to take money from my brother whenever he could.

My brother left Mexia some time after that and became a lifelong drifter, but he never came back to Waco. With his big heart and friendly personality, he never had any trouble getting jobs, a place to live, or friends. As recently as the fall of 2008, he was still living that way, drifting from job to job. That October, he suffered a massive stroke. He spent the next ten months in the Madisonville Care Center. He got married to a woman who was staying in the room across the hall from him. He is still in a wheelchair, but I am waiting to hear that somehow he is back on the road again.

When I think back on it, we seemed to have a normal life at the Home. We had transistor radios and the same things teenagers everywhere had in their homes. We loved to dance, and we played sports. We had TVs, although we didn't watch much, as we had so many other things to do. I do remember rushing home from school everyday to watch *American Bandstand*; that is how we learned to dance. We played the same games real-world kids played, like Simon says, red rover, and dodgeball. We had baseball diamonds, basketball and tennis courts, a gym, and a swimming pool. It was an open campus, and we were allowed to go into town or to Cameron Park. Sometimes our school bus took us, or we just walked.

The year we came to Waco, 1957, was the last year they had school on campus. Beginning that fall, we were all bused into town to attend school. It was the beginning of fourth grade for me and the beginning of my awakening to the potential that school held.

Teaching me to read is the only good thing my father ever did for me. I started with the funny papers at age four, and by the time I was five, I had read all of my brothers' and sisters' readers many times. By the time I started first grade, I was bored with Downy Duck and Dick and Jane. One day in fourth grade, our teacher was telling us about this place called the library, and we were going on a trip to visit it.

When I walked into that big stone building, I felt like I was in another world. Row after row of books in cool, quiet, dim sections. I was in heaven. In fifth grade, a town boy and I were allowed to read our own books during the time that the teacher read to the class. I was limited to the school library, so this boy would bring books from home to share with me. I read the entire Hardy Boys and Nancy Drew series in just a few months.

I haven't stopped reading since. Every time I have moved to a new town, the first thing I do is find the library and get a card. How anyone could live without John Grisham, James Patterson, Dean Koontz, or Stephen King is beyond me.

I have always remembered there being many incredible, fabulous things that happened to us, but when I try to tell someone about them, it just sounds so ordinary. It is difficult to relate an event and have it sound so super when a large part of it was in the feelings and emotional impact.

I still get a chuckle whenever I think about when I learned what "going to Waco" meant. It was the best thing that ever happened to me.

Phyllis Meacham Smith

1958–1961

I left home when I was fourteen. There were nine girls in my family, and conditions were such that I just could not stay there anymore. I moved in with a friend, and her parents were awarded custody of me by the court. They owned a dry-cleaning business in Alvin, Texas, and had three daughters of their own. They were struggling financially and about to lose their business, so I asked if I had any other options for living arrangements.

We met with the chief of police in Alvin. He spoke with the judge. I met with a social worker, and she advised me that the Waco State Home was a better place to go than the Home in Corsicana. I chose Waco.

By this time, I was fifteen. The social worker drove me to Waco. We arrived in the middle of the afternoon on a school day. We were sent to the campus hospital and left with Della Burt, the nurse. I waited at the hospital because the girls were in school and it was the houseparents' free time.

Phyllis Meacham Smith, photographed by Ann Edwards Gilbert-Pulliam on the Waco State Home lawn, c. 1959. Photo courtesy of Phyllis Meacham Smith.

I was fine until the social worker left. I felt brave until I realized I was there all by myself. I started crying. Mrs. Burt was real sweet and tried to console me. It was very traumatic, even though I thought I was ready for this change. I saw the girls get off the school bus, and they were all laughing and talking. Mrs. Burt told me to go to the window. She said, "They don't look unhappy, do they?" I thought maybe it wouldn't be so bad.

I lived in only one dormitory, the big girls' dorm. I am sure we had a lot more freedom than the younger girls did. My first houseparents were Mr. and Mrs. Smith. They were wonderful. We called them Grandpa and Grandma. They didn't stay there very long. I think they became disillusioned with the place and left.

They put me in the room with two girls who were best friends and didn't want a roommate. It was one of the bigger rooms, and it was big enough for three, but they didn't want me in there. They wanted me to just disappear, preferably from the face of the earth. We just coexisted until they both graduated, which was the following May.

I made friends and roomed with several other girls over these years—some likeable, some not so likeable. When I was a senior, I returned to the same room where my life at the Home began in 1958. I roomed with Ann Edwards, and we became best friends. Ann was a very pretty girl. She dated the most popular guys. I remember Pat Cloud, who was Miss Texas at the time, came to visit Ann at the Home. How cool is that—when Miss Texas comes to see you? She was beautiful.

Mr. and Mrs. Gay became our houseparents. They were not popular. Only a couple of girls would say they actually liked them. I do not think they were qualified to be houseparents. They thought if you were not a Baptist, you were going to hell. The Gays didn't like it, but when I became engaged, I began attending the Methodist church with my fiancé. They encouraged us to go to the Baptist church and would

even drive you there. They were religious fanatics, but they did not practice what they preached.

If you didn't figure out how to get along with the Gays, you were in for a lot of trouble, so I tried to do whatever it took to get along with them. I learned to play their game. Whatever they said, I agreed with until their backs were turned. Ann did not like Mr. or Mrs. Gay. I thought they were mean to her, probably because she was so pretty and popular. I think they held it against her, but Ann was kind of hardheaded, too. She would argue with them, but it didn't take long to figure out that you could never win an argument with them. Ann and I both dated boys off campus, so we did not want to be grounded for any reason. That was motivation to get along with them.

While I was at the Home, girls never worked in the laundry room unless they were in trouble. Joyce and I skipped class one day, and they sent us to work in the laundry for a day. That was not fun. I learned quickly I wanted no more of that job.

When I came to the Home, we slept on starched and ironed linens. We had starched and ironed white tablecloths, too. We sent our clothes to the laundry, and they came back starched and ironed.

The jobs in the big girls' dorm varied. Your work duties were changed by the houseparents at their pleasure. You might have to mop, wax, and buff the hall floors or clear tables, wash dishes, and keep the rest of the dorm clean. These chores were in addition to keeping your own room and bath clean.

For a part of my senior year, I was assigned to work in the cafeteria where the younger children had their meals. We had to get up early in the morning and work late in the evening, doing the dishes and cleaning tables. It was a sweaty, dirty job.

Then the Gays decided that the senior girls would be the dishwashers for our dormitory. I was one of the four seniors, along with Ann, Betty, and Linda. Linda

When I came to the Home, we slept on starched and ironed linens.

was the one who helped the cook prepare the food. She also washed the pots and pans. We other three washed the dishes in huge stainless-steel sinks. The rinse sink had a gas burner underneath, so the water was almost boiling. Needless to say, it was a hot, steamy job.

Usually, the quality of the food was unbelievable, but we could always tell when it was budget time and they were waiting for appropriations. Instead of fabulous meals, they were using whatever was left in the pantry.

Most of the girls went home for summer and Christmas vacations, but there would be a handful left at the Home. I was always one of those. I never went back to my family. They were so poor they would not have sent me a bus ticket anyway.

I never returned to live in Alvin. Once the Gays took us on a bus trip to Galveston, and since Alvin was on the way, I asked if we could stop at my parents' house. I visited briefly with my mother and sisters.

During my senior year in high school, I was working at the Waco Safety Council for Herb Lanier. On weekends, I would visit at the Laniers' home with his wife, Dot, and their son, Charles. After I graduated high school, I lived with them until I married and moved into my own home. They were very kind to take me in. I will always appreciate them.

All I wanted to do was finish high school and leave the Home. I didn't want to pursue anything beyond high school other than business school. I had two scholarships for education beyond high school, which I used to attend Four-C Business College. If I had known then what I know now, I might have done things differently. Later I attended college courses at night, but I did not finish a degree plan. I retired from the Department of Veterans Affairs in 1995 as a medical rating specialist.

I still live in Waco, not far from the Home. Sometimes when I drive past the Home, memories of walking to Cameron Park on Sunday afternoons and other fun times come to mind. Living at the Home was a good thing for me.

Guadalupe Vasquez King

1958–1968

My two sisters and I came to the Waco State Home in September 1958. My father had abandoned the family when I was six months old, and my mother was too ill to take care of us. We already had one sister who had been adopted by our grandmother.

This was in Sweetwater, out in West Texas, in the 1950s, when there were separate restrooms for whites and blacks, but Mexicans were often not supposed to use either one. The schools for blacks and whites were K–12, but schools for Mexicans only went to fifth or sixth. My aunt said that was because they thought Mexican kids would be working in the fields by that age anyway.

My mother was in and out of the hospital because of depression, cancer, and heart problems. We lived an entire year without any adult supervision. My father refused to take us. We had a wonderful caseworker in Nolan County, Mrs. Duncan, but we were in three different foster homes. The problem was that we wanted someone who wanted to adopt us for who we

Guadalupe Vasquez King, after leaving the Home.
Photo courtesy of Guadalupe Vasquez King.

were, not in order to get money from the state. The one exception was an older couple we were with for a while. But they had just celebrated their fiftieth wedding anniversary, and when one of my sisters had appendicitis, they had no idea what to do. They had no idea what to do with young kids.

My older sister made the decision that we were going to stay together, so we got admitted to the Waco State Home. It was the best decision my sister ever made. I was eight years old, and she was only four years older.

We arrived at Christmas time, and, of course, people only seem to remember orphans at that time of year, so we had a lot of parties. Because we were different ages, we were separated into different dormitories, but I got to see my sisters every day in the dining room.

This was the first time I ever had my own bed, the first time my clothes were not hand-me-downs from my sisters. It was the first time I had regular food, the first time I had a lot of friends of my own.

> We were not allowed to speak Spanish at the Home or at school.

There were more Mexicans at the Home than I thought there would be. My older sister kept track of all of them until the day she died. We were not allowed to speak Spanish at the Home or at school. We were punished for speaking Spanish because they thought we were talking about them. To this day, I do not speak a lot of Spanish, even though I have a degree in Spanish.

I do not remember encountering much discrimination at the Home or at school in Waco, but because they were older, my sisters noticed a lot more. I could always produce good grades, and because of my grades, I actually had too many privileges. My younger sister did not have as many privileges, because she struggled in school.

In Waco, the public school teachers nurtured us. Anytime I wanted to do something extra, there was always a teacher to pick me up or take me home late.

It was just amazing. I learned that the trick to doing this was good grades. The staff loved it. In fact, the entire staff attended my college graduation at Sam Houston State.

A lot of the girls worked in the dining room or helped in the laundry. The laundry was probably one of my favorites. You got to see people as they brought in their laundry. You ironed the younger kids' clothes, and as you got older, you ironed your own. We washed the sheets every week and ironed them. I loved the laundry facilities. I actually have bought some laundry equipment for my home that we had there at the Home. I like everything very starched and pressed, like they had it there.

Pulling weeds was one of our punishments. Punishment at the Home was rough, but I only got three paddlings in my life with the old baseball-bat paddle. You only needed one or two swats, and you knew that you had done wrong. They also paddled kids or grounded them for poor grades. My little sister was always being punished.

Our teen years were the roughest. For me, especially when my sisters had left the Home, it could be difficult. I had no family in town, but fortunately the houseparents and teachers were always there for me. If I ever wanted to do extra sports, academic, or extracurricular activities, there was always someone available to pick me up or take me home afterward.

A lot of the houseparents barely made it through high school. In those days, education was not a requirement. You just had to want to work with kids. I had wonderful houseparents except for one that I did not like. I ended up transferring to a dorm where I cared for little kids. It was the first year the Home was integrated, the first year black kids were admitted. This was during, I believe, my senior year in high school, in 1966. I was working with three- to seven-year-olds because I knew how to braid hair. When I was growing up, there were no Mexican dolls, only black dolls and white dolls, so my mother taught me how to braid the black dolls' hair. Therefore, when the job opening came up, I said I could work with the little kids, which got me away from the dorm parent who was hassling me. I think the job paid ten to fifteen dollars a month.

Their philosophy was you played hard and you worked hard. They tried to keep you busy. We got up at five o'clock and made our beds, and you had to be able to bounce a quarter off it. We went to breakfast, did our chores, caught the bus at eight o'clock and went to school, came home, did chores, did homework.

We had a minimum one-hour study period. Because of my grades and the extra schoolwork I was doing, I could sometimes go till ten. Then, in my room, I would use a flashlight to finish my homework.

Baylor University came out at least two or three times a week to help us with homework. They loved to come out on Sundays and Wednesdays because we had the dairy and homemade ice cream. We had all the tutoring we wanted.

My favorite subject was Latin. I loved Latin and I loved English. I took a lot of speech and drama, not because I was shy, but because I had such a Spanish accent. We only had trouble when we went to algebra, and one of the other houseparents would help me.

I played a lot of sports. I played in summer fast-pitch softball for the Waco State Home and went to state. I also played softball in school, back before women could letter. Then there was what they used to call "aerial speed ball" [soccer], baseball, tennis, and basketball, even though I am only five foot five. I could guard well, but I could not shoot. I still cannot shoot.

I was president of many organizations—the Girls Athletic Association, Latin Group, Spanish groups, and Farsgard Service Club. Farsgard was one of three or four service clubs at Waco High. I was always interested in mental illness because of my mother's depression, so I would volunteer. I certainly could not do any therapy, because I was not trained, but I could do things like bake cookies for the groups as a volunteer.

My senior year, I organized a drive to get Waco State Home residents to collect presents to be distributed by the Hogg Foundation in Austin.

The nondenominational chaplains at the Home were wonderful. I attended the First Mexican Baptist Church in Waco. Someone from the church would come pick me up every Sunday. I know it is unusual, but when I was four years old and we were attending services at both a Catholic church and a nondenominational church—my mother said we needed two services, not just one—I told my mother I did not want to be a Catholic. In fact, between my junior and senior years in college, I went to Mexico as a missionary for the Baptist Church. After that trip, however, I decided that was not what I wanted to do.

There was a lot of patriotism at the Waco State Home. If you passed the flagpole and they were raising the flag, you had to stop. We observed all the patriotic holidays, and to this day I still wear red, white, and blue on Fourth of July, Memorial Day, and so forth. Many of the guys volunteered for military service. Quite a few of them volunteered to fight in Vietnam.

I graduated from Waco High when I was eighteen. My mother lived in California with my aunt for much of that time, and my aunt would bring her to Waco to visit whenever she was able. My mother died on my twenty-first birthday, September 20, 1968, which also happened to be the day I left the Home.

I met my father about thirty years ago for the first time. I have since learned that he fathered fifteen children with three or four different families. He believed in spreading the wealth.

I graduated from Sam Houston State University with a degree in criminology and psychology and a double minor in Spanish and sociology. Originally, my first choice was the University of Texas at Austin, but Mr. Ludwick, who was the superintendent at the time, knew some people at Sam Houston, and so I went there on his recommendation and on faith. I had never visited any schools; I just went. I had a great time there.

After that, I came to Milwaukee and was accepted

in an MSW [master of social work] program the first day I was here. I worked as a therapist at a maximum-security prison for men—the first female to be so employed—worked as a probation and parole officer for four years, and worked on four doctoral programs, including two at law schools.

Currently, I teach psychology at Milwaukee Area Technical College, which is the second-largest community college in the country.

I have been married to Daniel Patrick King thirty-seven years. We have no children, but we have two Afghan hounds. We stay busy. We go to Europe every summer. Next week, I am going to New Orleans to judge Rolls-Royces and Bentleys in the Superdome. Last summer, because Daniel is a longtime member of the Royal Society of Arts, we were invited to a dinner at Buckingham Palace.

My time at Waco State Home was the best experience I ever had. I am very grateful for it. I have not attended a reunion since my sister died.

I believe that the free-love philosophy of the sixties and the changing of family systems led to many of the problems we have today. Here in the Milwaukee area, where I live now, we have one of the highest teen-pregnancy rates in the whole country. My first case here involved a seventeen-year-old who was pregnant with her fifth child.

I wish we had places like the Waco State Home now. I would be an advocate for it as long as the staff had proper education and training.

Nancy Wilkins Green

1958–1969

My mother, her sister, and two brothers lived in the Waco State Home before my brother and I did.

My mother's father was a war veteran, and her mother was a nurse at Goodfellow Air Force Base in San Angelo. They could not take care of the kids, because they were in the war. Then my grandfather got sick. One uncle ran away from the Home. The youngest brother was adopted when he was three, but made contact with the family again thirty years later.

My real father was in California and had mental issues. Mom was with my stepfather, and they had other children, but my stepfather was mistreating my brother. He was okay with the girls, but he mistreated the boys, especially the stepchildren.

Nancy Wilkins Green, with her brother David Wilkins, playing bingo as they waited to see a caseworker at the Waco State Home, c. 1964. Photo courtesy of Nancy Wilkins Green.

At first, we were put in a children's home in Beaumont, and then my mother drove us down to the Waco State Home. That was in 1958, when I was eight years old. I could not understand why my mother was going to leave me. She explained that she had lived in the Home, too, and that she thought it would be better for me. I was sad at first, but I think I got over it. My brother was not there very long. He was having a lot of problems with the houseparents, and they could not handle him. He does not talk much about it. There are some things that happened to him I never knew about. I did not even know he left the Home when he left. It was a bitter experience for him.

The caseworkers were like backstabbers. If you said something to them about the houseparents, they would go tell them about it. They protect children now, but back then they did not.

My brother played piano all the time out there. That is why everybody remembers him. He still plays piano.

I had a lot of issues that needed attention. At first, they were not aware that I had a hearing problem. I was failing in the younger grades, so they put me in the third grade and gave me a hearing aid.

I attended school off campus and graduated from Waco High. The Baylor students gave me a lot of tutoring, so it was a pretty good deal for me.

I would run away like everybody else and do little mean things, but there really was not anything traumatic about it. I ran away three or four times.

> I was sad at first, but I think I got over it.

We were just little mischievous demons, and we would get our little butts beaten. My very best friend there, Linda, and I ran away one time. We had an adventure, but we got our butts busted and were grounded a week when we got back. Linda has remained my best friend my whole life. We are still in touch. She lives in Washington, D.C.

Another girl had wooden legs. I remember she had no feet. They did surgery on her and fitted her with wooden legs. That girl could play football better than you and I could have. She would get out there and play football with us and beat the tar out of us.

When Vogue Beauty School started doing permanents, nine of us got our picture in the paper. They used us as guinea pigs.

I did not have a problem with the Home. I loved it. I was better off there than I would have been with my stepdad and my mother. I think I would've been abused. They took care of me at the Home.

I live in Waco now, down the street from the Home. My mother said when they were little, there was a little wading pool in Cameron Park. They used to walk there before they had a swimming pool at the Home.

For years, I have been trying to get the City of Waco to put a memorial there, but they have not paid much attention to me. It is all run-down and decayed now. We would like to have a little marker there for all the little children who used to walk down there because they had no other place to go swimming.

Boys working on one of the three Waco State Home farms, which covered hundreds of acres and produced vegetables for the Home and feed for the livestock. Harold Larson's private collection.

CHAPTER FOUR

The Sixties

The 1960s dawned with the nation once again at war, this time in Vietnam. Great social upheaval and cataclysmic changes were fueled by the youthful confidence and idealism of the baby boomer generation as well as by the demands of the nation's increasingly vocal disenfranchised.

Cultural icons included folk singers, Black Panthers, Motown, the Beatles, *The Sound of Music*, and hippie tie-dye.

It was also a time of great tragedy, with the assassinations of President John F. Kennedy, the Reverend Martin Luther King, Jr., and Senator Robert Kennedy.

Those who raised their voices for peace, civil rights, and other causes did not always march together, but there was a common theme in their agendas. Each called for justice and more responsiveness from American institutions.

President Lyndon Johnson's Great Society programs sought to create a more just society, with immigration reform, Project Head Start to help educate underprivileged youth, Medicaid to provide health care for the indigent, and Medicare to do the same for the elderly.

The hallmark Civil Rights Act of 1964 outlawed racial segregation in schools, public places, and employment. The Voting Rights Act of 1965 prohibited discriminatory practices that denied any American citizen the right to vote in federal or local elections. Funding for foster care paved the way for more alternatives to institutionalized care for dependent children.

Our stories of the last years of the Home reveal tumultuous changes. The farm-labor culture was gone by then, along with the canning plant, the sheep and cow barns, the acres of potatoes, and the hay fields. The children at the Home were more likely to come from urban rather than rural backgrounds, and African Americans were admitted for the first time.

In 1974, the barbed-wire fences were taken down and corporal punishment was abolished, and five years later, the Waco State Home was closed.

Bess Foster Tucker

1960–1962

I lived at the Waco State Home from January 1960 until June 1962, a short two and a half years. I have good memories of my stay there.

I remember traveling there by car from Austin when I was almost sixteen, along with my younger sister and two young brothers. While I don't know what they were thinking, I remember I was excited about the new life ahead of me. At the same time, I also felt a little scared and apprehensive. I recall looking back over my shoulder, afraid that my father was following and would somehow stop us.

We came to the Waco State Home by choice. Some of the kids at the Home, however, did not have a choice. The courts made that decision.

Bess Foster Tucker, age sixteen, at the Waco State Home, 1960.
Photo courtesy of Bess Foster Tucker.

I won't go into detail as to why I made this decision, but I just knew I could do better.

I lived in Dorm Five, the big girls' dorm. Mr. and Mrs. Eugene Gay were the houseparents. They were not the most ideal houseparents, but looking back, I think they did the best they could. At that time, just about anyone could be a houseparent, despite having no relevant education.

Punishment varied, depending on the severity of your youthful sin. It could mean a paddling from a wooden board with holes in it, or if the infraction was less serious, you might be grounded, sent to pull weeds in the flowerbeds, or forbidden to watch television for a week, which would mean missing *American Bandstand*.

It did not take me long to adjust to my environment. Dorm Five was a big, two-story brick building with a balcony in back. The building had beautiful old wooden floors, which we had to keep polished like glass. We buffed them with a big electric buffer, which we would ride on when the houseparents were not looking.

I don't remember how many other girls were in the dorm. We shared rooms, two or three to a room. At a very early time each morning, Mr. or Mrs. Gay would ring a loud bell at the foot of the stairs, which meant it was time to get up and clean our room and bathroom. Most of us had an additional chore each morning, depending on whether we were juniors or seniors.

Mrs. Gay would inspect rooms and bathrooms, and we would be grounded if we did not pass her inspection. We thought for sure she did this inspection with white gloves. If we were caught still in bed, there was a price to pay. I did get three licks for not getting up when the bell rang, but it happened only one time.

Breakfast was served downstairs in the dining room, and I was never late for that. The food was wonderful. We had our own cook, Mrs. Williams, whom we loved. We nicknamed her Puny, but I don't recall why.

We had electric sewing machines available, too, not the pedal ones I remember my mother using.

Somehow I was always late getting out of the dorm to catch the school bus, probably because of too much primping and too many chores. If you missed the bus, you were in trouble. I remember running as fast as I could to get on the bus, but I remember missing it at least once.

Mr. Gay, who drove the bus, would check the length of our skirts before we got on. If they were too short, we were sent back to the dorm and later punished. We thought Mr. Gay was a dirty old man for checking the length of our skirts. We learned much later what he was trying to tell us.

Each summer, the Gays would take us on a vacation. One year we went to Galveston. Another time we stayed in cabins at a camp near Austin. Those were the innocent days. We were carefree. That was when our great country was innocent, before JFK was assassinated, before we were attacked on 9/11.

We made those vacation trips and rode to school in a big yellow bus with WACO STATE HOME printed on the side in big, bold, black lettering for the whole world to see. As teenagers, we were embarrassed about being seen getting on or off this bus. As an adult, however, I have never been embarrassed about being at the Waco State Home. I have never felt sorry for myself for being there. I would have felt sorry for myself if I had not.

Prior to my arrival, the children attended school on the Waco State Home campus. The Home had its own hospital, with a wonderful military nurse named Della Burt, whom we all loved.

In my junior and senior years, I received a lot of honors. I was Spring Festival queen, homecoming queen, and spirit sweetheart. This was the same young girl who hid in the restroom in junior high in Austin because she did not have proper shoes to wear.

> I have never felt sorry for myself for being there.

I made a promise then that one day I would have 100 pairs of shoes to wear!

In our junior year of high school, we could double date, and in our senior year, we could go on a single date. In January or February of 1960, with a lot of snow on the ground, I met Buddy Tucker.

Mr. Al Burns, the houseparent in the big boys' dorm, called Dorm Seven, I believe, was pulling the boys on a sleigh behind his car. I bounced a snowball off one of the boys and started walking back to the dorm.

Suddenly, I was pushed to the ground, and my face was rubbed in the snow by Buddy. Well, it went from there. We started going together and upon graduation from high school, we were married. That was June 1962, and forty-seven years later, he is still the love of my life.

Divorce was never an option for Buddy and me, since we both came from broken homes. Perhaps that is one of the reasons our marriage has endured.

We have two children and three grandchildren. The old cliché rings true: "If we had known that grandchildren would be so much fun, we would have had them first."

I retired as a secretary from the Teacher Retirement System of Texas. How ironic that the State of Texas fed and clothed me for two and a half years at the Waco State Home and is now providing me with my retirement income each month.

I am truly blessed and never forget where I came from and where I am today. Life is all about choices. Life experiences should make you a better person and build character. It has made me the person I am today, compassionate and caring, but tough as nails when I have to be.

God bless this great country we live in, the land of opportunity. I show my love to my country, our troops, and our veterans by wearing my red, white, and blue every day.

Leroy Willeford

1960–1963

There were originally seven siblings who went to the Waco State Home. My four sisters and a brother went first, when I was three years old. My dad took my brother and me to Oklahoma, where we lived with my aunt and uncle for a time, but my uncle said he didn't want to raise us if he couldn't change our name. So my dad picked us up and dropped us on my grandmother, and she raised us for the next ten years.

We almost ended up at the Buckner Orphans Home in Dallas, and some people wanted to adopt me, but my grandmother didn't want to split us up, which is why we were taken to the Waco State Home. It wasn't an orphans' home. It was a home for dependent and neglected children, like us. Our parents were alive, but they just didn't take care of us.

So on January 13, 1960, Mrs. Janis from the Dallas County Child Welfare Department drove us down to Waco. I'll never forget that day. By then, the other five siblings had already left the Home, but one of them ended up coming back because my dad and my stepmother were abusing him.

Leroy Willeford, after leaving the Waco State Home,
c. 1975. Photo courtesy of Leroy Willeford.

The Home worked out great for me. Living there was the best three and a half years of my life. I had 280 brothers and sisters.

I was in the ninth grade by then, so I enrolled in University Junior High and then went on to University High School. There was a little bit of friction with the regular Waco kids because the Home almost always won all the sports activities, so they would split us up and put us on different teams. My sophomore year, I lettered in three sports, and my junior and senior years, I lettered in four sports—baseball, football, basketball, and track.

Normally, you moved on to a new dorm as you got older, but they made an exception for me. I stayed in Whigham's dorm the whole time I was there. In the big boys' dorm, you were allowed to smoke, but not in Whigham's dorm, which was better for my physical condition as well as my reputation. I was happy staying there. We got along real well.

Mr. Whigham was the punisher of the Home, a big discipline guy. You had to have the right attitude and the right frame of mind to live there.

I earned a football scholarship to college, and Freddie Lamb did also. He went to North Texas on a football scholarship and I went to Texarkana Junior College.

The Home was a place where you could learn to do things to support yourself after you got out of the Home. A lot of the kids did not take advantage of that. They just wanted to get out of the Home and get away. Some of them went into the military; some of them didn't turn out too well.

We had a nondenominational church service every Sunday morning. If you wanted to attend a specific church, someone would come to the Home and take you off campus to worship. The Baylor Bears happened to be in Waco, and they have a million Baptist churches in that town, so if you wanted to go to a Baptist church, there was one there for you.

Herbert Wilson was superintendent when I was there. He was a Shriner, a wonderful man, very kid oriented.

When you were in the Home, the state was responsible for you until you turned twenty-one. So from the Home you could have gone and gotten a college degree, but not many kids did that.

I left the Home with three hundred dollars in my pocket. The people who had tried to adopt me were then living in Texarkana, which was why I chose Texarkana Junior College over several other scholarship offers I had. They lived in Rowlett when we were growing up and living with my grandmother. I used to mow their yard and stuff like that.

After I graduated, I went to work at the St. Regis Paper Company in Dallas and started college at Arlington. I realized I needed to take the rest of the semester off and start again the next session. I discussed my plans with the dean, but after I left his office, he just tossed my Selective Service card in his out-box, so I got drafted.

That was during Vietnam, and if you could walk, they drafted you. I was in the army two years. I was in the medical corps and made E5 in twelve months. When I was stationed at Darnell Army Hospital in Fort Hood, two guys from the Waco State Home were patients of mine. It's a small world.

After the army, I went back to college, and when I left, I went to work a week later for the same company I work for today. As of June 5, 2009, I've been there forty-four years. They won't let me quit. I'm the national accounts manager for a food-packing business, and I ship about seventeen million pounds of products with national accounts around the country. I travel all the time.

I've been married before, but I've been single now for nine years. I have one son, who just got married in Austin. He and his wife graduated from high school

> Living there was the best three and a half years of my life. I had 280 brothers and sisters.

together. I took them to Hawaii a couple of years ago, and they got engaged in a cave under a waterfall, and then we celebrated at Willie Nelson's place in Paia. It was a real treat for me because he's my only child.

All my brothers and sisters are still alive and very healthy. Four of us usually come to the reunion every year. Two of the other siblings have a bad attitude about it. They think the Home was a bad deal for them, so they don't attend the reunions.

I was inducted into the Masonic Lodge in 1985. Normally, it takes three years to go through all thirty-two degrees, from the Masonic Lodge to Scottish Rite and the Shriners, but I did all thirty-two in one year. I got inducted in the Masonic Lodge in April 1985, and I walked on the hot sands, as they say, a year later at the Shriner temple.

I joined the Masonry because it's my way of giving back to the kids. The Shriners and Scottish Rite are all about kids. The money benefits the kids and the burn hospitals and bone centers. If you see us Shriners out there in September with our fezzes on, drop your money in that bucket, because it all goes to those kids and the hospitals.

I'm president of the Waco State Home Ex-Students' Association. I like doing it because it brings me closer to the people and my friends. It kind of plays to the skills I use in my regular job, too, making presentations and going out with clients. We had a great showing this year, 130 people, which is the most we've had in a while. The numbers have been getting smaller because we're dying, but we had people in their eighties, seventies, sixties, and fifties.

We used to go visit the kids on the grounds of the Home, but now that it's mostly a drug rehab center under the Texas Department of Corrections, most of us don't like to go there anymore. It's not home anymore.

We were meeting at the Lions Club for a few years, but we lost it one year when we didn't make the reservation in time, so the last few years, we've been meeting at the VFW hall, which has worked out real well.

We don't allow drinking during our meetings. You do have some tense moments sometimes because you get these kids coming back and the old, tense feelings from long ago come back to the surface. If you had people drinking, somebody might want to knock your lights out.

My life has been good. One thing I have as a personal goal is to go back and finish my college degree. I'm at the senior level, but I need to finish that. The company keeps telling me they're not going to let me retire, but I'm planning to do it anyway when I turn sixty-six. I'm going to play golf and enjoy life.

Angie B. Casarez

1960–1968

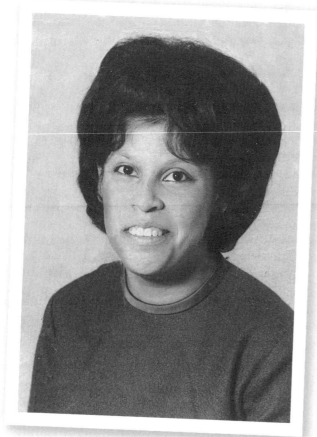

I was told that our neighbors reported on us. They said we were being neglected, that we weren't being taken care of, weren't being fed. The complaints went to the Child Welfare Department, and they came and picked us up. They put us in a children's home in Houston and kept us there for a couple of years, then transferred us to Waco. I had two sisters and a brother. I was ten years old when we came to Waco, and I stayed there until I graduated from University High in 1968.

My mother used to come visit us at Burnett-Bayland, and at the time I thought the man who was with her was my dad, but he was actually my stepfather. Years later I found out that my real father had been murdered.

All those years in Waco we never saw our mother. I heard that she tried to find us, but they would never let her know where we were. Years later she found us by accident. A guy they knew left the Home and went back to Houston, and one day my mother asked him if he knew any Casarez children in Waco. That's how she found us. I had graduated, left the Home,

Angie B. Casarez, age sixteen, Waco State Home class portrait, c. 1965. Photo courtesy of Angie B. Casarez.

and was already married by then, and my brother was in the service, but my sisters were still there.

So we never went home for Christmas, Easter, or Thanksgiving. I missed having holidays with a family. It was nice when the Shriners came on Christmas and gave us each a gift and some fruit. In the summer we got to eat watermelon on the slab, go swimming, go to camp and sleep in cabins, shoot bows and arrows, and things like that. We had fun.

I liked going to church in the morning and evening because we could sit with our siblings.

I came very close to being adopted by a lady who lived here in Waco, but it never happened.

My brother came to see me one time from Fort Hood. He had joined the army, and after basic training he was going to Louisiana, Germany, and then to Vietnam. At the time I was in the big girls' dorm, and I had gotten into trouble the day before, and they wouldn't let me do anything. My brother had come to visit me, and he was going to give me some perfume. It was called Jungle Gardenia. They wouldn't let me see him and made me stay upstairs. They gave me the

Thank God for the Waco State Home. I don't have anything bad to say about it.

perfume, and then I could see him walking up that long drive to where it ends at Nineteenth Street. Then he was gone. I didn't get to see him again for a long time. It made me so sad.

My brother always wrote me letters. He would tell me his friends were being blown up in front of him. He's been having problems ever since he came back from Vietnam. He's still my same brother, but he gets mad easier now. My brother's been through a lot. He doesn't talk about the war, but his wife bought him a set of films about Vietnam for Christmas, and he watches them.

I had a lot of friends at the Home, so now I try to keep up with them. At the last reunion I was saddened because there was hardly anyone from my generation there. Some of them are saying bad things about the Home, but why not leave the past alone and come be with your friends? I don't hold a grudge against the Home because they raised me. They kept us safe and gave us a home.

Thank God for the Waco State Home. I don't have anything bad to say about it. If not for the Home I'd probably be one of these people who are always in trouble with the law, doing drugs, and stuff. I don't do any of that. I have no regrets.

Juanita Johnson

1962–1965

AND

Virginia Johnson

1962–1969

Juanita: Our father was in the army. We were still with him in the early 1950s, when he was stationed in Panama, and I remember we had a black panther for a pet. His name was Catastrophe, and he was basically mine, because he really took to me. He was about the size of a German shepherd.

Virginia: He was half panther and half domestic cat. How that happened, who knows? We went to Panama and back to the States on a ship.

Juanita: I got in more trouble on that ship. My sister said she was going to feed us to the sharks.

Girls from the Waco State Home at camp, where Virginia Johnson was a counselor one summer. Harold Larson's private collection.

Virginia: At one point, they were looking for us all over the ship, and they found us in the garbage chute.

Juanita: We grew up on military bases. The first words out of my mouth were swear words.

Virginia: We were born at Fort Lewis [Washington] and lived at Fort Leonard Wood [Missouri], Scott Air Force Base [Illinois], and other places before the age of ten.

Mother and father divorced, and my mother couldn't take care of us. There were nine of us. We were living in Pasadena, Texas, and one night the neighbors called the cops on us. I don't know exactly why, but it was real late at night, right before Christmas, and we didn't have any heat. They took us to the Pasadena police station and asked if we wanted to see the cell our mother was in. We were just kids. It was hard.

I was eleven.

Juanita: I was twelve. Mother had another child in 1962, but we didn't meet her until she was seven or eight years old.

Our dad kind of washed his hands of us. When they went to court for custody, my dad told the judge he didn't want anything to do with us. He said he didn't want all those kids. Then he took up with a woman who had four kids.

Virginia: At the court in Houston, our father said, "None of those damn kids are mine. I'm not the father, and I'm not paying any child support." The judge said he didn't care what my father said. His name was on the birth certificate, and that meant he was the father and he was responsible for us. Dad told him he still didn't want any of "those damn kids." So the judge told him to be out of Texas by sundown or he'd throw him in jail. He took off.

Juanita looks just like him. I look like him some, but she looks like him a lot more. I found him in 1980. I bought him a plane ticket, and he came here on Thanksgiving, and we visited with him.

Juanita: The court took custody away from Mother, and we spent a year and a half at the Burnett-Bayland Home in Houston. We had the second-oldest sister there with us for a while. They sent her to nursing school. Two caseworkers from Burnett-Bayland took Virginia, me, a brother, and two sisters to the Waco State Home. It was the summer before school started. I remember we stopped by the side of the road and ate sandwiches and drank Kool-Aid.

The two youngest siblings went to foster care in Waco. Our brother was adopted by the foster parents, but our little sister ended up being in and out of the Home.

Virginia: Our mother was in and out of jail and prison because of blue-collar crime—not anything violent, just fraud and things like that.

Juanita: She never came out to visit us at all unless it was after I left.

Virginia: She came out in May 1969, two weeks before I graduated from high school. She brought us presents and took us out to eat. I asked her to stay and attend my graduation. When I got back to my dorm room, there were flowers and candy she'd left. I think I got one or two cards or letters from her after that. She died in 1986.

Our dad died in 1989. He never contacted us, never visited us, nothing.

Juanita: We had issues when we came out there. It was really hard to be taken from our mom. I was the oldest and very protective of my siblings. My daddy, when we were with him, raised me like his son. He made me responsible for the other kids, so right away I had an attitude. I was always fighting with other kids. I was their protector, so I was kind of a hellion.

Virginia: When we first got there, I was scared to death. I didn't know what to expect. I felt like I had to hang back for a bit to feel out the situation before I could get comfortable with it.

The first thing they do is they washed your hair with this nasty smelling stuff. It was awful. They'd stick your head over a big copper sink, cut your hair off, and then delouse you. They wouldn't let you have your hair past your collar.

One time in sixth grade, my hair got too long, and my housemother just chopped it off. It looked so bad. I took to wearing a headscarf, and my teacher, Mrs. Gunn—I'll never forget her—said something to a caseworker. She came to the school and made me take my headscarf off. All the kids in my class were so good. Even the boys who never spoke to me said, "Oh, it doesn't look that bad." They helped me out. That's when I realized that things were not that bad if you could be accepted at school and at the Home. I really didn't have a problem with the Home. I did pretty good.

Juanita: I had an authority problem, but only with the ones that were mean to me. One of the caseworkers hated me. She was cruel. She would take me up in her office and tell me bad things about my mom. She was very mentally abusive to me, which only made me act out more. She was physically afraid of me because I was strong. At thirteen, we were big, heavy kids. I weighed 150 pounds, and I was built like a grown woman. I had a reputation for being a little terrorist. A lot of the matrons were afraid of me. They wouldn't lay a hand on me. I'm not bragging; it's just how it was. My dad was in the army and he taught me how to fight.

I made good grades. I was a good student. I wasn't a hateful, mean person. I was just looking out for my siblings.

Virginia: A caseworker asked me one time if I thought I would be better off without my siblings. I said, "No, I love having a family like this." I didn't know what to think about that. I was very young. I think it was just a psychological ploy of hers, trying to scare people.

Juanita: For punishment, they beat us with those big old paddles and bruised our bottoms and our legs. The worst I ever got was three licks. I only got paddlings from people I respected. I wouldn't let anyone else whip me. If they were hateful to me, I wouldn't let them touch me. I would threaten them.

Another person I had trouble with was Mrs. Douglas. She was mean. One of the other matrons,

Mrs. Yarbrough, was good. She respected me. Ms. Anderson gave me three licks once, too, but if you said "ouch," and started crying, she would stop. She didn't even hit very hard. Another woman, Mrs. Brandt, had a swing like Willie Mays. She would knock your feet off the ground.

So those were the three times I got whipped, but I respected those women. The others, I wouldn't allow them to touch me.

Virginia: I got licks, too. They made us pull weeds in the garden, and one time I accidentally pulled some vines from a tree. My housemother said I did it on purpose. So they gave me five or six whacks with that big old paddle, and I was blue from my waist down to my thighs.

I think that incident was instrumental in getting Mrs. Canning, the superintendent, to change things around there. Mrs. Canning is now Mrs. Brumley, and I keep in touch with her. She's in Granbury now.

I didn't have a problem with the Home because if you didn't have anything better to compare it to, it was good. We got to eat every day, we got to go to the movies, and we got clothes and shoes. So for me, it was great.

Juanita: I didn't appreciate those things until I got older.

Virginia: We got to go to good schools.

Juanita: I got in trouble and got expelled for threatening to beat up a teacher. I was a very angry child. I didn't like this one teacher, who was condescending to me. I threatened her, and they expelled me and sent me to West Junior High. I studied hard and still made good grades and maintained a B average in school.

Other than being a hellion and fighting all the time, I had some fun times. Occasionally, they'd be shorthanded for the boys in the field, and they'd pick some girls to go out in the field. Because I was a big, strong girl, I was always chosen.

When it was hot, the boys' dorm leader, Mr. Hollingsworth, took us swimming after we worked in the fields. It was fun. We went to the lakes, and we went to Six Flags or the state fair in Dallas every year. There was a big swimming pool at the Home, a tennis court, and a baseball field. There were a lot of good, solid activities for us.

They put the girls in the dorms with a kitchen so we could learn how to cook. I'd do the cooking on days when our cook wasn't there. I already knew how to cook because my dad got me started when I was six.

Virginia: During the summer when I was fifteen or sixteen, I was one of the recreation people for the younger kids. Every day we'd take the little boys out and do something with them, and in the afternoon we'd take the little girls. That next summer, I was a camp counselor, and I went to camp on the lake for six or eight weeks straight. We'd take the kids out and shoot BB guns or do archery or cook. We'd take them into town to see the movie, and I saw *The Incredible Mr. Limpet* about forty million times. We went to the Alamo, too.

The bookmobile was wonderful, too. It came once or twice a week in the summer because we had to read all these books for school.

Juanita: We had three hots and a cot, and we got to go to school and do things other kids didn't get to do.

Virginia: Baylor students used to come out there. That's how I met Mrs. Canning. She was one of my tutors. Three times a week after school, we would go up to the auditorium and sing songs and play the piano.

I was in choir in school and in Golden Voices, which was the top chorus at Waco High School.

We had parties so there would be chances for the boys and girls to get together and interact. They tried to introduce us to the opposite sex in a way that was chaperoned.

There were good things, but there were also bad things.

Juanita: In those days, they didn't have the laws to protect children that they do now. The matrons that they hired out there were not properly educated. I don't mean that they were stupid, but a lot of them

didn't have the right frame of mind to deal with kids, especially kids who don't respond well to authority.

As I got older, I realized the Home probably kept me from ending up in jail. In my life, I've never been in jail, never been arrested. I don't do drugs, and I don't drink.

I've still been a little terrorist at times, but that's just my personality. I do think if I hadn't been sent out there, life would have been more difficult for me. I probably would have been in more trouble. That place did give me structure.

Virginia: Juanita's right in that it did give us structure. I've never been in trouble either. I know when some of the kids left the Home, they just went crazy with sex and booze and drugs. Some of them wound up in jail or dead. But other kids are like us: law-abiding, tax-paying, good citizens that have never been in trouble. We've sowed our wild oats, sure. It was the sixties—you had to try things.

I had a couple of boyfriends at the school, but Juanita had more than I did.

Juanita: They always went for the hellions, especially the teenage boys. I wasn't promiscuous; I was just tough.

I didn't graduate. In June 1965, I married a boy from the Waco State Home. I was sixteen. Later on I got a GED, and I've had some college.

I think they were urging me to get married because they didn't want me there. Mrs. Douglas at one point tried to get me to sign a paper so they could put me in the juvenile detention center in Gainesville. I wouldn't sign it.

My first husband turned out to be an abusive alcoholic. We had four children. I got married again later and had two more children. I've lost five of them.

Virginia: I graduated from high school in 1969. I had a little bit of college, and I went to court-reporting school, which didn't work out. Looking

> We had three hots and a cot, and we got to go to school and do things others kids didn't get to do.

back, I think I should've gone with what I wanted to do instead of what somebody else wanted me to do. I wanted to go to work for the post office. Back then, you could work for them twenty years and retire, but I let someone else talk me into court-reporting school.

Other than that, I've had a pretty good life. We're not rich by any means, but we have a good life. We live in Pearland, in the county next to Houston.

Juanita is on disability, and she's had some problems lately. We told her, "You're staying with us. When we buy a house, you're moving in. Just settle in. You're not going anywhere." My husband is fine with that.

Juanita: Over my lifetime I've had many, many jobs. I've done bartending, truck driving, and all kinds of work. I've had a hard, hard life, but when I look back, our life makes us what we are. I've had a lot of knocks, but it's made me very strong. I'm a good person.

Virginia: We've had our losses and our gains. People call me the glue that holds the family together. I've heard that from my brothers, my sisters, and my best friends. Juanita told me that this morning.

I don't have any kids, but we have cats. One died the day before I went to the homecoming in Waco. She was my baby, a scrawny little thing with a cropped-off tail. She adopted us from outside. We were out there one night, and she came up and put her paws on my shoulder and licked my cheek. What would you have done? We took her in and named her Bobbie.

I've been married several times. This one I've got now is better than all the other husbands and boyfriends all rolled into one. He's just wonderful. He's very good to me. He's number four and the last one. We've been together twenty years. I'm done kissing frogs!

James Hartley

1963–1966

I was born in 1957 in Bessemer, Alabama. At my age, I guess it is about time to step up to the plate and get all this stuff out. This will be only the second time I have ever told anyone this, so you should feel lucky. I never told anyone before, because I was afraid I would get beaten again.

I was about five years old when I first went to the Waco State Home, and the first dorm parents were pretty mean to me. At the second dormitory, they were all right. Then I moved to the dorm under Mr. and Mrs. Holmes. I guess they did not like me.

One day on the playground, this guy punched me in the back of the head. I pushed him and he fell. Mrs. Holmes grabbed me by the hair, pulled me

James Hartley and his sister Jan in San Antonio, many years after they left the Waco State Home, c. 1995. Photo courtesy of Mary "Liz" Westbrook Benton.

inside, and beat me. She and her husband called me all kinds of names. They told me I was stupid. They would say, "You little bastard, you retard." They told me I would never amount to anything.

I saw other guys get beaten, but not like me. I was beaten every day for the two years I lived in that dorm. I was seven years old, a baby. The other guys were ahead of me, yes, but they had no right to call me retarded and beat me. I got into fights because kids would say, "Look at that retarded kid. Look at that titty baby." This happened all the time.

I had knots on my head and bruises on every part of my body from the beatings by Mr. and Mrs. Holmes. They would kick me in the stomach and my ribs. Mrs. Holmes would grab me by the ear and pull me until my ear bled. They would make me stand in the corner and shove my face into that concrete wall. My nose would be bleeding, blood running down my shirt.

I would ask if I could go to the bathroom, and Mrs. Holmes would say, "Shut up and piss in your pants like you always do, you retarded idiot." So I soiled my pants.

Soon I began to believe I actually was retarded and stupid, but I had nobody to turn to. If I told anybody, they would beat me even more. For a long time, I said, "I am retarded. I am stupid. I am a bastard." It went to my head.

Have you ever been hurt and you cried every day until you could not cry anymore, but you still cried inside? That is the way I was when I was at the Home. I hurt so bad I wanted to kill myself.

What really hurt me was that they took me away from my family. I could not tell my sister Jan about it. I could not tell anyone, or I would get beaten again.

I was not only beaten by dorm parents, I got beaten by Mr. Pharr, the assistant superintendent. He beat me with a belt so bad on my back, my neck, and my legs.

> Have you ever been hurt and you cried every day until you could not cry anymore, but you still cried inside?

This is the trauma we kids had to go through. It is just so sad.

I was treated badly before I was sent to the Home. My mom died of a brain tumor when I was a baby. Dad went on a drinking spree and from woman to woman. He was a drunk. My dad is dead, and I should not say it, but he beat me.

I guess I got used to being beaten, but I would rather have been beaten by my dad than those people. They beat me much worse than my dad ever did, and he never called me a "retarded little bastard."

I had four sisters and one brother. We were all sent to the Home except for Francis, the oldest.

They kept me separated from my family. The dining room was the only place I got to see my sisters. If I raised my hand to say hi to my sister, they would beat me.

Francis and her husband came to visit me. Later, after my sister left the Home, she came back to visit once, but Mrs. Holmes told her, "No, he can't have any visitors. He made me mad." I had not done anything. She was just in one of her moods.

People do not know what happened out there.

After two years, they said they were sending me to the Mexia State School for evaluation and they would come get me in a week. I was there for eleven years. They never did come and get me.

At Mexia, they treated me with respect. The psychologists and the counselors told me, "You're not retarded. You're not stupid. You're just a troubled kid."

I was troubled because nobody wanted me and because of the beatings I took when I was in the State Home.

I played baseball, football, basketball, and did swimming. We competed in the Special Olympics and won trophies and gold medals. I was so happy at Mexia because those people did not beat me. We got punished. We would get demerits. When I got in trouble, I had to mop the floor, clean the dorm, the commode, do the laundry, and make the beds. But they did not beat me.

I got out of Mexia in 1975 and joined the army. I proved to everybody, even myself, that I was not retarded. I was not stupid. I was in the army six years. I lived in San Antonio, Houston, and Waco.

My life has been just up and down, up and down. Once I left the Waco State Home, I did not get beatings anymore. That is the only peace I have had. I guess the grace of God just told me, "We'll make it. We'll make it."

My brother died in 1974. My sister Jan died in 2005, and Francis died three months later. One sister was sexually abused at the Home, and she is still troubled. I have not seen my other sister in over thirty years. I guess they are still alive. It has been so long since I last saw them, I do not know for sure.

When I was in the Waco Jaycees, I was in the Gunfighters Club. After the Home closed and became the Waco Center for Youth, we would do our gunfighting show in lots of different towns—Temple, Austin, Waco, Mexia—and all the money went to the Home. We did a Christmas show, too, and when the guy who was supposed to play Santa Claus got sick, they asked me to do it. I am over six feet tall and skinny, so I was a funny-looking Santa Claus.

It helps to talk. I have kept this inside for so long. My friend Liz Benton, who was best friends with my sister Jan, is the first person I told. I never told my sisters. I did not know how to say it. I did not even tell my psychiatrist at the Mexia State School. I did not want to get beaten again.

When Liz got the letter from Sherry Matthews, I thought, boy, have I got something to say. Maybe they don't want to hear it, but it is time to step up and say what happened at the Waco State Home.

I just want to apologize to all the kids who were there and went through what I did. It was not our fault we were there. Our families just did not want us. When your family does not want you and you get beaten for no reason, called retarded and stupid, nobody has the right to do that.

No matter who they are, they do not have that right. There is enough bad in the world already.

Fernando "Freddy" Reyes

1964–1972

My name is Fernando Reyes, but most people at the Home knew me as "Freddy." I first came to the Waco State Home with my two sisters and a brother. I was the oldest.

Mom and Dad had split up, and they couldn't take care of us. We had been in an orphanage in San Antonio since I was in the third or fourth grade, but we outgrew that orphanage, so we were taken to the Home. I was in the sixth grade by that time. I had three younger brothers who were adopted in San Antonio.

A couple from San Antonio, Mr. and Mrs. Tapia, would come to Waco twice a month and bring us back to San Antonio for the weekend. They had

Fernando "Freddy" Reyes, left, *his sister Hope, and his brother Jimmy in 1973 at the Waco State Home. Photo courtesy of Fernando Reyes.*

kids our age. We were like part of their family and kept contact with our aunts through them. They tried to work out a way to get custody of us, but they couldn't, because they already had too many kids of their own. Once, they took us to meet my father, who was living in a kind of halfway house, but after that they quit coming.

My mother went back to Kansas with an addiction. Her brother and everybody helped her recuperate. She stayed there, remarried, and had other kids.

When we first came to the Home, I kept wondering when my parents were coming back to get me. But when I got involved with all the activities and learning they had for us at the Home, it didn't seem an orphanage any longer. I just started concentrating on what I needed to do with my life.

I had a really bad lisp, and I had classes for that. They taught me how to improve my speech.

My view is that everything went well for me at the Home. We were pretty well sheltered from the troubles outside.

We had plenty of activities each season. In the winter, there was deer hunting. During the summer, we would team up with girls in our age group and go to the coast or to an H-E-B camp near Marble Falls.

At Christmastime, we got clothes. We got new suits, we had shoes, we had food—we had nothing to worry about, really. We had each other. It got to where you actually thought this was your family.

It was awesome. Some people were traumatized from their experiences at the Home, but I never experienced anything bad.

We were allowed to go to Cameron Park on the weekends and venture down the trails and cliffs by the river. Sometimes we'd go to baseball games by Cameron Park. If you caught a home-run ball and brought it back, they'd give you a snow cone. It was fun.

> My view is that everything went well for me at the Home. We were pretty well sheltered from the troubles outside.

I didn't work the dairy. They had some cows and pigs out in the pasture. I remember them going out to castrate the little pigs. There were times we would go to other people's fields to hoe weeds and stuff like that. I really enjoyed that.

We had a barn where they parked the ten or twelve buses that took us to school. There was a big fire one day, and the barn burned down. There were mattresses in the upper level of the barn, and it was rumored that the fire was caused by one of the boys who was up there smoking cigarettes.

Al and Mary Burns were houseparents while I was there. Mr. Burns really encouraged us to get involved in our schoolwork and activities around the Home. When we had to do our chores, he would get us enthusiastically involved so we wouldn't dwell on personal problems. He was always on the go.

Some of them were strict. Mr. Whigham was supposedly the meanest one out there. He was also a baseball coach. Every summer he would have tournaments between different dorms. When it came to homework and chores, like yard work and garden work, he would really get on us about doing it right. If you got into trouble, he would instill a little fear into you to let you know that you needed to do right, which was good. We all needed discipline as we grew up, and I think a lot of us turned out pretty well.

Mr. Whigham was a large man, tall and bald-headed. His wife was like a woman from *Little House on the Prairie*, a real country woman, very down-to-earth.

I remember the time he sent three of us to his room to get spanked. Mrs. Whigham was there, and she grabbed a belt and told us, "I hope you are crying when you leave here."

We had our hands on the bed frame, but she beat the bed instead of hitting us. She just slapped the bed. I don't remember what we did wrong—maybe we got bad grades or something—but when we came out, we just couldn't keep from crying. In my opinion, the Whighams weren't as bad as everyone makes them out to be. What I experienced was mild.

I made a lot of friends, and I'm trying to keep in contact with some of them through the Internet. I've met a couple of people so far that way. They live close to me here in Athens, and one of them, a woman named Nora, operates a little place at the First Monday sale they have in Canton, Texas.

I finally graduated from Waco High School in 1972 after repeating one year. Though I just needed one English credit, I was in the band, choir, and all that stuff that last senior year because I had to keep the whole day occupied.

After I left the Home, I flunked out of the Marine Corps and then took different jobs. I've been working as a nurse's aide for the past eighteen years.

One sister has passed away. She turned out to be an addict, and they found her body in front of a Sonic drive-in.

My other sister lives in Waco. She has kids and grandkids and is doing really well.

I don't know where my other three brothers are, because they were so little when they got adopted.

I met my first wife at the Home. We had four kids, and now we have sixteen grandkids. She lives here in Athens, where I live, and is remarried. We still talk, and it's all good. We're here for the kids and the grandkids. My brother joined the army when he left the Home and now lives down in Austin and works for the IRS.

I'm with my third wife, Penny, or as she says, "third and last wife." Between the two of us, we have a total of twenty grandkids.

We do gospel singing at the Catfish Palace restaurant here in Athens. Every other Thursday night, we invite friends and sing while people are eating. We have a good time.

Linda Prather D'Agostino

1965–1974

As I walked down the seemingly endless hallway, I wondered how I'd gotten here and why. It was a strange place, a scary place, and I just wanted to go home. Before this, I had been living with my aunt and uncle, and my biggest joy in life was learning to ride my big, new bike. I felt like I had almost gotten the hang of it. I was able to keep my balance and maneuver through any pathway. Just a few more days, and I would look like a pro.

But now I was here, surrounded by little girls I didn't know. I was led into a large bathroom and ordered to shower. How could I shower in such a foreign place, amid strangers? As I stepped into the shower, unwilling to

Linda Prather D'Agostino, second from right, with other children atop a Ford pickup truck. Photo courtesy of Linda Prather D'Agostino.

remove my full slip, so as not to be naked and vulnerable, my mind was flooded with a myriad of feelings: fear, confusion, anger, embarrassment, loneliness, and sadness.

Where are my parents, I wondered?

I couldn't remember how things had gotten to this point. My two older brothers, my sister, and I were all in this Waco State Home. I had heard stories about my parents and their inability to care for us, about my aunts and uncles trying to step in, but I never really knew the truth. When you are only nine years old, certain conversations are not held in your presence, and others, you feel you should not listen to.

I had been put in a foster home in Leander when I was five. I recall my brother telling me we had been there more than once. I have only a few faint memories of that life and only one of them is positive. I remember the trampoline and jumping on it for what seemed like hours at a time. Perhaps it was my only escape from the horror I was living at the time.

I remember my brother David being treated so badly that even at five years old, my heart ached for him. He was always very tough, and to this day, I am envious of the strength he showed as a six-year-old being tormented and beaten.

I quickly adapted to life in the Waco State Home, even though it was nothing I had ever experienced. It was like a prison. One of the first things to happen when you arrived at the State Home was to be deloused and have your hair cut. When I went into the Home, I had long, beautiful hair down the length of my back. Mrs. Luedeke sent me to get my hair washed for lice and to get it cut. It was cut just under my ears, straight across the nape of my neck.

I was devastated, and when I saw David, I could not control the tears that streamed down my cheeks. I was so upset that I had to get my hair cut off. Big, brave, strong, ten-year-old David went to Mrs. Luedeke and cursed at her for cutting my hair. He threatened to beat her up. David was afraid of nothing.

We were awakened very early in the morning, ear-lier than any child at that age even considers waking up, to perform chores before school. We were allowed to go to public schools, but that was the only normal part of my world. Our minds were molded to think as the dorm matrons wanted us to think, to remind us that even the simplest of acts could result in a beating.

I was ten years old when I got my first beating. I was in Mrs. Chrisman's dorm, and her anger exploded without warning. Mrs. Chrisman was a big woman. She was tall, built like a man, strong and extremely intimidating to a child. I had been outside earlier in the day on the swings, talking to a couple of girls on the swing set. We had a disagreement. How serious could it have been at ten years old? I told one of the girls to shut up. Unbeknownst to me, the girl went inside and told Mrs. Chrisman what I had said.

A few minutes later, Mrs. Chrisman called me inside to the bathroom. She asked me if I told one of the girls to shut up. I said yes, but I had no idea why she was so angry. The conversation outside was nothing more than two kids talking, and I had already forgotten it.

When I replied yes, the violence began. She grabbed me by my ears and began beating my head against the metal lockers. I don't recall the entire conversation, but with each word, my head was slammed against them. The more she talked, the more my head took a beating. It seemed as if the tirade lasted for hours, but eventually she stopped. She spun me around and put her fist into my back, hitting me as hard as she could, and I went flying across the room. Her last words as she left the bathroom reminded me that I would never tell anyone else to shut up.

The girls were assigned to the dorms by age, and I became friends with several of the girls. We moved from dorm to dorm as we grew, and they became my sisters. I depended on them, I had fun with them, I accepted them, and I loved them. Josie, Wanda, Alicia—may she rest in peace—Melissa, Diane, and the others became my family and gave me wonderful, positive, funny, and loving experiences that I might never have had if I had not been in the State Home. We argued sometimes, as siblings do, but they were my makeshift family, and I loved them dearly.

The "Homers," as we were called, looked out for each other. We may have had our differences on campus or in the dorms, but in the public eye, we were like glue. If one of the outsiders picked a fight with one State Homer, he or she picked a fight with all of them. We made sure that no one was hurt by anyone that was not one of us.

Even though school was an escape for us, allowing us to leave the State Home campus for a while, it became a source of angst for me when I went each day. I felt as if I were not as good as the outsiders, since I was in a state institution and did not live with my parents.

One of the most horrific moments for me was arriving at school each day and hearing the words "here come the State Homers." Looking back, I know it was just a statement, and maybe even a term of endearment, but it was the most embarrassing thing I can remember. It singled me out as being different and inferior in my mind, and it called attention to my existence every day. You could not miss the buses—large, bright yellow, emblazoned with the words WACO STATE HOME. They were symbols of a life no one deserved.

Evelyn and Homer Wright were dorm parents. Although she ruled with an iron hand and he was a little odd, they were the closest things to role models I ever had. I remember she always carried herself with dignity, with a calm, almost motherly demeanor. I was terrified of her, but I respected her at the same time. Homer's claim to fame was the orange slip-on canvas shoes he always wore. I recall seeing him around campus, and even from a distance, you could tell it was him by the bright orange shoes. Mr. and Mrs. Wright taught us manners, respect, and how to be young ladies.

Their methods seemed as extreme as some of the other dorm parents, and often we found ourselves being punished for reasons we did not understand. One Sunday, we were all in trouble for something. I don't remember what. Before we left for church, Mrs. Wright told us since we were restricted, no boys could walk us back to the dorm from church.

After returning to the dorm, I had not even had time to change from my dress when I heard Mrs. Wright call for "all the girls who had boys walk them home from church." I felt sorry for the girls who had blatantly disobeyed her. I knew they were in for more of the never-ending punishment she could inflict.

A couple of minutes later, I heard her call my name, and when I responded, she asked, "Did you have a boy walk you home from church today?" I said that my brother did, and when she replied, "He's a boy, isn't he?" I knew I was in trouble. I meekly said, "I thought you meant boyfriends, not brothers," to which she replied, "I meant all boys."

We were taken into her office and told to pull up our dresses, and the spankings began. She was furious that we had ignored her. The strength with which she dealt each blow told us just how mad she was.

Spankings were not the only form of punishment we endured. One of their favorite assignments for girls who disobeyed was to make us "edge" the sidewalks with our hands. We had to sit out in the sun for hours and pull the grass and weeds a full inch away from the sidewalk. Sometimes there were stickers in the grass, sometimes there were thorns on the weeds we pulled, and our hands were stained and bloodied by the time she allowed us back inside the dorm.

My mom and dad came to see us once in a while. They brought us sodas, candy, and other treats we were not allowed to have, but their visits seemed forced, and the experiences were bittersweet. We always knew they would eventually have to go home and we would have to go back to the dorm. It was extremely difficult to see my parents for an hour or two and then watch them drive away. I can remember standing at the dorm window after they left and trying to get one more glimpse of them, even though I knew they were long gone.

The visits also allowed me to spend time with my sister and my two brothers. Because we were in different dorms, I did not get to see them very often. I knew very little about their lives at the Home and the hell they must have been going through.

We had been wild kids growing up, with very little supervision. I can remember skipping school several times and running amok on the streets of Austin even as very young kids. We ran up and down the capitol steps and rode the elevators for hours on end. We ran along Town Lake and in and out of the Sheraton Inn on Congress Avenue and First Street.

We roamed around Woolworth's for hours at a time, usually with no money to spend. The sights and sounds of Austin were our babysitters, and the freedom of the streets was usually a lot more appealing than hanging out in the bars, which was our regular routine.

We swam in a creek that had water moccasins, and we had no fear. We grew up long before our time. Our vocabularies consisted of words that no child our age should ever hear, much less repeat.

We roamed as a pack, we four kids. I was in awe of my oldest brother, and I worshipped him. When we had Cokes at the bar, he would always put peanuts in his. I never knew why, but he did it every time. When his Coke was almost gone, he would ask me to trade with him. My Coke was still almost full, yet I happily traded with him every time. I ended up with only a few sips of peanut-laden, flat Coke, while he had a new, almost full bottle, but it never bothered me. I only wanted to make the older brother I adored happy.

We were strength in numbers, and when we went to the State Home and were separated, it tore our bonds apart, and we were never able to regain that closeness

again. I know very little of my sister and brothers now, other than the humor we use to try and deal with the past. Our jokes and sarcasm mask the sadness in our hearts for the years we can never get back.

My brother and sister tell a story of being on the bus one morning, waiting to go to school. The buses lined up every morning in front of the administration building, and dorm by dorm, the kids went to the bus that would take them to school.

Barbara was saving a seat on the bus for my brother when Mr. Wright came over and told her to let someone else sit there. Saving seats was not allowed, he told her. She stood her ground and refused to move or let anyone else sit there. She was saving the seat for her brother, she told him, and when he realized she was not moving, it infuriated him.

When my brother got on the bus and sat in the seat she had saved for him, things got out of control. Mr. Wright, orange shoes and all, came down the aisle of the bus, started yelling at her, and slapped her. He grabbed her by the hair, dragged her to the front of the bus, and physically threw her off. He threw my brother off the bus as well. Why? What harm would have been done by letting a girl sit by her little brother on the way to school? It was one of the few minutes of time we were able to see our siblings, and it seemed the adults delighted in taking those away. My brother got in trouble for missing school that day. My sister lived in Mr. and Mrs. Wright's dorm at the time, and her punishment was swift and severe.

As young kids, we assumed the dorm parents were state employees, since the Waco State Home was a state institution. It didn't seem to us that any of them enjoyed their jobs or that they cared about the kids. It was always just a paycheck for them, we believed, and nothing more. They seemed to delight in inflicting pain on us—mentally, emotionally, and physically.

When I was fourteen years old, Mrs. Wright

> Our jokes and sarcasm mask the sadness in our hearts for the years we can never get back.

called me to her office and told me my dad had died. I remember seeing him earlier that year, and he did not look well. He was not eating much, if anything, and was losing weight.

Once when we went to Austin for a visit, we went to the hospital to see him. He was so thin I almost didn't recognize him. We had to wear face masks when we were in the room with him, and I was so saddened by his terrible condition that all I could do was stand there and cry. There were no words to describe how much my heart hurt, and I just looked at him through tears. I felt in my heart that he knew what I wanted to say—that I loved him and I wished things had been different. The look on his face as he lay there in bed, dying, reassured me he knew all those things.

I still wish I had said those things I felt, all those years ago, because I will never get the opportunity again. He was always a big man, well over six feet tall, and one of the strongest, funniest, handsomest men I had ever seen.

I remember we tried to get him to eat something when we visited him that summer, but he didn't have much of an appetite. Had I known that less than six months later he would be dead, I would have tried anything to get him to eat and take better care of himself.

They let us out of the State Home to attend his funeral, and the reality that I would never see him again, even less than I had when he was living, was almost too much to bear. Knowing that someday I would leave the State Home but would never be able to live with him again and make up for all the years I had missed with him was enough to send me into a deep depression.

Birthdays and Christmas were difficult times, as would be expected. Usually, we could go home to visit our families, but the visits were far from Norman Rockwell celebrations. My parents would go to bars, and we were given five dollars each to go shopping. The gesture was not so much to celebrate Christmas or a birthday as it was to get us out of their hair. It must have been hard to support four children and even harder to give them a Christmas or a birthday party.

Birthdays in the State Home were disappointing as well. They usually consisted of a cake and the other kids begrudgingly singing "Happy Birthday." The memories of those birthdays are anything but pleasant and did not give us a reason to anticipate them.

I can remember one Christmas before I left the State Home when someone sponsored our dorm for Christmas. We were asked what one thing we wanted more than anything that year. The girls went crazy asking for things they had longed for: an AM/FM radio, record player, albums, and all the things their parents either could not afford or would not buy for them.

When it came my turn to request my gift, I knew exactly what I wanted—a photo album. The other girls laughed at such a cheap gift, but I did not care. It was all I wanted from this stranger who was trying to give me a Christmas. It was a seemingly insignificant gift for a seemingly insignificant child, but it was a way for me to assemble the few happy memories I had in pictures. I wanted to look at the pictures I so carefully put in the photo album and filter happy memories apart from the negative realities.

I could look at pictures of my mom, dad, sister, and brothers and dream of a happy, loving story, one that included all the things people took for granted: dinners at the table together, kisses at bedtime, games and songs to celebrate holidays and birthdays. I wanted to escape my horrible existence, if only through the pages of a photo album.

My oldest brother ran away from the Home when he was seventeen and managed to avoid being caught. Once he turned eighteen, they would no longer search for him, and he was free to do as he wanted. He came back a while later to visit us, and when he left, he took my other brother with him. I'm not sure why my younger brother never came back. Did they not search for him? Did they not care that he was gone?

My sister graduated high school, and then she was free to leave the Home, too. I don't even remember the day they told me I could leave. Those memories have been blocked out of my mind like so many others that I can't bring myself to recall. I don't even know what day it was. I just know they allowed me to move back to Austin and live with my mother.

My family would never be together again—not that we ever were. I've heard stories of being homeless, living under the bridge when I was five. Does that count as living together as a family?

Moving home was the saddest thing that ever happened to me. My dad was gone, and my mom had a boyfriend. All of my friends were in Waco. My sister was living outside Waco with one of her friends from the Home. My older brother had joined the navy, and my younger brother was a phantom, living one day at a time with friends, relatives, etc., and I rarely saw him.

I sat on the couch at my mom's house and wondered what I was going to do now, and my mind was flooded with a myriad of feelings—fear, confusion, anger, embarrassment, loneliness, and sadness.

Ronnie Corder

1965–1975

My mother and father divorced when I was young, and he got custody of all the kids. There were five of us. He married again, and she had five kids of her own, so that made for a lot of kids in one house.

I remember my stepmother was crazy. She tied my sister and brother back-to-back and put them in a dark room. She gave me seventy-five licks with a fan belt off the car just because she caught me hanging upside down from a tree, trying to kiss my girlfriend. We were definitely abused.

My father was a jet mechanic for Braniff, and he was gone a lot. My dad had enough money, so it wasn't because of money that we ended up in the Home.

The Waco State Home swimming pool was a fond memory for Ronnie Corder, who served as a lifeguard. Photo courtesy of Ann Edwards Gilbert-Pulliam.

While he was gone, our stepmother decided to send us away. My grandmother took Thomas, the oldest, an aunt took my sister, Nancy, and somebody adopted our little brother, who was only about four at the time.

Someone came and picked up Randy, my twin brother, and me, and we ended up in a foster home. We didn't like the people, so we ran off and got caught and were put in juvenile hall in Dallas. Then they put us in another foster home, and we didn't like that one either. So they took us to the Waco State Home.

I felt I was better off in the Waco State Home than those foster homes, but I just hate that they split us up, and we still can't find our little brother. They won't ever let us know where he is. The papers are sealed.

> I remember when they took down that fence the last year I was there. We were free!

The first time we came to the State Home, I saw that barbed-wire fence and said, "Hey, Randy, we're gonna be in boot camp. Look at that fence. Looks just like a prison." Randy's quiet, and he didn't say anything.

When we got to our dormitory, it was like an army barracks with all those metal beds lined up row after row in one big room.

Years later, when I moved to the Senior Dorm—it was almost new—we had rooms we shared with just one other person. Randy and I were split up. Maybe we wanted to be in separate rooms. I'm not sure now.

I remember being put out there in the fields to work on the farm. They handed me a swing blade to cut the weeds.

In the early days of the Home, the principal of the school gave spankings with a wooden board. I don't think I was beaten, but we did get spanked. We had to turn around, put our feet straight, clasp our ankles, and bend way over. You could get a spanking for not doing your chores, for lots of things. I had my share of trouble.

One night, six of us sneaked out. We climbed over that barbed-wire fence they built to keep us in and broke into that little gas station near the entrance of the Home. We hauled out boxes of beer and hid them on top of a building. Unfortunately, the next day an inspector came, found the beer, and hauled it back. We didn't ever tell anyone we were the ones who'd done it.

My brother Randy was talking to me just last night, and he told me something I'd never heard before. Two of our friends who'd gotten the beer with us ran away and were found beaten to death in a boxcar near the railroad tracks, not far from the Home. Randy told me he'd run away with them but decided to come back. The next day, we were all told what happened, but Randy didn't say a word about being with them that night.

One summer when we were at the Home, a couple came and took us on a vacation to Pike's Peak near Denver, Colorado. We hiked in the mountains and really liked being out in the fresh air.

I can remember a canoe trip down the Brazos, too. We paddled fifty miles, turned over five or six times, lost our cooler and gear, but it was fun. I was so sunburned I couldn't even walk when we got back.

We rode this green bus everywhere, and everybody knew it was the State Home kids who were arriving, even if it wasn't marked.

We traveled in that bus to games. I was a lifeguard at the State Home swimming pool and played many sports—basketball, baseball, and football. We once played the Methodist Home in basketball, and I scored fifty-one points in one game. I got a plaque, but I don't know what happened to it. It used to sit in the trophy case right inside the front doors of the headquarters building.

I remember when they took down that fence the last year I was there. We were free! We could get across anyway, but taking it down changed the whole environment. It wasn't like a prison anymore. We felt part of the community for the first time.

I was also in the play *Oliver!* though I hadn't really been interested in plays before. I remember Mr.

George Weaver asking me if I'd play the part of Bill Sikes. He told me, "I think you can sing this song." I said, "I can't sing anything." He said, "Well, we can practice together," and we did.

I remember standing up on the podium, singing solo, and everybody looking at me. I'll never forget that. We traveled around, went to the Huntsville prison to put on the play, even got on television.

Oliver! changed my life and made me think somebody really cared. The whole group, we all felt special. I could relate to Oliver being an orphan, for my father didn't want me.

The next summer, I was in *The Two Gentlemen of Verona*. I really had a good time in those plays. I was thrown here and there most of my life. I didn't really feel I belonged anywhere. Being in those two plays made me feel part of something for the first time.

When I was seventeen, I left the Home and went into the Job Corps for two years and got my GED. I found out when I was fifty-one years old that the GED I got in the Job Corps wasn't real—it was falsified.

So, I still don't have my high school diploma, but I've done all right.

After two years in the Job Corps, I moved to Louisiana with Margaret, we had two sons, split up, and I married someone else.

I worked for Coca-Cola for twenty years, then a marketing company and retired. I was in Tennessee when my two sons came and brought me back to Louisiana, where I saw Margaret again. So we're back together. She always was the love of my life. I guess when you love someone, things have a way of working out.

I finally found my mother after I got out of the Job Corps, and I helped take care of her. She had health problems and had a heart attack and died in her fifties. My stepmother died ten years ago.

I've asked my dad about being sent to the State Home. He's in his eighties now, and I think he feels guilty about it. He says he doesn't remember what happened or why. He likes to see his grandkids, so we try not to talk about it much.

Mary "Liz" Westbrook Benton

1966–1967

Mom died in 1965, right after I turned fifteen. She broke her hip in a fall. She was in the hospital, expecting to come home Monday morning, but Sunday night she developed a blood clot and died. We lived out in the country on a farm north of Waco.

I just could not go back to the farm after my mother's death. I wanted to stay with my sister, who lived in our house in Bellmead, a suburb of Waco, but my dad wanted me on the farm. He just could not see past his own grief. My sister understood me and tried to reason with him. It was a stupid thing to fight about, and there was no real reason for it other than pride and stubbornness, but that is how I ended up at the Waco State Home.

By then, my father had married another woman, and they were running a bar. I guess it all adds up in the end.

I attended school at University Junior High. The following fall, I started

Mary "Liz" Westbrook Benton's school portrait taken in 1965, a year before she arrived at the Waco State Home. Photo courtesy of Mary "Liz" Westbrook Benton.

Waco High School. I lived in Mrs. Story's dorm, which was the last one before the big girls' dorm. Mrs. Story was a widow, a very nice woman, very religious. I missed being around my family, but I made friends pretty quickly. Janice Hartley became my best friend. Everyone called her Jan. She and I would watch television with Mrs. Story. She liked to watch the Billy Graham crusades.

I suppose Mrs. Story let me get away with some things. For one thing, your hair was not supposed to be longer than shoulder length, and mine was a little longer than that. I guess she overlooked the rule because I took good care of my hair.

But Mrs. Douglas, the matron in the big girls' dorm, seemed to have it in for Jan and me. As soon as we walked in the dorm, she said, "I'll tell you one thing: I'm not having any prima donnas here. First thing you're gonna do, Liz Westbrook, is get that hair cut."

The first day, she had one of the girls who was going to beauty school take me upstairs and cut my hair to the bottom of my ears. She just chopped it off. She wanted to make a point.

Mrs. Douglas's husband was a retired Baptist preacher and nice. But she was a real bitch, and that is putting it mildly. Maybe Mrs. Douglas hated us because she thought we were Mrs. Story's pets.

Your work assignments were rotated every week. I did not mind the work per se. However, if you got sick and had to stay in the campus hospital, you still had to work. Once when I went on summer vacation with my sister for two weeks and came back with the mumps, I went straight into the hospital. Every morning, after I bathed and dressed, I had to mop the bathroom and clean the ward. Mrs. Burt, the nurse who lived there, was mean.

If you were on the laundry, as soon as you woke up, you were expected to throw on your clothes and get down to the laundry room. One morning when I had laundry duty, I woke up with my period and had to go to the bathroom to clean up first. I was only a few minutes late. I was sitting on the toilet when Mrs. Douglas came in and started hitting me with the paddle. I tried to explain but she did not want to hear it. She was practically foaming at the mouth.

There were houseparents who molested the kids, others who severely beat them. Mr. Pharr, who I believe was the supervisor at the time, beat the kids terribly. He beat one girl with a paddle until she had bruises from head to toe.

Some of the social workers in the office also abused the kids. A male caseworker made a girl perform oral sex on him when he was giving her driving lessons. She was the sister of a friend of mine. The emotional damage to this woman has been devastating. She has been in and out of hospitals, and the aftermath has been terrible.

One of the male houseparents was transferred from a boys' dorm to one of the young girls' dorms. He was caught in the shower with a seven-year-old girl.

Some of the dorm parents were wonderful. As for the others, perhaps if they had been subjected to the same treatment they gave the kids, they might have changed their ways.

Mr. and Mrs. Hollingsworth had the big boys' dorm. Mr. Hollingsworth was nice, and everything I heard about him was good except that he used to take boys out to the drive-in so they could pick up girls. Perhaps he thought he was giving them an education. His wife was a quiet person.

After the incident in the bathroom, I was angry, upset, and hurt. I ran away, partially because of the incident but also because I thought, "To hell with this place, I'm getting out of here." I wanted to see if I could get away with it. Another friend came with me.

The rule was that after the third time you ran away, they sent you to Gainesville, the reform school for girls. I thought, "Hell, one time's not going to get me sent there." My cousin took my friend and me to my sister's house in Bellmead. My sister wanted me to call the Home and tell them I was all right. Although I resisted at first, I called Mrs. Douglas and told her I just wanted her to know that I was okay and I would come back in the morning.

John, my sister's husband, was a firefighter in the air force. He was on twenty-four-hour duty that night at Connally Air Force Base, so morning was the soonest he would be able to drive me back to the Home anyway. Mrs. Douglas just screamed at me, "You get your butt back here right now." I finally had to hang up on her.

The next morning, when John and my sister took me back to the Home, they went straight to the superintendent's office. They brought up the bathroom incident and warned the superintendent not to lay a hand on me. They already had a lawyer because they had been trying to get me out of the Home. Child welfare was working with them, too.

Probably because they were aware that there was a lawyer involved, I not only escaped a beating, but things began to get a little better for me. After a while, Mrs. Douglas seemed to actually take a liking to me.

When I got caught smoking with a bunch of other girls in a bathroom, she slapped us all in the face. Later that night, Mrs. Douglas told me she knew my roommate and I smoked in our bathroom every night after supper. "As long as I don't catch you, I'm not going to worry about it," she said. "But when somebody comes and tells me, I've got to do something about it."

One of the tragic things about an experience like this is that it destroys your ability to trust people. I had an uncle who worked in the boiler room at the Home, but I never told him anything, because once you are put in a place like that, you cannot trust anyone. This is what happened to me, and I was there only a short time. Think about the kids who were out there all their lives.

The horrible thing is that so many of these kids had

already been abused before they were admitted to the Home. Jan told me that her father abused them, too.

I think everyone who was out there was harmed in one way or another. There is trauma when you have to leave your family and go in a place like that, and then there is more trauma once you are in there, cut off from your family. Then comes the abuse and the aftermath of that abuse for the rest of your life.

I did not have a lot of bad experiences personally, but if something bad happened to one kid, the whole dorm heard about it. They talked about it. You could see the effects of what happened to that person.

Some people say everything was wonderful at the Home, that these things did not happen. I guarantee you that that is not true.

It took a lot of effort and persistence to cut through the red tape, but my sister and brother-in-law got me out of there. Sometime in early 1967, I left the Home and went to live with them.

I got married the day after I turned eighteen and moved to Pennsylvania. My husband and I have been married forty-one years now. We have four daughters and ten grandkids. I raised my own kids the way my mom raised me. I would say that my life has been okay. I made my choices, and things have been different for me.

My sister and John moved to Ohio, then to Pennsylvania, and we have remained close over the years. Dad and I finally made up. Every year, we went to Texas to visit him and my aunt. He got to know my kids before he died, which was good.

I have recently been in touch with several people I knew at the Home.

I have not been to any of the reunions. I was planning to attend in 2005, but then Jan died, and I said to hell with it. I probably would not know anyone there anyway. Until Jan's death, we remained the best of

> One of the tragic things about an experience like this is that it destroys your ability to trust people.

friends and visited often, even though I live in Pennsylvania and she lived in San Antonio.

At one time, Jan had started a book, but when she passed away, the family lost the notes. Her husband threw everything out. It is a shame because she and her brothers and sisters lived at the Home for several years and she had an awful lot to say. Not all of it was good, either.

Jan's brother, James Hartley, lived with us here in Halifax for about a year, but he's in Texas now, where he has nieces and nephews.

I cannot say that my entire experience in the Home was bad, because there were a lot of good times and I met a lot of wonderful kids. They fed us balanced meals. We did things that were fun. We would do things with the big boys' dorm. We would go to movies, the state fair, and summer camp. It was not all bad, not every day, not all the time.

Once a year they took us to Sears and bought us three dresses for school. We were supposed to wear our skirts to the middle of our knees. We didn't always do that of course. We would pull them down to our knees, but once we got on the bus, we would pull them up. Those types of restrictions you can live with. But some of the people out there were just mean, and that is an entirely different matter.

I wish to God that Dr. Phil had been around back then. That place would have been shut down in a heartbeat.

Vincent Galaviz

1968–1974

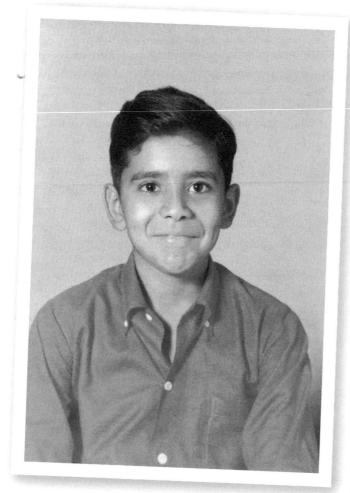

I remember when my mom and dad were still together. They were both working, so we were at home, and we were playing with one of those open heaters with flames. We were sticking paper and stuff in there and watching it when it caught fire and caught the clothes on fire, and then the house burned down. Everybody got out except for my little sister who was just a baby. The firefighters wouldn't go back in, but my dad ran in there and got her out and saved her life.

My mom and dad split up, and my mom couldn't take care of the four children, so we were taken to the Burnett-Bayland Home in Houston. Then we were at St. Mary's in Galveston, and they were going to close it, so we went to Waco. My sister and brother were there first, and they didn't take us for a year or so. They wanted to split us up. They were talking about taking us to Boys Town, Girls Town, and we said, "No, no, no." We wanted to stay together.

Vincent Galaviz during his first year at the Waco State Home, 1968. Photo courtesy of Vincent Galaviz.

I was eleven when I got to the Waco State Home. It seemed like a big place to me. I didn't know where to turn at first.

All the kids in dorms that didn't have a kitchen would eat in the cafeteria, and each dorm had its own table. But that was when I could see my sisters and brothers come in and go through the line, and that gave me some relief. Just seeing each other made us feel better.

Life was good. They treated us pretty well. I know some people had hard times, and I did, too, but not as bad as some. People who didn't have any brothers and sisters were more vulnerable. They found out I had a bigger brother there, and I didn't get picked on too much. I had a couple of fights there, because if you don't fight, they're going to pick on you all the time.

There was a grassy area behind the cafeteria where you would go if you had a conflict with somebody. We called it the "problem solver." That meant you would go over there and fight. We'd take guys over there and say, "If you've got a problem, here's where you work it out. If you win, you win. If you lose, you lose. But we're all brothers."

You always have to watch what you say and what you do. When we went to church, you had to wear a suit and tie. You couldn't loosen your tie or unbutton your coat until you got back to the dormitory and touched your locker. If you did it before that, you got your butt whipped.

Some of the dorm parents were pretty cool, but some of them were just looking for any excuse they could find to bust you. A busting was a whipping.

I ran away when I was fifteen because I wanted to see if I still had parents. I just wanted to know. The night we ran away, everybody was dressed up to go to a concert. I had some money in my pocket already because I used to sell my lunch every day. One guy always bought my lunch for fifty cents, and I saved the money until I had fifty dollars or so. But somebody squealed on us, and when we were getting on the bus, they told us to get off the bus.

They had us undress and put on our pajamas, and then they took us to the hospital where the nurse, Mrs. Burt, stayed with us until about midnight. She said, "Well, I don't think you're going anywhere tonight," and sent us back to the dorm. But we did. We all put on an extra pair of pants and left. I had only about two dollars because they had taken my money. When they got back from the concert, we were gone.

We got a couple of rides, but we walked most of the way to Yoakum, where one of the other guys came from. I baled hay on a farm, getting paid three cents a bale, and saved enough money for a bus ticket to Houston.

When we got to Houston, we stayed on the streets for two weeks, just scrounging. Sometimes we had to steal.

I didn't really know where to look for my parents, only the general area where we had lived. I had gone to De Zavala School when I was little, which is around Harrisburg and Navigation. There was a Spanish radio station on Alameda. I talked to the guy there and told him I was looking for my parents. He said he'd put me on the radio.

So I announced on the radio who my parents were and all that. Sure enough, that night my mom came down and I got to meet her for the first time in years. When we were up in Waco, she couldn't afford to come see us. My friend and I had been staying with my mom for a week or so when this man we knew came and said, "Your dad wants to see you."

That was a shock because I thought he was dead. I went to see him, but I couldn't tell my mom because she would have kicked me out in a heartbeat. My dad was a paint-and-body man. I kept in contact with him. I don't know what happened between my mom and dad, but he was a good guy.

One day the guy I ran away with got homesick and called his mom in Wichita. She called the Home in

> People who didn't have any brothers and sisters were more vulnerable.

Waco, and they came to my mom's apartment and caught both of us.

Back in Waco we got our butts busted. They were surprised we had run away. They put us out in the fields and made us cut the grass with a sickle. That was our punishment.

We used to go down in those underground tunnels to the girls' dorms. You would open the lid, hop in there with a flashlight, and take off down there. The tunnels supplied the return lines for the heating system, and it would get real hot down there, but it was fun. Sometimes we'd find a different route, so we'd mark it for next time. You pop up somewhere, look around. When you're young, you're curious. It was almost like Tom Sawyer and Huckleberry Finn.

I joined the Boy Scouts and went all the way to Eagle Scout. It was one way I could get out of the Home, and I could go on adventures and get familiar with the woods.

I'm still an outdoors person. I love to go hunting, but it costs too much, so we go fishing.

When I was in the tenth or eleventh grade, my stepsister came to the Home and got us out. That was in 1974, so I was about seventeen. We went back to Houston, and I attended school for a while, then eloped with my wife. Guess where we went? Right back to Waco. I stayed with my sister there until I got a job, then we got our own place. At the end of July this year, we'll have been married thirty-four years. My wife's name is Filippa, but we call her Gigi.

I'm glad I did get to go to the Home. They gave me more respect for myself and for others. They taught me a lot. The only thing I didn't like is that they didn't prepare me for life, for the outside world. When I got out, I didn't know which way to go. If they had explained things about the outside world, I think a lot of people would have reconsidered what they were going through and picked another path in life. That was the worst thing about the Home.

Life has been pretty good. It took a while for me to find what I wanted. Right now I'm a union plumber, and that's what I do for a living. It's mostly new construction. It's been good for me. I've got two kids and two grandkids.

We used to go see my mom at least twice a month until she died. We saw my dad even more. He just recently passed away.

My older brother passed away. He used to paint electrical towers, transformers, and stuff. One day he got electrocuted. It's a dangerous job.

My little sister works at a sheriff's department, and my older sister works at the Waco Center for Youth, which used to be the Waco State Home. I told her, "I always said you were going to stay there forever." I like to mess with her.

Billie Ceaser

1968–1976

I was eight years old when they sent my two sisters and me to Waco State Home. I was born in Dallas in 1960 and had been in a foster home since I was ten months old. My mother started having kids when she was young. There were ten kids. She and my father split up, and he moved to Florida.

Two of my sisters and I were in a foster home in Dallas, and the couple was elderly. It wasn't bad, but they were just too old for us from the beginning. I sort of remember that the foster mother had an accident, a fall or something. My mother had sisters in Dallas, but there were just too many of us for anybody to take on, so we got split up all over the place.

I don't even remember my real mother. She died in 1970. When I was older, I saw a picture of her. We didn't even get in touch with our father until we were older, and then he passed away.

Fifteen-year-old Billie Ceaser in her tenth-grade class portrait from
Waco High School, 1975. Photo courtesy of Shirley Ceaser Taylor.

Being so young, we were scared when we first got to Waco. We went from living in a home to an institution. The foster parents were the only parents we knew. I remember my sisters were separated into different dorms.

Two of my sisters were in a foster home, and two of my brothers were in foster homes in Dallas. Their foster mother would come get us on holidays and during the summer. They were the only people we had to visit. We were able to be with our brothers and sisters, but then we stopped wanting to go there. My sisters and I never talked about the reason, but it was because her husband always wanted to touch people. He had a hand problem, you know. It was nice to know our brothers and our sisters, but it wasn't nice to go through that.

I had friends at the Home. There were other African American kids there who had been in the Home before I got there. I don't remember any discrimination or prejudice. I think the Home helped me a lot because where I live, it's mostly black people, but I get along with all people because I was around them in Waco.

We had a lot of activities. I learned to swim at the pool on campus, and that was good, learning to swim at a young age. We used to go skating, and I remember going to rodeos.

We used to go on camping trips at Marble Falls, then we stopped going there and we went to a place called Leakey.

We definitely attended church, but I don't remember which one. There was no sleeping late on Sunday morning.

We had to make our beds and clean our rooms, and I think we had kitchen duties, like washing dishes.

My sister and I were talking about the infirmary the other day. I had to stay in there when I had chicken pox. It wasn't that great because the nurse, Mrs. Burt, was so mean. For some reason, I remember having apple juice and toast there.

It wasn't the most horrible place in the world.

When I was about fifteen, I had friends who got sent away after getting pregnant. They would have the baby, and then they would come back. I think the babies got put up for adoption. One friend went away, and when she came back, she told me she had a son. Another girl had two babies put up for adoption. I remember saying, "Oh, God, I sure don't want to go through that." I just never wanted that for any kids of mine. I didn't start dating until I left there.

I think I was more of a quiet kid—went to school, did what I had to do. I didn't get beatings, or at least I don't remember any.

I still keep in touch with a friend from the Waco State Home named Jimmy. He was a student at Baylor, and he worked at the rec center at the Home in the early seventies. Jimmy is still in Waco, and he's doing a lot now, has the Mission Waco place. They have church services under the Interstate 35 bridge, and he sent me an e-mail when he was in a TV special in Dallas. I even lived with Jimmy and his wife in Waco for a while.

I remember Rebecca Canning being superintendent, but the main reason I'm familiar with her name is that Jimmy talks about her a lot.

When I was sixteen, I quit school and went to Job Corps. I don't know why. Two friends and I just decided to go to Job Corps. I got my GED there, and they sent me to college. I came to New York in 1987, and except for a student layoff for a couple of years, I've worked in banking ever since. I worked at Bank One, then JPMorgan Chase. I was a loan officer in the mortgage department, and I loved my job, but then everything went bad, and the mortgage industry collapsed. Don't blame me—I wasn't the boss at JPMorgan Chase. I got laid off, and now I'm at home, collecting unemployment and looking for another job. I don't know if I need to do banking anymore, but that's all I've ever done.

I still talk to one of the girls who went to Job Corps with me. Her name is Jeanetta, and we're friends on

MySpace. She's still in Waco and sees people from the Home.

I have three children and one grandchild. I love my children.

I think about those days in Waco, and I guess it was okay. Like I said, it helped me. It wasn't like having a mother and father, but, I mean, it wasn't the most horrible place in the world.

Epilogue

Waco State Home, c. 1924 Harold Larson's private collection.

CHAPTER FIVE

Overview

Stories from alumni of the Waco State Home are remarkably honest and inspiring, often funny and entertaining, sometimes angry and tragic.

The stories tell us how the children of the Waco State Home coped with adversity early in their lives. They reveal how the many opportunities at the Home far exceeded their own expectations and were often superior to what was available to other children during the Depression and Dust Bowl years in Texas. These are stories of children who were branded "dependent or neglected" but went on to enjoy successful careers and, perhaps more important, to become loving and nurturing parents of their own children.

The Waco State Home had many much-loved teachers, matrons, and other staff members. We learned the names of employees who went beyond their designated roles to personally mentor children, provide hugs, offer love and encouragement, and even shepherd them into college and rewarding careers.

But what about the employees who sexually exploited children under their watch, or the so-called disciplinarians who inflicted savage beatings for even minor infractions of the rules, such as waving at a sibling in the cafeteria?

What happened to them?

A yearlong search of the Texas State Library and Archives Commission (TSLAC) and, more recently, the examination of archivist Harold Larson's vast library, some of which is now housed at Baylor University in Waco, produced boxes and boxes of disheveled papers, photographs, letters, and barely legible copies of documents. The documents and interviews map out a damning trail of abuse and of failures at the highest levels to protect the children.

OVERSIGHT OF THE HOME

Our research into the history of the Waco State Home revealed that when allegations of abuse and other complaints were investigated, the inquiries were conducted in secret, as if the general public had no right to know about them. This approach avoided not only negative publicity for the state, but also any grand jury hearings that might have resulted in criminal charges.

Secret hearings to investigate abuse were held at the Home in the early 1940s, after which a few employees were fired, asked to resign, or not rehired, but policies were slow to change. Corporal punishment at state institutions and schools was legal (as it is still today in Texas and about a dozen other states). When cases of sexual impropriety and abuse against children were discovered in places like the State Home, the allegations were usually covered up and the guilty parties were quietly shuffled out of town, their pensions and reputations intact.

In the beginning, the State Home was under the supervision of the Texas State Board of Control, which was also responsible for all state charitable institutions—state schools, hospitals and sanatoriums, orphanages, and juvenile training schools. The board even oversaw the Alabama-Coushatta Indian Reservation and the State Cemetery.

The board's primary function was to oversee operations and budgets, not public welfare—and certainly not dependent children, which meant that the equivalent of the office supply clerk for the state was placed in charge of dependent and neglected children.

The oversight authorities changed over the years, occasionally at the whim of the governor. Sometimes they were paid, full-time employees; sometimes they were unpaid, part-time, politically connected appointees; more often they were state employees who were pulled from other departments and had little or no training in child development.

The superintendents of the State Home therefore had substantial freedom to run its operations, hire and fire employees, and establish rules and regulations to "keep the children under control." More important, superintendents were held responsible for operations and finances, and that meant balancing the budget. If they could demonstrate that the dairy, cannery, livestock, and farmland were being put to use to feed the children; that it was cheaper to educate the children at the Home rather than pay the Waco school district to do it; and that such goals could be met by using limited- or minimal-wage staff members and unpaid volunteers, they were considered successful and were likely to be reappointed.

A review of the minutes of Board of Control meetings over the years shows that when the board met, the focus of the meetings was the budget or supplies or, in one instance, the quality of the coffee served to staff at the Home.

THE COFFEE DEBACLE

While children at the Home were waging a private war to stop the bloody beatings and avoid sexual abuse, another battle was being waged by the Board of Control. The subject was the quality of coffee—yes, coffee. During a Board of Control meeting in December 1954, the minutes reported: "We had received complaints from the Waco State Home concerning the grade of coffee purchased for that institution and they had requisitioned a better and more expensive quality be purchased for them . . . Mrs. Miller was further instructed to write other states and secure a complete break-down and specifications on their methods of purchasing coffee for state institutions."

The board's investigation of coffee took three months.

A final decision was made on February 4, 1955, after the board members and secretary conducted blind taste tests on the coffees and judged the coffee already being used at the Home to be the best.

These records perhaps help explain why more important and relevant issues related to the care of the children, such as beatings and sexual abuse, did not get the full attention of the board.

CHAPTER SIX

Abuse

In addition to the Board of Control or whatever entity was responsible for oversight, there were many who were in a position to help stop abuse at the Home. Staff members, law enforcement agents, the district attorney, judges, state legislators, caseworkers, psychologists hired to counsel the children, ministers who came to conduct services, volunteers from the community, and others had opportunities to observe and report abuse.

There were many reasons nothing was done. Some, including state officials, confused poverty with immorality, and parental failure with children's worthlessness. State documents referring to the children as "inmates" and "little orphans" reflected the prejudices of the times.

Children who were sent to the Waco State Home were there either because their families could not provide for them or because the state declared them dependent or neglected. Some had lost one or both parents. In most of the children's cases, district courts had ruled that the family conditions were so dire that there were no options other than the State Home. In some cases, alternatives could have been pursued, and questionable admissions, which were difficult to reverse, did take place.

In 1940, Governor W. Lee "Pappy" O'Daniel used his radio address to urge "the good citizens of Texas" to take "a little orphan boy or girl" from the Home for Christmas. He referred to the children as "inmates" and praised the Waco State Home and the State of Texas for their "tenderest care."

These little tots in their original abode and environment might not have been so attractive to prospective foster parents, in fact they may never be discovered by prospective foster parents but after being taken over, cleaned up and dressed up and given proper attention by such schools as the Waco State Home they become very attractive and very desirable . . .

It should make the hearts of all Texas citizens swell with pride to know that these little dependent and neglected children receive such splendid care.

—Governor W. Lee "Pappy" O'Daniel, radio address, December 1940 (TSLAC)

Not all public officials shared Governor O'Daniel's opinion of the state homes during those years. One of the harshest descriptions of Texas's charitable and reformatory institutions was found in a legislative report in 1943: "We found conditions in some institutions to be so foul and rotten we cannot print them." The specific mention in the report on the Waco State Home indicated that new management had elevated the school to "standard," and that the "unrest" among employees and children had been corrected to "some extent and conditions much improved" (*Journal of the House of Representatives*, February 1943, Legislative Reference Library of Texas).

The "unrest" referred to the brief but terrible period in the history of the Home during the term of Superintendent Arthur C. Wiebusch. Weaver Baker, a former lawyer, schoolteacher, and district attorney, was appointed chairman of the State Board of Control in 1942 and oversaw the firing of Wiebusch.

ARTHUR C. WIEBUSCH, 1941–1943

One of the first warnings of problems with Superintendent Arthur Wiebusch came from Mrs. T. P. Moser, a teacher at the Home. Mrs. Moser, who had recently been fired by Wiebusch, personally appeared before the board to complain about him and an abusive "disciplinarian" named Roy Lawrence.

Mrs. Moser reported that Wiebusch was a "militant dictatorial" man who fired able and sympathetic employees and openly stated that the children of the Home were inferior and could not be rehabilitated. Many of the children were not allowed to attend school, she said.

She described bloody beatings by Lawrence and said he had formerly worked at the Gatesville State School for Boys.

She said she personally saw a very small child "unmercifully" whipped because the child did not willingly submit to a hypodermic injection, that the child was virtually thrown into spasms, and that two hypodermic needles were broken in the process. When she complained, Mrs. German, the nurse, told her that the child "had to be thus treated because its parents were no account."

Mrs. Moser further reported that many prominent people in Waco were aware of the situation and were displeased with the administration. She said she was not an applicant for Wiebusch's job, that she would not under any circumstances return to her job under prevailing conditions, and that she was ready and willing to testify and could produce several other people who would do likewise.

The report noted that Mrs. Moser was the sister-in-law of Price Maddox, a member of the Department of Public Safety Commission.

Baker sent Wiebusch a copy of Mrs. Moser's complaints, offered to defer any action until Wiebusch replied to the charges in writing, and advised him to keep the inquiry strictly confidential until the board took action.

On September 22, 1942, Baker sent a stern warning to Wiebusch regarding his penchant for transferring boys from the Waco State Home to the Gatesville State School for Boys. He said Wiebusch had no right to transfer children without a court ruling.

The board began an investigation into the beatings and other complaints by interviewing staff and children and soliciting information on what was going on at the Home.

BEST PAL: DON'T GIVE ME AWAY

Hearings were scheduled for October. Before they started, a profoundly sad, poignant letter from a young boy was found among the documents:

Dear Mr. Baker,
I was getting along fine until this morning when Lawrence came to the dish room and started

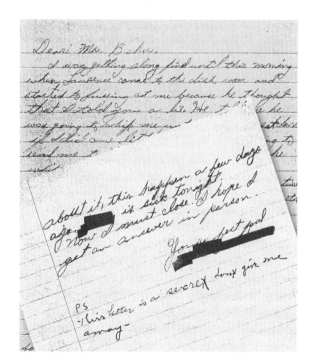

A letter solicited from a child at the Waco State Home during State Board of Control investigations of abuse during the 1940s; the letter was sent to the boy's abusers, despite a plea for secrecy. Texas State Library and Archives Commission.

fussing at me because he thought that I told you a lie. He told me he was going to whip me until I couldn't sit down, if I did one little thing, he is going to send me to the Reform School after he whips me.

Did you tell Wiebusch that if I stepped out of line one time to send me to the Reform School? He already has someone to take reports on me closely so he could do so.

Seven girls and four boys ran away since I came back. All of the girls that ran away got whipped. Lawrence got drunk and burned up his mattress while I was gone. You could write to Mr. Bridwell and find that out for yourself.

[Deleted] made a sandwich and ate it at the table, the dining room matron reported him to Lawrence and he almost beat him to death, just ask my matron about that. She was so hurt about it, this happen a few days ago. [Deleted] is sick tonight.

Now I must close. I hope I get an answer in person.
Your best pal
[name excised]
PS This letter is a secret. Don't give me away.

—A young boy to Baker,
October 1942 (TSLAC)

Baker sent the child a brief, friendly, pat-on-the-head letter:

Dear [deleted],
I was mighty glad to get your letter, and will talk to you the first time I am up there at the school. Be a good boy and study hard, and everything will come out all right. Any time you feel like writing me, do so.
Your friend,
Weaver H. Baker

—Baker to a young boy,
October 12, 1942 (TSLAC)

The fate of the young boy is revealed in letters sent by prominent citizens of Waco to the board barely two weeks later. One reads in part:

Dr. Kovacs says the Board of Control knows of the situation and has for some time. Some of the boys have written letters to them. The letters were returned to Mr. Wiebusch and the boys were beaten. Employees did the same thing and they were dismissed. So it does look hopeless, except that too many people know about it and it can't be quieted now without some action. So you may expect some fireworks in the near future.

—Sarah Snare to the Texas State Board
of Control, October 26, 1942 (TSLAC)

SECRET HEARINGS AT THE HOME

Wiebusch appeared before the board and denied all charges, also claiming that the evidence of a bloody beating was actually a ruptured boil.

Finally, on October 29, 1942, a private hearing was held at the Waco State Home; present were state representative Eugene McNamara of Waco, state senator Kyle Vick of Waco, Judge Douthit Young McDaniel of McLennan County, and members of the State Board of Control. Witnesses included several children who had allegedly been beaten, as well as current and former staff members.

Dr. William H. Mansfield, the pastor of the Austin Avenue Methodist Church, Waco, was the first to testify:

I have heard of the whippings of five boys. They told me about the boys and showed me a strap and showed me the blood on clothes and it looked to me as if it was done pretty severely. I examined one boy and there were bruises . . . of the buttock, one side was blue and hard and there were stripes on it. I would say it was about the size of the palm

of my hand, that is about three inches square . . .
The skin wasn't broken on the other side at all, but
on the other side you could see the stripes and it
was blue but there was no blood there but it was
pretty severe.

—Hearing, Waco State Home, report dated
October 29, 1942 (TSLAC; this report is the
source for the testimonies that follow)

Dr. Seylor B. Kovacs, chaplain of the Home, who
had already been quoted in an abuse-complaint
letter to the board, testified: "As I came up one time
I heard a sound and they said it was a boy being
punished. I understood it was a slat being used and I
heard the groans of the boy . . . and I made the statement that it sounded like the boy was punished with
a barrel stave or something of that nature . . . I think
that much of the punishment meted out is completely unwarranted."

Mrs. Lillian Horton, a matron at the Home, graphi-
cally described beatings of the children as well as
Wiebusch's indifference to staff complaints:

(Child) was black and blue and I was just plumb
sick. I called him to me and felt of him and he
had fever—he looked to me like he was sick and I
told him to go over and get in bed and I said in the
morning if you are not better we will have to have
something done for you and the next morning I
felt of him and he was still hot . . .

. . . We went in there and pulled his clothes
down and his whole bottom was just as black as
this man's clothes and had a great long gash cut
and he was bleeding . . . They are treating them
like they do in Germany.

. . . Mr. Wiebusch just kept on saying that he
didn't think that I was loyal to him . . . He got pretty
mad and talked pretty loud to me and I talked
pretty loud and he told me that he wanted loyalty.

There were lots of little girls whipped and I

think Mr. Lawrence whipped them too hard. I
have punished them, too, but not too hard. There
were four little girls he whipped and the next
morning one of the little girls was still black and
blue and one girl said that it hurt her very much.

Not all staff members who testified were willing
to criticize Wiebusch's policies. Mrs. Luella Elam,
the head matron, said: "I suppose it would be my duty
when a report comes in of a girl being whipped to see
about her and I usually try to. As to the number of
whippings administered to the girls in a week I don't
think there are so many."

One of those who defended Wiebusch and Lawrence was Mrs. Anna Mae German, a practical nurse
who worked at the Home. She had been accused of
breaking two hypodermic needles in the arm of a resistant child, and she claimed that the boys were not
beaten at all: "When this boy came down the other
day he had a place on his back and this place looked
to me like he had skidded on either gravel or a plank
or something like that . . . I didn't think it was from
a whipping. I know the boy and I think he would do
anything in the world and lay it on somebody else."

The school principal, J. O. Robinson, defended
his own use of corporal punishment: "The paddle I
use is made of ply-board. That's the only instrument
I use. I think Mr. Lawrence uses a strap. I would say
it was about . . . thirty inches long. I would not know
just how thick it was. I saw him whip one child and I
would say the strap was something like an ordinary
razor strap, rather heavy . . . The whipping I saw him
administer, I think was severe."

The recreational director, Roy Lawrence, "after
having been duly warned," defended himself:

I have never felt like that I was being brutal or
being severe or punishing to the point of being
brutal to these children and if I ever did it was just
ignorance on my part because . . . I always had an
interest in the kiddies . . .

. . . I will say there are lots and lots of weeks that I don't whip any . . . I never have given more than 42 licks, if I have, it was necessary . . . I never gave any as many as a hundred. I gave [deleted] and [deleted] 42 and the other boys 25 licks and that was for running off . . .

When I use this strap I hold it that way (indicating).

Then the children who had been beaten were brought into the hearing room, physically examined, and asked to testify.

A fourteen-year-old boy gave this account:

The first time I ran away I got right to the outside edge of Waco and some soldiers picked me up and brought me back and I was sent to the hospital . . . and they shaved me baldheaded . . .

. . . I ran away the second time and there were four other boys the next time and that night . . . they put us in jail, and Mr. Lawrence came and got us and gave us a 'bustin.'

. . . They use a strap about that long and about that wide and about that thick . . . They gave me 117 licks . . . They whipped me behind there, you bend over and catch your ankles. (Witness shows how).

A boy, age seventeen, testified as follows: "I know that I am supposed to tell the truth here . . . Some of the boys said that I got 61 licks, I don't know how many. I did not count the licks on anybody else, I hurt too much myself to count the others. This 61 licks bruised me up. I think it left little places on me. I do not have any boils on me and I did not have at that time."

Another seventeen-year-old boy stated: "My mother is pulling cotton . . . I don't go to school any more—I just work here in the kitchen."

Another seventeen-year-old talked about not being in school:

I came out here in the 5th grade and I skipped and started in the 7th. I am not in the school now and don't know why I am not.

. . . When he got us back he whipped us harder than he ever whipped us before . . . When he was whipping there he tore a hole in my shirt.

A fifteen-year-old boy confirmed the punishment given to some of the boys who testified earlier, and provided another instance of a school-age boy being denied an education:

I tried to count the number of licks those other boys got and I proceeded to count them but I would not swear my counting was correct . . . As I counted they gave the first boy 117 licks . . . and the second boy got 61 licks and he gave me 54, and he gave the other two boys 49 licks and 57 licks.

. . . I would not mind letting you see at all. I try to change breeches every day but sometimes I don't. I changed breeches night before last. Most of the time the breeches are sent to the laundry to be laundered. I do not have any Sunday clothes.

If I went to school I would be in the 9th grade. I have four subjects and I made three A's and one A- . . . I got a whipping for talking in the dining room. We are supposed to whisper there—he doesn't approve of our talking.

Girls also testified to the brutality, as in this account by a fourteen-year-old: "I have been punished about a month or two weeks . . . by Mr. Lawrence . . . for stealing a pair of socks . . . He hit me 27 licks. This is the kind of strap he used . . . looks like it. He hurt me and he bruised my body." Another fourteen-year-old added: "I had two whippings from Mr. Lawrence. He gave me the first whipping for phoning but I didn't phone—I went over there for some other girls to phone."

The next day, October 30, 1942, Baker sent a letter to Superintendent Wiebusch, highlighting major findings from the hearing. The letter also confirmed the board's policies of forwarding to Wiebusch all complaints and of continuing to reveal the identities of those complaining:

An examination of [deleted] disclosed that even a layman could never have been mistaken about the abrasions in the skin on his body being considered from . . . a pimple or a boil . . . You intentionally tried to mislead the Board as to the facts in order to protect Lawrence.

It is your job to clean up your own situation there, and with that in mind, you may recommend to this Board the measures which you believe necessary to effect this purpose . . . But we expect from you, at all times, a full and accurate explanation . . . and we will reciprocate by giving to you a complete statement of any matter coming to our attention.

—Baker to Wiebusch,
October 30, 1942 (TSLAC)

Although support from the board members for the superintendent was clearly eroding, the beatings and other abuse would continue for another year before the board took punitive action against anyone. Meanwhile, since Wiebusch received a copy of every complaint sent to the board, he continued to systematically fire "disloyal" teachers and staff members.

On November 21, 1942, Wiebusch wrote the board, promising that corporal punishment in the future would be given only under the direct supervision of the superintendent and with a doctor or nurse present, and agreeing to fire Mrs. German, the nurse, and Lawrence, the disciplinarian.

On December 2, 1942, Chaplain Novacs wrote Baker, claiming that despite admonitions to Wiebusch not to punish those who had testified at the hearing, Novacs had been fired. He asked whether his firing was the wish of the board. Apparently it was, for he was not rehired.

Letters of complaint to the board continued to come in throughout the winter and into the next year. Finally, on March 13, 1943, Mrs. L. E. Williams and Mrs. W. P. Sheffield, both teachers at the Home, traveled to Austin to confront the board. Baker sent a letter to Wiebusch, informing him of their testimony. Excerpts from the testimony of Mrs. Williams and Mrs. Sheffield indicated that little had changed at the Home:

Last week Mr. Robinson, the principal of the High School there slapped a girl student, [deleted] age 17, completely down while she was on the stairway. Mrs. Williams later protested to him about the action and he stated that he should have stomped her instead of slapping her.

About two weeks ago Mrs. Kennedy, another teacher there, had witnessed Mr. Robinson whipping some little 6th grade girls, and had asked her to examine them; that upon examination she found that they had large clear blisters raised by the board used by Robinson . . .

Some time ago from out of Mrs. Williams' room [deleted], [deleted], [deleted], and [deleted] were severely punished by Robinson because they did not get some laundry. Mrs. Williams examined [deleted] and found that she was beaten to where she had large purple and black spots on her body . . .

These teachers say that the children never are encouraged, but are constantly reminded that they are no good and came from disrespectable parents, and this Miss Guynes told a young girl last week in the presence of her classmates that she was no good and should be in a hog pen. Robinson says he had rather give them a licking than eat ice cream . . .

Teachers are forbid to talk to the children and both of these teachers have been told to not let the children stay with them at all, but to run them away from their rooms when not in school. The children are never permitted to talk to each other while they are eating, but are required to remain quiet and are severely punished when they do talk. One little boy was whipped until he was ill because he put a piece of meat in a biscuit and started out of the room. While all of this goes on the matrons talk to each other and often pack food off in the presence of the children.

Some 12 girls have been sent over to N.Y.A. (National Youth Administration) where they work for $10.80 per month and their board; that they have Saturday afternoon and Sunday off at which time they are usually attended by a gang of soldiers. These two teachers are very much concerned about their welfare.

—Report from the Board of Control, March 13, 1943 (TSLAC)

Two weeks later, Mrs. Williams again wrote to Baker:

I again write to you concerning the present conditions at the Home. When you come to investigate do not be fooled by the too assuming attitude that all is running smoothly. For, Mr. Wiebusch is making a desperate effort, stopping at nothing, to have ready a perfect camouflage of an atmosphere of joy and contentment in and around the Institution for your observation. He and Mr. Robinson will stoop to anything if they thought they could score a point.

I earnestly pray that these less fortunate boys and girls will be given a fairer chance to meet life.

—Williams to Baker, March 30, 1943 (TSLAC)

Baker's reply was similar to most of his letters in answer to complaints: "As you know matters of this kind must be worked out slow and we must be sure we can prove what we say before we begin. May I thank you again for your assistance. Will you kindly continue to do what you can in the best interest of the children" (Baker to Williams, March 30, 1943 [TSLAC]).

Two months later, Mrs. Williams wrote another scathing letter to Baker about conditions at the Home, saying that she "had rather make an effort to right the gross injustice being done these children, taking a chance of losing my position as a teacher, in order to try and help their cause" (Williams to Baker, May 25, 1943 [TSLAC]).

On the same day of Mrs. Williams's letter to the board, another letter arrived, this one from Wiebusch, requesting the board's approval to fire Mrs. Williams (and Mrs. Sheffield, who had joined Mrs. Williams in previous appearances before the board). The board informed Wiebusch two days later that it would not support the firings of either teacher.

Shortly afterward, a letter arrived at the board office from the new State Home chaplain, Dwight Baker, who had apparently been criticized by citizens for his role in protecting the abusers. The chaplain was outraged by the "insubordination" of other employees who encouraged students to write letters to the board: "They have resorted to the lowest form of treachery and that is having these children do their dirty-work. I do not blame the youngsters in any sense but pour my contempt on any group who will hide behind a group of children and pour their filthy propaganda into a stream that has now become a river with an undercurrent that is affecting the attitude of each and every child here that is old enough to drink from the dirty dregs" (Baker to Board of Control, June 23, 1943, Harold Larson's private collection; hereafter cited as Larson private collection).

LAWRENCE'S BIG MISTAKE

As for Lawrence, even though he was fired as disciplinarian in December 1942, after the hearings, he still visited the Home and somehow had access to the children, at least the teenage girls. Lawrence made his big mistake in the summer of 1943 when he kept a seventeen-year-old girl away from the Home overnight. Mrs. Sheffield was one of the teachers who reported the incident to the board and forced Wiebusch to notify the district attorney. The girl's testimony is excerpted here:

> Mr. Lawrence and I went to the Southern Club and drank and danced. I drank two glasses of beer and he drank beer also. We stayed there somewhere about midnight and left. We drove around town for while and then he took me to the home of [excised]. I stayed there the rest of the night, and Mr. Lawrence came by the next morning and picked me up and carried me back to the Home. Mr. Lawrence made no improper advances toward me at any time . . . So far as I know Mr. Wiebusch didn't know anything about my going out with Mr. Lawrence.

> —Statement,
> June 7, 1943 (TSLAC)

Lawrence fled to Louisiana, and on June 11, 1943, the McLennan County district attorney notified the board and Wiebusch that he would not seek to extradite Lawrence, since giving alcohol to a minor was only a misdemeanor: "I do not feel that we are in a position to prosecute this man so long as he is in the State of Louisiana" (McLennan County district attorney Stansell Bryan to Board of Control, June 11, 1943 [TSLAC]). The abusive disciplinarian Lawrence was finally gone, not only from the Waco State Home but also from the entire state.

When the young woman involved, now in her eighties, was asked about the incident, she said she did not think her "fifteen minutes of fame" caused the termination of Lawrence. "It was the other girls," she said, but declined to explain further, except to say that she knew about other incidents involving his taking girls from the Home and "other things."

LAST STRAW FOR WIEBUSCH

About a month later, and sixteen months after the first documented complaint against Wiebusch, the Board of Control sent Wiebusch a condemnatory letter that detailed the lengthy list of complaints stemming from the hearing the year before and from information provided by alarmed citizens. The letter noted how the board had given Wiebusch every chance to correct the listed abuses: "We believe any fair minded person will say, after knowing the record in this case, that you have received the indulgence of this Board far beyond what is usually accorded any superintendent" (Baker to Wiebusch, July 3, 1943 [TSLAC]).

On July 15, Wiebusch sent, as requested, his answers to the complaints identified in Baker's letter and strongly denied that he was guilty of any of the charges. On behalf of one of the boys who had been beaten and had testified at the earlier hearing, Wiebusch produced a statement by the boy and a campus doctor that the boy had not been beaten by Lawrence but by another student.

A few weeks later, Mrs. Williams again complained to the board:

> A boy student at the Waco State Home was hit over the head by Mr. Davis, the farmer, and severely hurt, and that [deleted] was given 150 lashes yesterday with a bat.
> . . . The ones in authority were whipping the children severely, going so far as to injure the boy's jaw to the extent of a fracture . . .
> Judge Baker, I wonder if you would be in a position at present, to tell me if my services as a teacher at the Home for the coming school term will be in order?

> —Williams to Baker,
> August 9, 1943 (TSLAC)

Baker's letter to Mrs. Williams was again typical of his replies:

We are making inquiries with reference to the brutal treatment of the children at the Waco State Home, and thank you for the information.

Until a new Superintendent is appointed, there is nothing we can do about telling you about your job for next year. Personally, I want to thank you for the assistance you have rendered us over the months.

—Baker to Williams,
August 11, 1943 (TSLAC)

On August 20, 1943, Baker wrote Wiebusch a terse letter asking him to vacate the premises by September and notifying him that Ben S. Peek had been elected superintendent. Unfortunately, the board's problems with Wiebusch were not over. Within a month after he left, the board was looking at evidence of embezzlement by Wiebusch. His former secretary testified that he had stolen money sent to children from their families and destroyed the letters. A letter from the investigator to the board said, "I am confi-

dent there have been other cases of misappropriation of funds and can be easily traced. Some of them will be Federal cases if proven true" (Senter to Baker, September 27, 1943 [TSLAC]).

We could find no record of any criminal charges being brought against Wiebusch. But they almost certainly should have. Some alumni discovered, when they retrieved their State Home records, that their families had in fact sent money they never received.

An alumnus who discovered such letters, which mentioned not only money but also requests to take him home for Christmas, which were denied, said, "I was shocked to discover all those letters, sent month after month, year after year. I never saw a letter from my family, and I never got any money. I thought nobody cared."

Documents show that Mrs. Williams, despite her valiant and somewhat successful efforts to stop at least some of the abuse at the Home, eventually lost her job. She was not listed among the employees during subsequent superintendents' tenures.

CHAPTER SEVEN

Control

State documents reveal many battles over control of the Home, with superintendents and staff battling state agencies, district courts, legislators, concerned citizens, parents, alumni, and even the children. One of the most powerful superintendents, who created an excellent school system and at the same time a self-sufficient, working farm, was the educator Ben S. Peek, Sr.

BEN S. PEEK, SR., 1943–1954

In 1943, the *Waco Times-Herald* glowingly welcomed the new superintendent, Ben S. Peek, Sr.:

> Not in a long time has a Texas administrative act exceeded in value the appointment last week of Ben Peek . . . Those kids out there have needed a break for a long time, and now they've got it. The former superintendent of South Junior High School will bring love and affection to them along with a very high administrative quality. Ben Peek is a good man. So far as those poor kids are concerned, God must have been hovering around the state board of control when it looked over Texas and finally said of Ben Peek "that's the man for them."
>
> —August 24, 1943,
> *Waco Times-Herald* (TSLAC)

The abuse of children unfortunately did not end with Peek's arrival. The notoriously abusive, bat-wielding C. B. Whigham, cited dozens of times in alumni stories, served under Peek for nearly ten years. This was a surprising turn of events, since Peek had been involved in the yearlong investigation of brutal beatings under Wiebusch's watch.

During his first year, Peek produced a report on the Waco State Home. He spends two pages of a three-page document on the workings of the farm:

> The problem of providing food and feed has been receiving special attention and our agricultural program has been expanded with the addition of 200 acres of bottom land. The feed bill is being reduced by pasturing 35 head of our dry cows and calves on the new acreage while land adjacent to the institution has been converted into pasturage for the dairy herd. Twenty acres of oats have been planted on the new farm for feed, six acres of Irish potatoes and 40 acres of corn have recently been put in to help solve the food situation . . . Fifteen hundred chicks . . . have been added to the flock of four hundred laying hens.

Toward the end of the report, he discusses the work to be done directly with the children:

> The attitude they presented on my arrival . . . was one of distinct suspicion, animosity and general distrust.
>
> . . . To lead the thinking of warped minds to accept normal standards of thinking and living is not easy, but some success has been attained.
>
> —Ben Peek, "Resume of Work Done,
> Waco State Home," a report to the
> Board of Control, April 11, 1944 (TSLAC)

The staff of the Waco State Home numbered fewer

than twenty in 1944, which meant that the children supplied nearly all the farm labor.

Baker praised Peek in letters, signing them "Your friend":

Perhaps I should not take too much pride in what you have done up there, as I cannot do so without engaging in a species of self-serving thoughts, but when I think back a little better than three years ago of the status of that school there, with the children in holy fear of the Superintendent and other employees, being unmercifully beaten up on occasion by those who admitted most of their time was spent in honkytonks, with a school unrecognized by any accredited agency, with a political superintendent supported by the entire legislative setup in McLennan County, I cannot

but feel the utmost satisfaction in what you have accomplished up there.

Certainly, we know on this Board to whom credit is due. All we did was elect you and you did the job, and you have certainly done a good one. Your friend, Weaver H. Baker.

—Baker to Peek,
June 7, 1945 (TSLAC)

COMPLAINTS AGAINST PEEK

Even though Peek, a former Waco superintendent of schools, built what many alumni called "an outstanding school system" on campus, there were complaints against him. Children who had left the Home and returned as adults to visit siblings or staff, as well as

In 1944, the Waco State Home had fifteen hundred chickens, four hundred laying hens, forty acres of corn, twenty acres of oats, and six acres of potatoes, all worked by the children of the Home. Harold Larson's private collection.

parents who came to see their children, were often denied visitation. Usually, no reasons were given for the decision.

Peek fought contentious battles with the board and the courts. He continually pushed the board and the attorney general's office to grant him more autonomy, including the ability to approve adoptions without parental consent and to transfer children to penal institutions and state hospitals. One of the most shocking cases documenting Peek's transference of children involved an alumnus who was transferred from the Waco State Home to an "epileptic colony," even though he never had a seizure in his life.

The man, who did not want his name revealed, said that conditions under Peek were "awful, a living hell," and he often ran away with his older brother. "They beat the shit out of my brother and me at the Waco State Home," he said. When the alumnus was nine years old, Peek arranged for a doctor to sign papers claiming that the child was epileptic and transferred him to the Abilene State Hospital, originally called the State Epileptic Colony. He was forced to stay there until he was eighteen, even though schooling stopped at the eighth grade.

According to the man, the Abilene institution was worse than Waco. "They damn near stomped me to death, broke my hip, and jammed a stick in my eye," he said. "I've still got scars all over me from the things they did to me at those places."

The man managed to finish high school, served in the Marines, married, and had a successful career. He said he avoids talking about the Home because it is too painful, but he was happy to hear about the book and hopes it will expose the truth.

Baker, apparently aware of such cases, sent a stern warning to Peek, again signing it "Your friend": "You will be cited for contempt . . . and if found guilty, punished severely. I mention this, Ben, simply because I am afraid you do not understand the danger of failing to obey the trial courts in matters relating to the children committed to you . . . You simply must pursue

that policy, or you will surely come to grief in the days ahead" (Baker to Peek, September 4, 1945 [TSLAC]).

Despite reprimands from Baker, Peek repeatedly defied court orders, the police, and caseworkers, and he ignored pleading letters from parents who had improved their family conditions and wanted their children back.

A MOTHER'S PLEA FOR CUSTODY

One example of Peek's arbitrary use of power was the case involving a distraught mother who wanted her children back.

During a bitter divorce in 1940, the mother lost her two children temporarily to their paternal grandfather, who, without her knowledge, took them to the Waco State Home. After she married a "fine man" with a "good permanent job," she began working with the courts to bring her children home, visited them regularly, and sent money and clothes.

When the mother complained to the board that she was not allowed to take her children from the Home for visits, Peek's response was brief but firm:

> These letters explain why we are forced to exercise care in letting parents have their children to carry out in town.
>
> . . . I have found it quite necessary to have visiting parents come to the office for a short visit with me before allowing them to visit the children. We are trying to secure in this way a pledge from the parents to assist us in building in the minds of the children a love for the home.
>
> —Peek to Baker, September 20, 1943
> (Larson private collection)

His letter to the mother was very clear:

> We are doing our best to make the children satisfied with their home life here. I trust that you may

be able to assist us by writing cheerful letters to [excised].

. . . Too much company upsets the children and causes them to want to get out.

—Peek to mother, September 27, 1943
(Larson private collection)

Excerpts from the mother's letter to the Board of Control detail her battles with Peek during the six years her children were in the Home:

I have never given up hopes of being happy with them once more . . . The probation [officer, who was probably involved because of the daughter's history of running away] writes Mr. Ben S. Peek . . . asking him to release the children to me through the Summer . . . I rented a larger place and did everything in my power looking forward to their coming. Mr. Peek absolutely ignores this letter and when I went to Waco for my children he just told me that the children weren't allowed to leave the Home for the Summer not giving me any reason at all. He seems to think he can run things his way. Well, I did all that was left for me to do. I came home broken hearted and left my children.

—Mother to Baker,
June 7, 1946 (TSLAC)

A year later, the daughter ran away from the Home and went to her mother. After seven weeks, the mother appealed to local authorities to help her regain custody. A probation officer gave the mother permission to keep her daughter and notified Peek, asking him to release the children to the mother.

Instead, Peek threatened to have the police pick up the daughter and put her in jail until he could arrange to get her back to the Home. (Holding runaway children in jail was a common punitive action taken by many superintendents.) The mother stayed at the probation office with her daughter until the State Home patrol car picked her up.

Then, as the mother sought legal help to get her children back, Peek filed charges against her for influencing the daughter to run away, leaving the mother with a $100 fine.

The answer to the mother's plea for help from the board was a brief letter from Baker: "Your letter . . . will be referred to . . . Peek. You may rest assured the matter will be given full consideration." Baker's letter to Peek about the case was even briefer: "The enclosed letters are self-explanatory of the subject matter" (both letters dated June 10, 1946 [TSLAC]).

Although no other records were found, an alumnus who knew the two children said that when the girl was sixteen, she and her brother left the Home with their parents. He said he never heard from them again.

REFUSING MINORITY CHILDREN

While African American children were denied admission to the Home until passage of the Civil Rights Act of 1964, Hispanic children had been legally admitted under Peek's predecessors. However, in August 1946, a social worker in El Paso complained that Latin American children were being refused admission to the Home. Baker's warning to Peek was brief and clear: "You are advised that Latin-American children and Anglo-American children are on an absolute parity, insofar as our admission rules are concerned, and hereafter you will admit Latin-American children when they are duly committed, in just exactly the same manner as you would an Anglo-American child" (Baker to Peek, August 19, 1946 [TSLAC]).

PEEK'S FINAL YEARS

That was the last letter from Baker to Peek that we found in the records; Baker was killed in Austin in an automobile crash on September 22, 1946.

Even though his friend and supporter Baker was no longer on the board, Peek continued to seek ways to increase his power as superintendent. In January 1947, Peek won a ruling from the Texas attorney general that he could, without parental consent, arrange for the adoption of children at the Home if the committing authorities granted approval.

The annual report authored by Peek in October 1953, a little more than a year before he was fired, reported many "proud accomplishments." The report was sent to John H. Winters, the executive director of the State Department of Public Welfare, and was passed on to all legislators.

The first page set the tone for the remaining twenty-nine pages:

> Let the facts be heard and evaluated! In the decade from 1943 to 1953 there have been 853 children cared for at the Waco State Home.
>
> . . . From the ugly green caterpillar emerged a beautiful butterfly and today's child at the Waco State Home is indistinguishable from any happy, normal child!
>
> . . . We have canned in one year as much as 6,000 gallons of good vegetables and fruits for consumption. We raise all our pork.
>
> —Peek, annual report, submitted to John H. Winters, executive director, State Department of Public Welfare, October 23, 1953 (TSLAC)

Peek was suddenly fired from the Waco State Home in 1954, but there is no official explanation for it in any state records, including the board minutes the week of his termination. Newspaper reports and documents from Larson's private collection suggest that Peek fought the Board of Control over its plans to close the campus school system.

According to the Waco city directories, Peek must have left the city for several years, although his wife was working in Waco. In 1958, he was listed in the city directory as a night clerk at the Town House Motel and Hotel.

SUCCESSION

Superintendent Peek was followed by Acting Superintendent James Lands and Superintendents Herbert Wilson, James McNabb, and Jewell Ludwick, who collectively served from 1954 to 1974, before the reform years. Although few state records about their administrations exist, they had noteworthy creden-

Superintendent Ben S. Peek. His fierce battle to retain the outstanding campus school system he built may have cost him his job. Harold Larson's private collection.

tials and were recognized in the media for improvements to the Home. Alumni, however, reported continuing sexual and physical abuse throughout their terms.

Wilson (1955–1963) was a former caseworker for the Waco and Corsicana state homes and deputy commissioner of the Department of Public Welfare. During his tenure, he built two residential cottages, closed the campus schools, enrolled the children in public schools, allowed children to return home to visit their parents, and hired additional caseworkers to counsel and interact with the children.

McNabb (1963–1965) was the former superintendent of the Texas Baptist Children's Home in Round Rock.

Ludwick (1965–1974) had served as school principal of the Waco State Home under Peek and was a former superintendent of public schools. He was cited by alumni for helping them get into college.

The terms of Peek, Wilson, and Ludwick were certainly tarnished by the abusive "disciplinarian" C. B. Whigham, who beat boys with a baseball bat until they were bloody.

Pop Taylor, who sexually abused young girls, was mentioned in alumni stories during the fifties, when Peek and Wilson were superintendents.

James Hartley's horrifying report of abuse took place during McNabb's brief term.

Abuse at the Home was rarely reported by anyone, including children who left the Home early, and the experience in 1949 of alumnus John (Gifford) White may explain why.

White said that the day before he and his sister (ages thirteen and fifteen) were released from the Home, an official picked them up in a car, drove them away from the Home, and then warned them, "If you ever say a word to anybody about anything that happened to you or to anybody else at the Home, we'll find you and bring you back."

White said he and his sister never talked about the Home, even after they became adults, because "the last thing we wanted was to go back to that place."

Even Waco State Home archivist Harold Larson inadvertently played a role in covering up the abuse, for he served as protector of the Home's public image. In fact, he attempted to bribe one superintendent to prevent "any bad news getting out about the Home." Larson's almost obsessive efforts to protect the image of the Home stemmed from a promise he made to Peek and Ludwick in 1950. If he were allowed to organize an ex-students' association, he would never use its collective power to "cause trouble" for the Home. He kept his promise, for his records of child abuse at the Home were discovered after his death with a warning that they could "hurt a lot of people" and should never be made public.

CHAPTER EIGHT

Reform

THE TURNING POINT: JUDGE WILLIAM WAYNE JUSTICE'S RULINGS

The real turning point in the history of the Waco State Home came from the landmark decision by federal district judge William Wayne Justice in *Morales v. Turman*, a federal civil rights case filed in 1971. Dr. James Turman was the executive director of the Texas Youth Council (TYC), which supervised the Waco State Home and all juvenile penal institutions in Texas.

Justice found that a number of practices—including arbitrary beatings, solitary confinement, and the use of drugs to control behavior—routinely practiced at TYC facilities constituted cruel and unusual punishment. He ordered the immediate closure of the Gatesville and Mountain View juvenile facilities, and as a result of his ruling, the Waco State Home was eventually closed as a facility for dependent children. The many court decisions related to the case became a rallying cry for those seeking to transfer children out of institutions and into foster or adoptive homes and to improve local services so that families could keep their children at home. It also sent a message that abusing children under state care would no longer be tolerated. Unfortunately, recent reports of long-term physical and sexual abuse at TYC facilities suggest that abuse of children under state care has not ended.

REBECCA CANNING, 1974–1976

The final transformation of the Waco State Home took place under the leadership of Rebecca Canning (now Brumley), who was superintendent from 1974 to 1976.

A thirty-one-year-old former secondary-school teacher, Brumley had tutored children at the State Home as a college student in the 1960s. She also wrote her master's thesis on the Home. With the knowledge that claims of abuse at the Home were genuine, she recognized that the system itself called for an overhaul.

Superintendent Rebecca Canning (now Brumley), who reformed the Home, abolishing corporal punishment and developing individual treatment plans for each child, c. 1975. Used with the permission of the Waco Tribune-Herald.

Brumley immediately announced a ban on corporal punishment and put the Home on a path toward individualized care, a homelike environment, community opportunities, and positive programs for academic and personal development.

She established a treatment-team approach for each child, involving every staff member whose job touched the child, from social workers to cooks. Team members met regularly to coordinate efforts, and each child was invited to attend and discuss plans or goals in a positive, supportive manner.

Although new policies were implemented under the directives of a federal court order and with the support of Ron Jackson, the new TYC director, Brumley faced significant challenges. The more progressive members of the staff welcomed the proposed changes, but most other staff members seemed incapable of offering direction and discipline to the children without the threat of physical punishment. Some were resistant, defiant, and even hostile. The children tested the new boundaries by running away, often only briefly.

Acting quickly to signal a new era of positive care, Brumley removed many of the physical symbols of institutionalization, including the fences that surrounded the grounds and reinforced its prison-like atmosphere. The yellow buses emblazoned with WACO STATE HOME were painted dark green and left unmarked. The Home purchased vans and cars so that children could travel in small groups. Existing buildings were converted into centers for student activities, learning, foster care services, and community services. The commercial laundry was closed and replaced with residential laundry equipment in each dormitory.

The remaining dormitory barracks were phased out, and the cottage-style dorms were updated. For the first time in the history of the Home, some of the housing was arranged so that siblings of vastly different ages could live together in a family setting with a set of "parents." The opportunity for siblings to live together was a far cry from the days when they were punished for waving to each other in a segregated dining hall.

Brumley also established two "Senior Houses" on campus for older teens; six lived in each residence, and cars were donated for their use. The staff helped set up the most realistic family settings possible so that graduating seniors could learn to cook and manage a home on their own.

Brumley's ultimate goal for each child was to find the most appropriate homelike living situation possible, on or off campus.

Rehabilitation counseling was established to help reunite children with their families. Some of the children at the State Home had at least one living parent, grown siblings, or other relatives who could provide homes. Parents were encouraged to interact with their children through special family functions on campus.

"If own-family reuniting was not appropriate or possible," said Brumley in a recent interview, "alternatives were sought or developed along a continuum of care through which the child could thrive."

At the top of the list were adoption and foster-home care, the most significant programs for moving dependent children out of institutions, according to Brumley. She also arranged for contract placements with vocational halfway houses, specialized small-group homes, and other alternatives.

Under Brumley's direction, the children were offered a proliferation of cultural, recreational, educational, and vocational opportunities, both on and off campus.

To increase community involvement, she organized a Citizens Advisory Council as well as Special Friends and Friend Families as ways to allow for visits, trips, and activities and to encourage family-oriented relationships. The campus church services were shut down, and children participated in the religious experiences of their choice in Waco churches, assisted by community volunteers who picked up and returned the children, often including them in Sunday meals with volunteer families.

The educational programs were expanded to provide counseling in cooperation with public schools, supplementary educational tutoring, study groups, and federally funded vocational training.

Staff turnover increased under Brumley's tenure. She worked to increase the percentage of professionally trained staff, and she beefed up staff development with national conferences and workshops, consulting, and visits to other residential care facilities in Texas and other states.

Brumley's goal of individual care had been largely accomplished by the time she left the Home in 1976. Most of the children were residing in homes or other community-based placements. She remained involved in the deinstitutionalization plan and the legislative process leading to the transfer of the Home to the Texas Department of Mental Health and Mental Retardation.

The Waco State Home was officially closed in 1979. It reopened as the Waco Center for Youth, a psychiatric residential treatment center.

Brumley's attitude toward the institutionalization of children was articulately summed up in an article she wrote in 1979: "Until the foundations and functional contradictions of the 'structured environment' itself are critically challenged, we will continue to send needy children away to places where we would never send our own" (Rebecca Canning, "Homes of Last Resort: The Never-Lands We'd Like to Forget," *Baylor Line*, November 1979).

Brumley is now executive director of the Red Oak Foundation, a nonprofit charitable organization based in Fort Worth.

CONTINUING CHALLENGES

While conditions have improved since the late Judge Justice issued his compassionate directives, there is still much to be done for dependent children. The website for Children's Rights, an advocacy group for dependent children, reported in 2010:

Many child welfare systems are underfunded, understaffed, beset by serious systemwide problems, and lacking the leadership necessary to fix them. They compound the trauma that abused and neglected children have already experienced by:

- Bouncing children from one unstable placement to another, uprooting their lives repeatedly and without warning, and drastically reducing the chances that they will ever end up in permanent homes.
- Failing to protect children in foster care from further abuse and neglect.
- Failing to provide adequate medical, dental, and mental health services to ensure children's health and well-being and help them cope with the abuse and neglect they have endured.
- Failing to move children quickly into permanent homes through either safe reunification with their families or adoption when reunification is not possible.
- Warehousing children in institutions, group homes, emergency shelters, and other "temporary" and non-family settings.
- Overmedicating children to control their behavior.
- Neglecting children's educational needs.

—www.childrensrights.org, February 2010

CHAPTER NINE

Conclusion

The most disturbing fact that emerges from this collection of first-person stories and the documents confirming abuse is that boys and girls at the Waco State Home were repeatedly subjected to severe beatings and sexual exploitation during most of the Home's existence, no matter who was superintendent, no matter who was providing oversight at the highest levels of state government. Superintendent Rebecca Canning ended corporal punishment and sexual abuse at the Home immediately after she arrived in 1974, five years before the Home was finally closed.

An obvious reason for indifference toward the abuse of dependent children was simply prejudice against poverty. It existed then, and it exists today. Poverty was a theme in the children's lives before they arrived at the Home. And the kiss of death for a family already in poverty was a criminal record. A review of the files of children whose parents had a history of crime shows that such children were rarely returned to their families, and that visits or any other forms of communication were strongly discouraged, even if the parents' crime had been to steal food for their children.

PASSING THE TRASH

Another explanation for the continuing abuse at the Waco State Home lies in the term "passing the trash," jargon often associated with orphanages or children's homes. It refers to the common practice of quietly firing abusive employees from one facility and then passing them along to another institution rather than ensuring that they are not allowed to continue the abuse.

The infamous C. B. "Buddy" Whigham, allegedly one of the most abusive of the staff members in the history of the Home, worked at four different children's facilities in Texas.

Whigham and his wife, a dorm matron, worked at the Home on and off for nearly twenty years, from the 1940s until 1970. He was employed at the Boys Camp and the Gatesville State School for Boys (both penal institutions) before he came to the State Home.

He was first hired by Superintendent Ben Peek, who fired him after nearly ten years when a group of students organized a protest in response to the particularly bloody and brutal beating of a classmate. Whigham stayed in Waco and worked at the Methodist Home for Children.

He was rehired a few years later by Superintendent Herbert Wilson for another nearly ten-year term. During that time, a group of junior high boys in Whigham's dorm came to the rescue of a severely disabled classmate who was being beaten by Whigham. Although the boys left Whigham beaten and bloodied, they were not punished but instead moved to another dorm and said they never saw Whigham again. The records are not clear about who was being protected—Whigham or the boys.

Whigham finally retired about five years after the incident but not without a send-off from the State Home and other public officials.

Even the local newspaper, apparently unaware of Whigham's abusive history, reported on his career in laudatory terms:

Mr. and Mrs. Charlie Whigham are retiring after being "Mom and Dad" to thousands of children over a period of 20 years at the Waco Sate Home.

there were also courageous employees who risked their jobs during tough economic times to defend the children.

Mrs. L. E. Williams, a teacher at the Home during the Wiebusch term, emerged as a tireless champion of the children. She defiantly fought to stop abuse, even though Wiebusch tried to get her fired, and she stayed on staff and continued to complain until Wiebusch was gone.

Some staff members and concerned citizens also joined Mrs. Williams in her crusade. One dorm parent, Mrs. Ratliff, apparently stood up to Whigham and did not allow him to "beat her boys" when she was around to stop it. A former student's letter said:

> Mrs. Ratliff was the only dorm parent that would take up for us. She was a loving person and not the least bit scared of Whigham.
>
> The first time [I got beaten], as soon as Whigham let me go, I hauled ass for the dorm. Mrs. Ratliff had just stepped outside . . . [She] advanced towards Whigham, who retreated. I heard, "Don't you ever lay a hand on one of my boys." When we heard what she said, we knew we had a friend."

—[name withheld] to Harold Larson,
June 1996 (Larson private collection)

Not everyone who was concerned about the children was willing to go public with their complaints. Some, like Mrs. Mabel Legg, one of the most beloved teachers of the State Home and one often mentioned in the alumni stories, chose to get along with Wiebusch but did what she could to help the children by being an excellent teacher and giving them loving, caring support in the classrooms.

There is clear evidence that she did not like Wiebusch and often intervened on behalf of the students. She stopped him from sending one of her students to the Gainesville State School for Girls "for no reason in the world except she didn't dry a stew pan," she

. . . He has lived, worked and played with boys. "We just seem to fit together," he said.

"I have more children than anyone," he said. "They run in thousands." Whigham said he had never worked with girls but "loves them just the same."

—*Waco News-Tribune*, November 7, 1970
(Texas Collection, Baylor University)

DEFENDERS OF THE CHILDREN

Just as the history of the Home is peopled by abusive staff members abetted by public indifference,

---

C. B. "Buddy" Whigham, a dorm parent at the Waco State Home for more than twenty years. He is mentioned in many stories for his brutal beatings of the children with a baseball bat. Harold Larson's private collection.

said (Mabel Legg, interview by Harold Larson, undated, Larson private collection).

At critical moments, even Mrs. Legg was caught up in the complicity of silence maintained by much of the Home's staff. When she was asked by Mrs. Williams to accompany the group to Austin to take its case to the Board of Control in 1943, Mrs. Legg refused to go.

She explained in a taped interview with Harold Larson several years before her death:

I said I am not going to Austin with you tomorrow and they said, why not, and I said Mr. Wiebusch has given me my job. I said it may not be perfect but he has given me my job and I said as long as I work for the man I'm going to be loyal to him . . .

. . . The teachers began telling the students that Ms. Legg was against them. She was for Mr. Wiebusch, when that wasn't true at all. And they found it out sooner or later. And so, at the end of two years, his term was over so didn't do too much harm.

—Mabel Legg, interview with Harold Larson, undated (Larson private collection)

THE REAL HEROES

The purpose of this epilogue is not to diminish the power or question the truthfulness of the stories shared by the more than fifty alumni who trusted that their memories would be treated with respect. The purpose is to look behind their stories, to examine the system as it existed at the time and consider its implications for today.

An inside look at the fifty-plus years of operation of the Waco State Home, which was staffed by many compassionate, intelligent, and educated caretakers and overseen by well-meaning state authorities, demonstrates how challenging it is to uncover abuse and stop it. Despite the presence of those with good intentions, there was a long history of misguided management as well as a lack of oversight and controls. It is difficult to look back and not be appalled at the failure to stop the abuse, much less to nurture the children. The system seemed designed to keep them under control by inflicting brutal, humiliating, and meaningless forms of punishment.

This book is a chronicle of courageous people, but it is also an indictment of a system that failed to protect or nurture children who had committed no crime

Mrs. Mabel Legg, a much-loved and respected English teacher at the Waco State Home for many years, with her husband. Harold Larson's private collection.

nor done anything other than have parents who could not provide a home for them.

The children at the Waco State Home, who were first failed by their own families or communities and then by the state that claimed them as wards, deserved better than they got.

When you look at the collection of stories, most of the alumni strongly believed that the Waco State Home was preferable to their other options. Their resilience and successes in many areas of their lives do not support the notion that growing up in a children's home is necessarily a setback for life.

I am grateful to all of those who searched their memories and their hearts to share their stories. We owe them our profound respect for their willingness to revisit the past, for it was not always a joyful journey. In fact, many said that it was painful, despite the fact that most of them focused on the happier memories of life at the State Home.

The stories from the alumni celebrate the collective and personal strength of the thousands of children who lived at the Home, their determination to overcome tremendous challenges before and after living at the Home, and their amazing ability to make the best of what they were given and move on with their lives.

As one alumnus said, "The children of the Home are my heroes." Indeed, they are heroes for us all.